Dedication

This book is dedicated to all residents of the town of East Brookfield, past, present, and future. To those who are proud to live in a small, rural community; to those who proudly respond, "Podunk" when asked where they live; and to those who work to make our community a kind, caring, wonderful place to call home.

Cover Photos, clockwise from top left:

- Connie Mack, while manager of the Philadelphia Athletics. Thompson, Paul, photographer. Connie Mack, mgr., Phila. Am. Jan 7, ca. 1911. Image. Retrieved from the Library of Congress, <https://www.loc.gov/item/2008678872/>
- Hodgkins Building, photo by author, 2017
- East Brookfield Baptist Church, photo from the collection of East Brookfield Historical Museum
- Depot Square, photo by author, 2017
- Union Hall; artist drawing, from the collection of East Brookfield Historical Museum
- St. John the Baptist Catholic Church on Connie Mack Drive. Photo by Carolyn Kowalski, from the collection of East Brookfield Historical Museum
- Governor Coolidge signing bill making East Brookfield a town, 1920, from the collection of East Brookfield Historical Museum
- District 3 School House, Podunk, from Silliman Family collection
- East Brookfield Depot, approximately 1950s. Photo from Quaboag Valley Railroaders.
- Keith Block: Emerson, Paesiello. Keith's block. 07 Apr 1906. Web. 11 Oct 2017. <http://ark.digitalcommonwealth.org/ark:/50959/4t64hh66r>.
- Franklin Stone, photo by author, 2017.
- East Brookfield Post Office, photo by author, 2017
- Podunk road sign, photos taken by the Massachusetts Department of Natural Resources and gifted to Alva and Helen Silliman in appreciation, December 23, 1959.
- Podunk Chapel, photo by author, 2017.

© 2019, Heather Gablaski

Acknowledgements

The very best part of writing this book was meeting new people and hearing memories from so many current and former residents. I hope to have accurately represented their memories here. In particular, Larry Gordon, Jeanne LeBeau, Louise Meyerdierks, Eva Perron, Jean LeDoux, Joan Bedard, and Wayne Boulette were always interesting to speak with and their recollections of lifetimes in East Brookfield were invaluable to deepening my understanding of that history of our town and what a special place it is. Terry Travers, from Spencer, and Brandon Avery, from North Brookfield, are both such a wealth of information about nearly every historical event in the area, that I found myself wishing their knowledge were available for download.

In a definite example of how we are all connected if we look closely enough, after an unsuccessful bid on Ebay to acquire the diaries of Mary Ann Harrington, who lived in the house across the street from the one in which I live today, I connected with the person who purchased them. After emailing and speaking on the phone we discovered that our great-great-grandmothers were sisters! Courtney Clements has generously shared the diary entries with me and you will see a few noted in sidebars in this book. The hard work that comprised life in the late 19th century was quite evident in the years of journals she shared.

Dr. Louis Roy's *History of East Brookfield* was an invaluable starting point for topics to include and events to research. If you don't have a copy of this book, I highly recommend it to learn more about the history of our town.

As far as sources, I relied on newspaper accounts, personal accounts, photos, maps, and any historical artifact I could find. Due to the age of sources, types of sources, and in many cases lack of sources, I did the best I could with some topics in piecing together events. Throughout this project I wished many times that people would write more things down. Things you don't think are important today will be forgotten tomorrow unless they are written down.

Finally, I would like to thank those who gave me feedback on the drafts of this book: Larry Gordon, Louise Meyerdierks, Glen Silliman, and Jordan Gablaski. Thank you for helping me make this book something to be proud of!

Table of Contents

Chapter 1 Introduction ....page 4
Chapter 2: Early Inhabitants .... page 7
    Section 1: Pond Dwellers .... page 10
    Section 2: The First and Second Settlements at Brookfield............ page 16
    Section 3: Life in the Easterly Section .... page 30
Chapter 3: Separation .... page 69
Chapter 4: Our Town: Then and. Now .... page 77
    Section 1: Town Center ....page 78
    Section 2: Lakes .... page 111
    Section 3: The Flats .... page 134
    Section 4: Podunk .... page 142
Chapter 5: Notable Events and People .... page 159
    Section 1: Notable Citizens .... page 160
    Section 2: Podunk Sends a Tree to New York City .... page 180
Chapter 6: Development in the late 20th and Early 21st Centuries....... page 185
Chapter 7: Remembrances .... page 204
    Section 1: FaceBook .... page 205
    Section 2: E.B. Historical Commission FaceBook Page .... page 213
    Section 3: Journals, Notes,. and Interviews .... page 218
    Section 4: Newspaper Clippings .... page 226
Chapter 8: In Summary .... page 235
References
Index

CHAPTER 1

Introduction

The history of East Brookfield, though it is the youngest town in Massachusetts, is one that parallels the history of our country; almost a microcosm of U.S. History within the borders of our town. When the first humans crossed the Siberian land bridge and spread throughout the Americas, many groups eventually settled in the region which would come to be known as New England. Their footpaths through the wilderness were widened as the English began to use them with their horses and then wagons. Some of these same footpaths are the familiar roads and highways we drive along in our cars today. As the Europeans settled in the "New World", the native population was decimated, first by exposure to disease and then by warfare as these two cultures clashed over use of the land. The English would succeed in their determination to expand the settlements that had begun along the coast, but only after costly battles with native tribes. This region was then part of the Revolutionary War, leading the rebellion against English rule and establishing an independent nation.

All the changes that occurred in our nation over time would impact life here as well. Different modes of transportation - stagecoaches, trolleys, and railroads - figured prominently in the development of our town. Mills and other industries flourished here as well. Men and women from East Brookfield would make their mark on the world. The game of baseball would not be the same without the influence of a man from East Brookfield. Roller skates were improved upon and became a popular past time. Thousands of animals would be helped by a local shelter.

Looking forward to when our small town would turn 100, I decided to take on the task of chronicling our town's history and notable people and events for the celebration. As a life-long resident with a long family history in this town, I've always enjoyed spending time looking through my grandparents' attic at the artifacts they collected over the years. Newspaper clippings, old books, and family photo albums told not only my family's history, but the history of the town in which they lived. Growing up in East Brookfield, I remember being proud of its small town culture. As I researched more, I was surprised to learn of the industries that had flourished in the past and the social events that defined the town. Our "baby town" was once a major industrial and manufacturing hub in New England.

A Note on Process

In thinking about this book and what I wanted for it, I began by re-reading Dr. Roy's book, *The History of East Brookfield,* noting key details I felt should be a focus of this updated work. I then moved on to reading several books on related topics such as King Philip's War and American Indian groups; journals and magazines from the 20th Century related to the various industries in East Brookfield; annual reports and other government documents of the towns of Brookfield and East Brookfield from the 1800s to today; and local newspapers. Wonderful photos can be found in Dennis LeBeau's *The Brookfields: From the Collection of William Bullard.* Other sources that are listed in the bibliography at the end of this book are valuable sources of information for those who want to delve deeper into the history of our town.

My favorite part of the research process by far was reading local newspapers from the years 1873 to 1953, which are digitized and available on the website *BrookfieldsResearch.org*. Reading through these searchable newspapers truly made the time period come alive. In reading the weekly papers, I felt transported back in time and increasingly nostalgic for the simplicity of life in the late-nineteenth to early twentieth centuries. It seemed like a place where everyone knew and cared about their neighbors: who was ill, who was traveling, or who had visitors; a place with a great sense of community. Hundreds and even thousands of people would gather here for a variety of reasons, from ice skating and horse racing on the lake in the winter, to vaudeville shows and sporting games in the summer. I found myself wishing I could travel back to this time period for just one day to experience this way of life for myself, though an 1876 account of laundry freezing solid before it could be hung on the line to dry made me thankful for modern-day conveniences!

Another important and enjoyable aspect of writing this book was talking to many residents about their memories of life in our town. Many anecdotes from these conversations, as well as comments from the Historical Commissions' FaceBook page, have made it into this book.

The research process at times felt like putting a puzzle together. Different resources added to what I already knew of the town's history or contradicted what I thought I knew, sometimes adding more detail to incomplete stories. That said, though I did my best to substantiate facts and anecdotes, I am certain there will be some details that readers remember differently or on which they have a different perspective, or some things readers may think are missing from this book. History is indeed a story and changes with additional voices that are added or resources that are uncovered.

This book is arranged both chronologically and thematically. The beginning summarizes events during the first settlement in the area and describes what life was like in the "Easterly Section." This was the name of the village of East Brookfield while it was still part of the town of Brookfield. After a section on how the separation of the towns came about, the book moves to a more thematic review of the main sections of the town: the town center, the lakes, the Flats, and Podunk. There is some overlap between these sections and the section prior to separation. I hope it is not too redundant in describing those places and businesses which straddle the time of the incorporation of the town in 1920.

This book is meant to be accessible for readers of all ages who want to learn the basic history of East Brookfield. My primary hope is for readers to find this a book that is engaging, informative, and promotes pride in our town. I hope you enjoy reading this book as much as I enjoyed writing it!

To another one hundred years!

"Tribal territories of Southern New England tribes about 1600," Nikater, Wikimedia Commons, 2008.

CHAPTER 2

Early Inhabitants

In driving, walking, or biking through East Brookfield, one cannot help but notice the natural resources that make this area attractive for all kinds of recreation and economic pursuits. Today, people enjoy boating, swimming, fishing, and ice skating on Lake Lashaway, Lake Quaboag and South Pond, hiking and hunting in the Podunk section of town, and there are small commercial farming businesses on the Flats. These same resources made this area attractive to people throughout the history of North America, from the Native American tribes who lived here prior to English settlements, to the earliest English colonists who moved here from the coast, to people today who enjoy the relative peace and tranquility of this small town that is still close enough to major cities to provide jobs and entertainment opportunities.

Some historians estimate that the native population encountered by English settlers in New England in the 17th century was about ten percent of the population that inhabited the region prior to Columbus's "discovery" of the

New World. The introduction of diseases from Europe had decimated groups of people who had no immunity to diseases like diphtheria, malaria, typhus, and influenza. Smallpox in particular was deadly to Native Americans and an epidemic between the years of 1617 and 1619, shortly before the Mayflower landed in Plymouth, was particularly devastating.

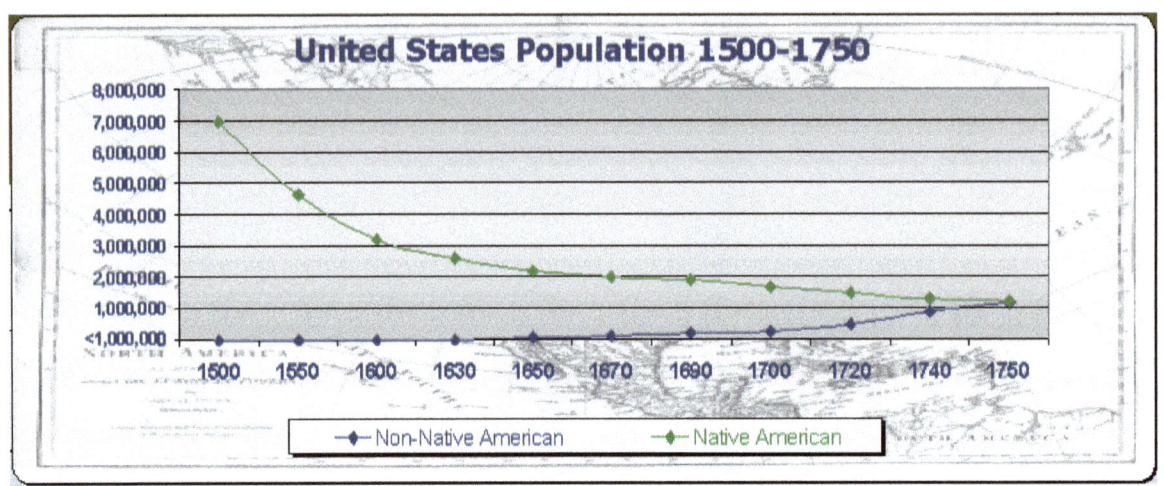

Steen, Francis F. ""The First European Contact"." Local California Chronology. UC Santa Barbara, 31 Mar. 2002. Web. 12 July 2017. <http://cogweb.ucla.edu/Chumash/>

The Pilgrims, who accidentally landed on the coast of New England in 1620 after being diverted by weather from their original destination in the Hudson River Valley, would work hard to learn how to survive off the land in the sometimes unforgiving climate of New England. Not only would they would have help from natives, who were interested in the trade goods the English had to offer, but they were the unknowing beneficiaries of the decimation that diseases brought by previous Europeans. As the newest European settlers arrived in Plymouth and the Massachusetts Bay Colonies, they spread out and found lands that had been cleared for agriculture but were not as populated as they had been just a few decades earlier. They gradually moved onto this land, purchased it from remaining native leaders, or sachems, and built their own permanent settlements. The English found none of the gold and silver the Spanish did when they colonized areas in the Caribbean, South America, and southwestern portions of North America, but the villages they established along the eastern coast would gradually grow into towns and cities, spreading first along rivers and then overland throughout the region.

Established rivalries among Native American groups, along with a lack of understanding of each other's cultures, would change the relationship between the English colonists and the Native groups in the area to one of mistrust and animosity. Eventually all out war would erupt resulting in the establishment of

English domination in the region. The area that was first the Quaboag Plantation, then Brookfield, and finally, hundreds of years later, East Brookfield, was one of the key regions in New England where a cooperative relationship between natives and settlers became one of animosity and then violence.

"File:Brookfield1.jpg." Wikimedia Commons, the free media repository. 5 Jan 2015, 09:13 UTC.12 Jul 2017, 13:19

Part 1

THE POND DWELLERS

While the density of native populations was greatest near the sea, where the weather was generally more forgiving and food sources were ample, other groups settled and thrived along the many inland rivers, lakes and ponds. The land along the water provided a fertile soil that was loose and easy to work with the tools of the time, mainly made of shell, bone, stone, or wood. After spring floods deposited rich soil along the banks of the rivers, natives would plant there. While they relied on hunting and fishing for food, they also planted corn, beans, and a variety of squashes. The fertile soil and ability to control their food supply allowed for semi-permanent villages to be established across New England.

When the English landed on the coast of Massachusetts and started their own settlements, it is estimated that 20,000 Native Americans lived in Southern New England. Tribes were linked by a common language and intermarriage and had little understanding of the number and strength of the English and what their arrival would mean to their way of life. Travel among tribes took place on footpaths and along rivers in the densely forested country.

Native American settlement in this region dates back 8,000 years. According to the Massachusetts Heritage Landscape Inventory Program conducted in 2008, there are at least seven archaeological sites in the area between the Quaboag River, the southwestern shore of Lake Quaboag, and Lake Road in Brookfield. East Brookfield has eleven documented archaeological sites recorded with the Massachusetts Historical Commission. Nine of these are prehistoric and two are historic. (*Massachusetts Heritage Landscape Inventory Program: East Brookfield Reconnaissance Report,* Massachusetts DCR, CMRPC, North Quabbin Regional Landscape Partnership, Spring 2008, http://www.mass.gov/eea/docs/dcr/stewardship/histland/recon-reports/ebrookfield.pdf)

One or more of these sites is that of a Woodland Period inhabitation from between 3,000 to 1,600 years ago called the Adena. This settlement is located between Lakes Quaboag and Quacumquasit, or South Pond, in what used to be the Tobin Campground. This site is one of the easternmost locations of the Adena culture, which is part of a larger Native American group that traces its roots to the Ohio River Valley. They were known for their unique burial mounds. Burial sites were first found in 1963 during a construction project. The site was partially excavated by a local resident who found a variety of artifacts including spearheads, cooper beads, and stone pipes. (Bulletin of the Massachusetts Archaeological Society, Volume 27, Massachusetts Archaeological Society, 1965.) In 2017, the Massachusetts Archaeological Services Department began a study of this area with the purpose of surveying the area and creating a map of known and potential archaeological sites. There is no plan to excavate deeper than the topsoil so as to protect the site. (Flanders, Kevin. "Archaeology Specialists Coming to Tobin Campground." Spencer New Leader [Spencer] 27 Jan. 2017, XXXVIII, 4 ed., sec. A: 1 . Print.) Results of the study confirmed the presence of artifacts and burials related to the Adena culture.

Howard Drake, longtime resident of East Brookfield and amateur archaeologist, had a collection of over 3,000 stone tools that he found throughout the Brookfields, many along the shores of area lakes and in the Podunk section of East Brookfield. These artifacts speak to the benefits of plentiful fresh water that allowed for semi-permanent settlements.

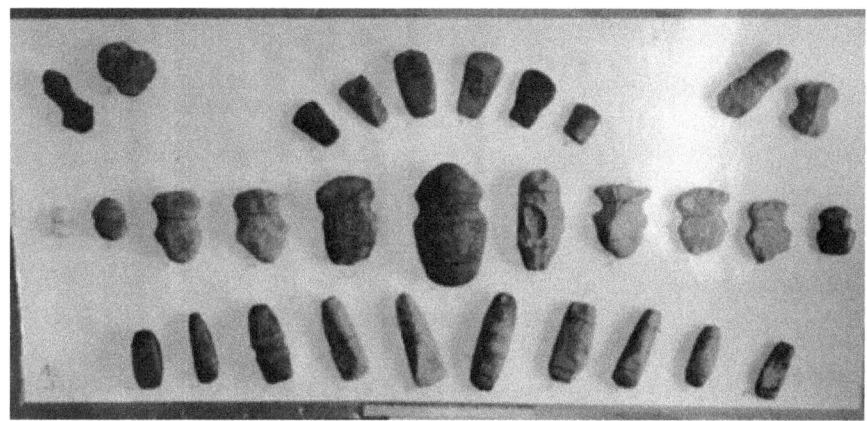

Photo of Howard Drake's arrowhead collection, EB Historical Museum Collection.

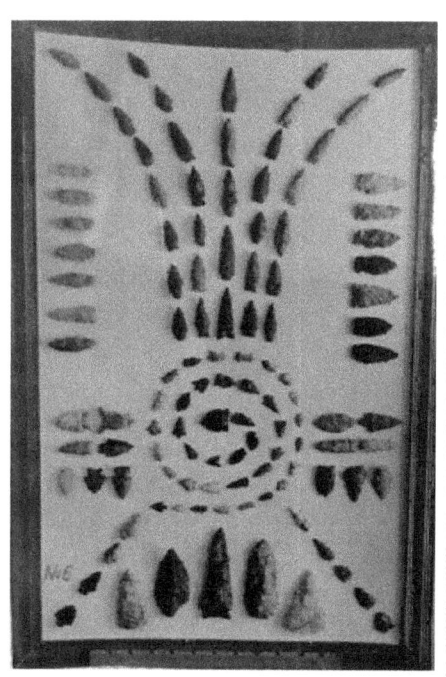

Photo of Howard Drake's arrowhead collection, EB Historical Museum Collection.

These settlements attracted those European settlers who wanted to trade with native groups and also those who saw it as their mission to convert them to Christianity. A Puritan by the name of John Elliot became convinced that his mission was to bring Christianity to the natives tribes of New England. He learned the Algonquin language and translated the Bible into Algonquin. He attempted to convert the natives not only to Christianity, but to convince them to change their culture to be like that of the English. By 1674, there were fourteen so-called "Praying Villages" across New England where natives who had been converted by Elliot lived. In approximately 1655, John Elliot came to the Quaboag area. There is no evidence that he was successful in converting any natives, but there is anecdotal evidence of his attempt, including a large rock on Andre Cormier's property near South Pond that is the site of his sermons. An early map notes the location of the "Praying Rock." Mr. Cormier's property has much evidence of Native American settlement and he has been working on creating an outdoor learning center here that will preserve the area.

John Elliot's Praying Rock, photo by author, 2019.

A later tribe located in the area that would become the Brookfields was the Nipmucs. Though whether the Nipmucs were the name of the tribe or just the name of the largest group among four closely related native groups in the region is difficult to determine. For the purpose of this history, the Nipmucs will refer to the groups of natives living in the area that would become Central Massachusetts. Nipmucs were part of the larger Algonquin nation and lived in the region between the Merrimack and Connecticut Rivers. Nipmuc translates to "freshwater fishing place," which accurately describes the major food source of the people. Their villages were basically self-sufficient, having very loose, if any, alliances with other villages. They built houses out of long poles covered with mats made of woven bark. As a small group, they paid tribute to larger native groups in the area, including the Mohawks, Narragansett, Wampanoag, Massachusetts, and Pequot. The Nipmucs joined other Native American groups during King Phillip's War, and virtually disappeared as a group after the war; some fled to Canada, others joined other native groups and moved further west, and others were sold into slavery.

In 1675, the first European settlers to the area called all the natives in the region Quaboags, perhaps based upon a name the natives called themselves. Each village had its own leader. The Quaboags numbered approximately 3,000 and lived in the area that today makes up New Braintree, Barre, Warren, the Brookfields, and part of Sturbridge. Main settlements were along the Quaboag River, and Quacumquasit (South Pond) and Quaboag Ponds. The Quaboag Indians lived a mostly agrarian lifestyle, planting corn and other vegetable crops, hunting and fishing to supplement this food source, and engaging in fur trade with Europeans. They were semi-nomadic, moving depending on the season and where food could be found, but generally returning to the same areas. Each tribe had its own leader, or sachem, and a council which would help make decisions that affected the entire group. They created alliances for protection and had within their power the right to sell land. It was from the sachem of the tribe that the English settlers procured a deed to the area that would become Quaboag Plantation in 1660, the precursor to the town of Brookfield.

Most history books tell of the conflicts that took place between European settlers and indigenous peoples. Lesser known, however, are the conflicts that took place simultaneously among groups of natives. In typical Eurocentric telling of history, the conflicts on the North American continent were reduced to an "us vs. them" story while leaving out the hostilities between different native groups. If not for these hostilities, the natives in the New England region could very well have joined together to fight against the English rather than remaining divided. The Quaboag Indians lived between two larger, sometimes hostile groups. The Mohawk to the west are depicted as a war-like group. They were known for sending small groups of warriors to raid villages, ambush hunters, take prisoners, and demand tribute be paid in deference to their superiority. When they expanded to the east and south into Connecticut, the Quaboags were between them and those they were fighting. There is some evidence, from limited reports to the English, that while the Quaboags more closely identified and allied themselves with native tribes to the east, the Mohawks from the west attempted to control the Quaboags by raiding and ambushing them at different times in the 17th century. In his book, *The Quaboag and Nipmuck Indians,* Donald Duffy gives an account of the Quaboag Indians requesting assistance from the governor of Massachusetts after three of their men were killed by the Mohawks. The governor declined to assist, citing a lack of resources and difficult relations with the Mohawk themselves. It is possible that the Quaboag Indians did not report the full extent of attacks by the Mohawks to the English, but were so desirous of help from the English that when the governor refused military support, they turned to John Elliot, the previously mentioned minister from Roxbury, to establish a presence in their village and teach them the tenets of Christianity. Perhaps they thought a closer relationship with the English though a shared religion would garner them support against their enemy.

More tensions among native tribes occurred when Uncas, a leader of the Mohegan Indians, attacked the Quaboags at their village at Quaboag Pond in

1661, perhaps in retribution against an enemy, Onapequin, who was born in Quaboag and possibly led raids against Uncas. Even though Onapequin was no longer living with the Quaboags, their village was an easier target and one that would most likely fall to Uncas's attack. At the time of the attack, the famous Massasoit was living at Quaboag, attempting to live out the rest of his life in peace rather than dealing with the conflicts arising from expanding English settlements and the fights among the natives. Not wishing a war with Uncas, Massasoit and the Quaboags asked the English for help after seventy of Uncas's men invaded Quaboag, killed three people and took five prisoners, including a woman and two children. Uncas released the woman in return for a promise of ransom, one of the prisoners escaped, and Uncas continued to threaten two remaining prisoners with death and enslavement unless his ransom demands were met. (Pembassua, Quaquequuunset, and Wasamagin. "Declaration of the Dealings of Uncas and the Mohegan Indians to certain Indians, the Inhabitants of Quabaug." Letter to Winthrop, John Jr. 21 May 1661. MS. Quaboag Territory, n.p.). After the attack, the Quaboag Indians were too fearful to travel far from their homes.

At about the same time, the Massachusetts Bay Colony had granted permission to men from Ipswich to settle near Quaboag Pond on a piece of land that measured six square miles. The English were welcomed by the Quaboags as they felt they would help protect their village from attacks by other native groups, or at least be a deterrent to further attacks. Earlier settlements in Massachusetts were along the coast or on water routes as these were easier to travel than the trails that led over land. Therefore, Springfield was settled fairly early as it was accessible via the Connecticut River. Overland travelers had to spend a night in the wilderness and were at the mercy of hostile natives, wild animals and the weather. A permanent English settlement in the area of Quaboag Pond would serve as a safe stopping place for those travelers and was seen as essential for the continued economic growth of the settlements west of Boston.

John Pynchon, founder of Springfield, had great financial interest in seeing an English settlement at Quaboag. He was a member of the Mass Bay legislature and was frequently in the Boston area. After getting assurance from the Quaboag Indians that they would be willing to sell land to the English, he recruited some men who were interested in settling the area. Once this land deal was in the works, Mass Bay officials were more willing to respond favorably to the Quaboag Indians' request for help. They sent a letter to Uncas demanding that he stop raids against the Quaboags and address any concerns to the officials of Massachusetts who would serve as mediators in solving the problem between the two groups. In return for their help, the Quaboag Indians had to agree to send either the returned captives or their children to Mass Bay Colony in order to receive teaching in Puritanism. A small contingent of three to five men were sent to Quaboag and announced the English protection of the area by shooting their guns each night. This brought a time of peace to the Quaboag Indians and the beginning of English settlement in the area.

Part 2

THE FIRST AND SECOND SETTLEMENTS AT BROOKFIELD

While the boundaries of the Quaboag Plantation included only a small portion of what would become the town of East Brookfield, if the town were to have an ancestor, it would be Quaboag Plantation. A brief history of this settlement is helpful in understanding the development of East Brookfield.

The first Europeans to settle in the "New World" kept mainly to areas in close proximity to water routes to facilitate travel by boat. The two most well-known of these Massachusetts settlements were established along the Atlantic Coast by the Pilgrims in Plymouth and then the Puritans in Salem and Boston. However, the Puritans also settled in the area around the Connecticut River, calling the settlement first Agawam and then Springfield. While trade was conducted via the river, there was overland travel between the eastern and western settlements, and gradually these travelers saw the potential for a settlement of it own in the region.

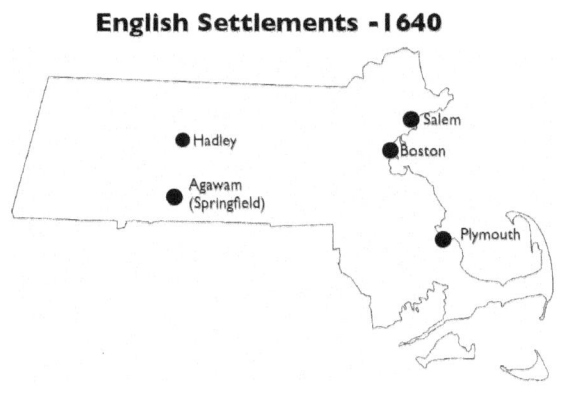

The conditions which made the area attractive to the Quaboag Indians, plentiful streams for fresh water and fishing, fertile land for crops, and forests filled with animals for hunting and timber for building, combined with the opportunity to cater to travelers through the establishment of taverns made the area ripe for settlement by the growing English population. Because the natives had used the land for farming, some of it was already cleared of trees when the first English settlers arrived. This must have added to the obvious potential of the area. Finally, the natives of the area enjoyed a peaceful and productive trade with the English, so the danger of attack seemed small.

John Pynchon, son of the founder of Springfield, was one of the men who saw the economic benefits of a settlement in this middle region between the two larger settlements of Massachusetts. He financed the original purchase price and the settlement costs of the plantation. These costs included building and maintaining a mill for grinding corn at the site. Pynchon purchased the area for 300 fadom of Wampaneage, the currency used by the Indians and made of black and white shells, making it possible to literally make money. Pynchon paid for the land and then English settlers paid him an average of one pound five shillings for each house lot. (Roy, Quaboag Plantation, p51)

The first English settlers to the area that would become known as Quaboag Plantation were from Ipswich and came to the area in 1660. These settlers were given permission from the Massachusetts General Court to purchase and settle on six square miles of land provided that twenty families and a minister be established there within three years. These settlers relied mainly on subsistence farming, hunting and fishing to eke out survival in this relatively remote area, far from larger settlements. The first concentrated area of settlement was on "Foster's Hill," in what is today West Brookfield.

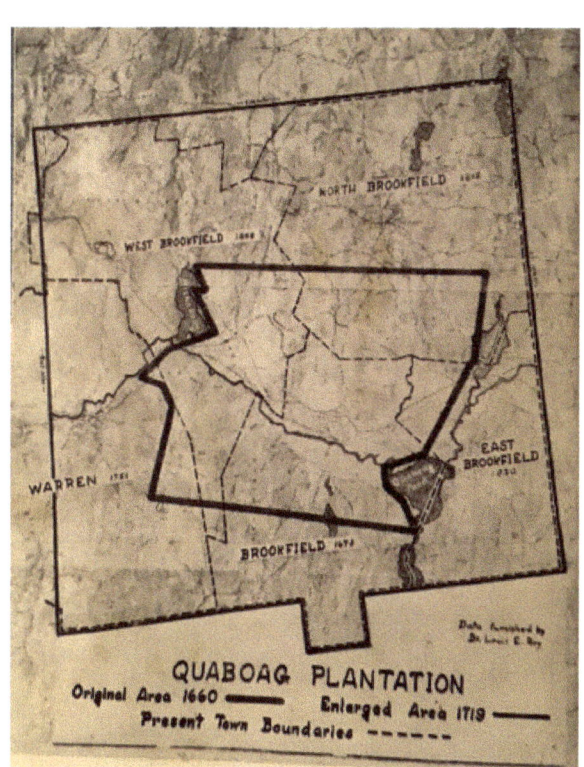

Map showing boundaries of original Quaboag Plantation boundaries and expanded boundaries. Note the original boundaries do not include major bodies of water. These were important to the lifestyles of the natives who needed to retain control over them as part of their food supply. Published on back of Quaboag Plantation's 300th Anniversary Souvenir Program, drawn by Dr. Louis Roy, 1960.

In his book, *Flintlocks and Tomahawks*, Douglas Leach describes the New England landscape of the late 17th century as one mainly covered in lush forests with a very few clearings where villages and fields were located. These sparse villages were connected by "woodland paths," similar to the trails and cart roads that can still be walked today on the Pelletier Woods Property.

Along with the encroaching English settlements, there were native camps in the area. The Wekaboag lived along the shores of Lake Wickaboag in present-day West Brookfield. There were two Nipmuc camps on Quaboag Pond in present-day Brookfield, and one at the fork of the Seven Mile River and the Five Mile River, formerly a steep hill leveled during construction on the East Brookfield railroad station and freight yard. As most of the English settlers settled in Quaboag Plantation, the area that would become East Brookfield continued to be home to many Native American groups.

This time in Massachusetts history was not a tranquil one as there were several small skirmishes with native groups. As the settlers learned how to better survive in New England, there was a population boom, instigating the settlement of more land to provide for the growing population. It took five years from the time the petitioners received approval from the crown before the land was purchased from Shattoockquis, the leader of the Quaboag Indians in November of 1665. It seems likely, based on future land deals with Native Americans, that the "sale" of land to the English for Quaboag Plantation was actually meant to be more of a lease. Native Americans did not have the same ideas regarding individual ownership of land that the English did and would frequently move their villages as game moved or as fields needed to lay fallow. Indians generally saw land deeds as a type of lease, to be renegotiated after the leader who signed them died. This would prove to be a mistake repeated many hundreds of times in North America and capitalized upon by the English as they pushed further and further west.

In his book, *The Quaboag and Nipmuck Indians*, Donald Duffy theorizes that while the written description of the land in the original deed to the settlement in Quaboag is extensive, there must have been additional, verbal agreements, which were never recorded in the deed. As evidence of this, he cites the settlers' request for more land when they had run out of meadows, even though there were meadows within the land outlined in the deed. Duffy believes these meadows must have been still in use by the Indians remaining within the perimeter of the land. Therefore, there must have been some agreement that the English could not use land that the natives were actively using.

In fact, in the fall of 1665, the Quaboag Indians were concerned enough about the new English settlement that they met with Lieutenant Cooper, who was negotiating the land deal on behalf of Pynchon, in an attempt to confine the English to areas that would allow for more space between them and native fields and villages. At the meeting were the chiefs of two Quaboag tribes, one who lived around Quaboag Pond and the other who lived along the shores of Weakapaug, or Wickaboag, as we know it today. This leader, Mettawompe, would later lead Indian forces during King Phillip's War. He was a highly effective warrior and would lead the attacks on settlements at Brookfield, Hatfield, Springfield, and Lancaster. The Indian proposal essentially cut the original acreage of the deed in half. Cooper did some surveying of his own to try to come up with a counter offer that would retain the total amount of the deed at thirty-six square miles.

Anything less and settlers may not come. This is the land that was ultimately in the deed and conveyed to the English to allow settlement.

By 1667, there were eight English families living at Quaboag Plantation. (A History of East Brookfield, Roy: 1965, p.37) While the original grant required twenty families in the first three years, Quaboag was not initially an enticing place for English families to move. The best land was still being used by the Quaboags, and it was prior practice of English to move to places recently vacated by natives as they then would not have to spend time and energy clearing the land; it was already done for them. In 1670, the settlement petitioned the English government to allow them to enlarge their area by six miles each way from the center in order to encompass more cleared land. The petition was denied.

Signs posted at boundaries of original Quaboag Plantation. Photo by author, 2018.

On October 10, 1673, the residents of Quaboag petitioned for township, which would allow them to establish their own government. Their petition was approved on December 19, 1673, the town was named Brookfield, and the land officially deeded to residents. Unfortunately, the new town would not be long-lived.

Tensions had been rising between the English and the natives for many years around a variety of issues. These included disputes over land sales, as well as the different ways in which the English used the land. The English farmers brought with them horses and cattle and often let them roam free, ruining natives' crops. Extensive agrarian land use by the English impacted the ability of natives to hunt in the forests, which were being cut down for farmland or firewood. Damming rivers to harness water power for mills impacted the natives' ability to fish in rivers which had provided a major source of food for them. In 1675, the mostly peaceful coexistence with native tribes and English settlers ended with the start of King Philip's War. At this time, Brookfield's population of twenty families was nearly triple that of newly founded Worcester.

War began further east from Brookfield, when, on June 20, 1675 in Plymouth Colony, a small group of Native Americans from the Pokanoket tribe raided English farms in Swansea. When an English farmer shot and killed a native, all out war erupted, spreading across New England. Over the course of three years, nearly half of all towns in Massachusetts were attacked and twelve were completely destroyed, including the settlement at Brookfield.

Wood carving showing the technique used to set buildings on fire during King Philip's War. By Artist unknown.Hugh Manatee at en.wikipedia [Public domain], from Wikimedia Commons

Brookfield's relatively isolated location made it an obvious target, even though residents of the settlement were convinced that their previously peaceful relations with the natives would protect them from attack. The Nipmucs were traditional allies of the Narragansett and Wampanoag tribes, who had begun the fighting to the east. In fact, the Quaboag Indians, who were part of the larger Nipmuc tribe, were related to King Phillip. His mother was a Quaboag Indian. Because of this, leaders in Boston feared that they would ally with the attacking natives. In August 1675, an armed contingent of British soldiers marched to Quaboag to assess the intentions of the Nipmuc Indians and petition them to ally with the English. The Indians did not come to the planned meeting. The soldiers set off for their camp early the next day, accompanied by several residents of Quaboag, who were not armed, attesting to their belief that their friendly neighbors were not in accord with those who were attacking other Massachusetts towns. The group rode into an ambush, known as Wheeler's Surprise, and eight men were

Historical marker honoring John Ayres, a found of Quaboag Plantation and killed during the 1675 attack on Brookfield. (Photo by author, 2016.)

Site of tavern on Foster Hill Road where Brookfield residents waited out the siege of 1675. (Photo by author, 2016.)

killed; three were Quaboag residents. The men fled back to the town and the entire population of 79 barricaded themselves in Ayres Tavern to wait for help. They held out for three days against an estimated 300 to 500 natives who tried repeatedly to set fire to the tavern. Once reinforcements arrived, the natives left the town, burning all the buildings on their way out. A total of twelve Englishmen were killed and ten wounded in the attack. About eighty Indians were killed and an unknown number wounded. The residents were evacuated and most returned to the towns where they had lived previously, never to return. The town of Brookfield was no more and the area remained empty with the exception of soldiers until 1686 when a second attempt at settlement was made.

King Philip's War brought to reality the perpetual English fear that natives would join together to eliminate their villages and towns. The attack on Brookfield, which had previously had friendly relations with neighboring tribes, was seen as an indication that natives were not to be trusted. This belief resulted in a changed relationship between settlers and natives. After King Philip's War, natives were either executed, sold into slavery in the West Indies, or relegated to reservations, in order for white settlers to feel at peace again. Mettawompe, who was part of the original land deal that resulted in the English settlement at Quaboag Plantation, was hung on the Boston Common. This precedent would be repeated throughout the growth of the United States as English settlers pushed native tribes off their land as they moved west.

While most American Indians who lived in what is today the Podunk section of East Brookfield migrated west after King Philip's War, several families remained and traded and worked among the white settlers, particularly at the Henshaw Tavern. Visitors who were passing time at the tavern in the midst of a long journey could be enticed into a betting game in which coins were placed on a post for a Native American to show their skill with a bow and arrow. If the arrow hit the coin, they kept it as payment. This, along with hunting, trapping and selling baskets to travelers made up the bulk of their livelihood. ("Historic Podunk: Written for Meeting of Historic Society, June 23, 1926, held at "Gray Ledge" alias "Indian Rock House" in Podunk," W.O. Terry.)

Settlement in Brookfield between the years of 1675 and 1686 was comprised of intermittent garrisons of troops and passing travelers between Massachusetts Bay Colony and Springfield. The plentiful natural resources ensured that this area would not remain wilderness for long and James Ford petitioned for a second settlement in 1686. In accordance with the law, if a group wished to resettle an area that was destroyed during King Phillip's War, they had to petition the governor or court in the area to ensure that the rights of previous landowners were protected. Therefore, the second settlement at Brookfield was located somewhat further to the east to make sure that previous landowners would not return to find their land inhabited by others. This second settlement included the area that is the town of East Brookfield today.

In 1690, the settlement consisted of two villages, three miles apart. The one furthest to the west centered around the garrison that was still in use to protect residents and travelers from native attack. The settlement furthest to the east was first settled by Joseph and John Woolcot. They built their homes at the sharp left turn in the Post Road at what is today the intersection of Slab City Road and East Brookfield Road at the North Brookfield town line. The Lawrence and Mason families built homes nearby. In 1693, forty Indians attacked the settlement. Having seen the Indians in the fields near their home, Joseph sent his wife and two young daughters to hide in the woods. When he and his young son left the house to follow, they saw a Native American in the yard. Their dog attacked the man, who fired at the dog

Monument on Slab City Road, placed by the Quaboag Historical Society, 1903. Photo from collection of EB Historical Museum.

while retreating. Joseph grabbed his son and ran for the fort, three miles away in the western part of the new settlement. His wife, Rebecca, and two daughters were discovered and killed. Joseph Mason's house was attacked and he and his son were killed, but the Indians took his wife and infant child captive. The infant was killed soon after their capture. Neighbor Thomas Lawrence was also killed in the attack, and his eighteen-year-old brother Daniel was taken captive. A third Lawrence brother rode the thirty miles to Springfield to get help from the troops stationed there as there were only six troops in the Brookfield barracks.

Forty-two troops set out to track the Indians and their captives, eventually rescuing Daniel Lawrence and Mrs. Mason and killing fifteen attackers. Daniel Lawrence left Brookfield and returned to live in Charlestown; Mrs. Mason and her husband remained in Brookfield. During this time, the residents of the eastern portion of Brookfield were ordered to evacuate their homes and remain in the garrison until the threat had subsided. A stone on the side of Slab City Road, just over the town line into North Brookfield, memorializes this event. The stone reads *"Near this spot, Thomas Lawrence, Joseph Mason and son, Mrs. Joseph Woolcot and two children were killed by Indians in 1693."* This marker is across from what was the site of Woolcot's Tavern, built in 1723. For many years, this portion of the Post Road was known as "Woolcot Corner."

Attacks by Indians continued sporadically over the next decades. In 1694, Indians attacked two men in the woods in the easterly part of town, killing John Lawrence, whose brother was killed in the attack the previous year. The 1704 attack on Deerfield so frightened the residents of Brookfield, that they did not feel safe working in their fields, their major economic activity. They requested permission from the governor to either abandon the settlement or be paid as soldiers. Even though it was expensive to keep the garrison at Brookfield and pay residents for their efforts in protecting the settlement, "to abandon Deerfield and Brookfield would be to leave the western frontier exposed to further surprise assaults." (Roy, History of East Brookfield, p 64). It appears as though the governor gave in as several landowners in what is today East Brookfield were also listed as soldiers in the Brookfield garrison in 1706, including John Perry, John Hamilton, Joseph Bannister, Edward Walker, Edward Kellogg, and Robert Eommons. (Roy, History of East Brookfield, p 69). In his book *History of East Brookfield*, Dr. Louis Roy included an account from John Woolcot of being captured by natives in 1708. John Clary and Robert Grainger were fired upon by natives while walking along the road in the eastern part of the settlement in August 1709. Grainger was killed instantly and Clary was wounded. Coincidentally, both men's families had been involved in Indian attacks in the past. Grainger was the brother of Rebecca Woolcot, who was killed in the 1693 attacks and ironically, the two were killed on nearly the exact spot. John Clary's father had been killed by Indians in 1688. John Kellogg, John Grosvenor, and Stephen Jennings were attacked and killed in 1710 while cutting hay. During this time, the residents must have been in a constant state of anxiety and fear.

These sporadic attacks were perhaps a reason why the second settlement at Brookfield did not attract many new settlers. The low population led to financial difficulties for the town and resulted in a petition to the General Court on May 26, 1701 asking for support in three ways. The first was financial support to pay for the services of a minister, the second was for permission to tax nonresident landowners for maintenance of the land, and the third was a request to expand the boundaries of the settlement to twelve square miles, centered on Foster Hill. As a result of this support, additional settlers were attracted to the area. Fifteen additional land grants were recorded, seven of which were within the current town of East Brookfield. Several of those who settled in Brookfield at this time were veterans of colonial wars and brought individual skills as artisans to the area.

Mills were essential in grinding grain to make flour and in cutting lumber, but during the time of the second settlement, there were no operating mills in Brookfield. Residents needed to travel to Springfield to use the mills there. There was great interest in building mills in the Brookfield settlement so people did not need to travel so far for this essential service. Those who were able to build mills for community use were rewarded. For example, on July 12, 1718, the Committee for Brookfield rewarded John Wolcott with forty acres of land due to the *"great expense...in building a gristmill: and now he is designing and has done considerable towards the building of a sawmill which is probably to be very benefitiall [sic] to the town..."* (Record Book of the Proprietors of Brookfield (Mass.), 1701-1772, Special Collections, University of Massachusetts, https://archive.org/details/PR17011772Part1, page 24.) Louis Roy, in his book *History of East Brookfield,* wrote that the foundation of the gristmill could still be seen off North Brookfield Road in East Brookfield, about 400 feet southeast of the junction of Old East Brookfield Road. Wooden remnants of this gristmill can be seen in the East Brookfield Historic Museum.

By 1718, the town of Brookfield was economically stable due both to the busy grist- and sawmills and the full taverns that catered to travelers along the road between the Boston area and Springfield. There were fifty families living in the community, the meetinghouse was mostly complete, and there was an established church with a minister. The requisites for creating a town were met and on November 12, 1718, the House of Representatives invested the residents of Brookfield "with all powers, privileges, and authorities to direct, order and manage all the affairs of ye said Township." (Record Book of the Proprietors of Brookfield (Mass.), 1701-1772, Special Collections, University of Massachusetts, https://archive.org/details/PR17011772Part1, page 252.) By the end of the year, the Committee for Brookfield, which had governed the settlement from Springfield, was disbanded and Brookfield established its own governing body.

In 1719, the original borders of the town were expanded, resulting in the town of Brookfield encompassing eight square miles. In the east, this expansion included Lakes Quaboag and Quacumquasit and a majority of the land that would become the village of East Brookfield. The area around the two lakes was once home to native Americans who, by this time were much diminished in number, having either migrated further west or been killed in King Philip's War. This allowed their former lands to be acquired by the English settlers. These lakes would become essential to the economy of East Brookfield, and perhaps gaining these valuable water resources was the reason for the expansion. Residents would fish in the lakes and hunt along the shores; pottery and brick kilns were built on the shores of both lakes, and later in the 1800s and early 1900s, they would be home to parks providing for the entertainment of residents and tourists.

As more settlers came to the colonies, King Charles II ordered the "King's Highway" or the "Great Highway," built to provide a means of faster travel and communication among English settlers in the colonies. This "Bay Path" was first laid out in 1673, mostly following existing trails. It began in Watertown, traveled through Framingham to Marlboro, then to Quaboag and on to Springfield. This route between Boston and Springfield was expanded upon and became known as the "Post Road" since it was the path used to deliver the mail. The first rider to deliver mail using this route started his journey in New York City on January 22, 1673 and arrived in Boston two weeks later after traveling 200 miles through a nearly unbroken wilderness with the potential of encountering unfriendly natives. The "highway" first extended from Boston to Marlboro and then extended to Brookfield and later Springfield and eventually all the way to New York City via Hartford, Connecticut. Initially, mail was delivered once per month by a rider on horseback who packed letters and small packages in saddlebags as he traveled from Boston to New York, through the Brookfields and then back again. Another duty of the early post riders was to direct travelers to the best trails and taverns along the route or even act as a guide. It also fell to the post rider to designate places along the road where he would pick up letters and packages for delivery.

As the Bay Path followed mainly established trails, its route was often circuitous. To avoid hills that would tax horses and oxen, the Bay Path's route through the east village of Brookfield was shaped like an "s." Travelers would come from the east and down what is today Gleason Street to Route 9. The road then turned down what is today Cottage Street, almost to the Seven Mile River, then continued on its way west by leading behind where the Baptist Church now stands. From there, the road straightened out again. It was the building of the dam across the Five Mile River in 1825 that eventually straightened the road. The new lake formed a barrier but the earthen dam served as a crossing point for the road. (Hodgkins, Martha A. "Address to Quaboag Historical Society." East Brookfield, 3 June 1903.)

When forest trails developed into wider paths, the lone riders were replaced by horse-drawn wagons and stagecoaches. With these forms of transportation, more passengers could make a journey between Boston and New York or anywhere in between. As a result, inns and taverns grew up along the Post Roads to provide food and lodging for the carrier and the passengers. Over time, the so-called "Post roads" expanded until there were three: the Upper Post Road, Middle, and Lower Post road were later added. All three Post Roads converged in New Haven and from there traveled to New York City. The Upper Post Road corresponds to what is today Route 20 until Worcester, when it follows the present Route 9 and Route 67 in East Brookfield. The road then turns left onto Slab City Road in North Brookfield and eventually reconnects with Route 9.

In 1751, Benjamin Franklin was appointed to the quite elaborately-named office of "Joint Deputy Postmaster and Manager of His Majesty's Provinces and Dominions on the Continent of North America." He and the other deputy were charged with improving the mail service to be more consistent, secure and efficient. In 1753, Franklin spent over two months in New England to help mediate complaints between post riders and constituents over the cost of sending mail. Post riders were estimating distances and charging accordingly. The cost of mail delivery was determined by its weight and the length it needed to travel. (Lamoureux, Danielle. "What Paved the Way for Route 9?" Spencer New Leader 27 Sept. 1995: 6-7. Print.) According to the original story of the Post Road, Franklin invented an odometer to measure out distances more accurately. This device was attached to a wagon wheel which made a "click" at each revolution. The noises were then counted to measure out a mile.

In 1971, the editor of the Benjamin Franklin papers at Yale called into question the veracity of this seemingly well-known historical detail. He wrote, "Not one document in this very substantial mass of contemporary documents has been found to contain so much as a single reference to roadside

Post Road Marker built into stone wall on Main Street, East Brookfield. Photo by author, 2016.

Boston Post Road Marker, or "Franklin Stone" on North Brookfield Road. Photo by author, 2016.

milestones, erected by Franklin or by any other persons." ("The Boston Post Road Historical Markers That Get The Facts Wrong." New England Historical Society, 2016,) As a result, sometimes these markers are referred to as 1767 Stones instead of Franklin Stones.

Regardless of whose idea they were, these markers are familiar relics of life in colonial Massachusetts. According to local historian Bob Wilder in 2006, the longest continuous stretch of markers could be found in the eighteen miles between Leicester and Warren. At that time, the lettering on some had nearly faded away due to rain or salting in the winter. Local historical commissions installed signs near each of the mile markers in 2006. In East Brookfield, there are two markers; one on Route 9 and one on North Brookfield Road. Both are on the National Register of Historic Places. The marker on Route 9 is in embedded in the stone wall in front of 318 Main Street, on the westbound side of the road. The one on North Brookfield Road is across the street from the aptly-named Bay Path Golf Course. Following the Post Road route will give travelers an idea of what travel was like for early residents of our town.

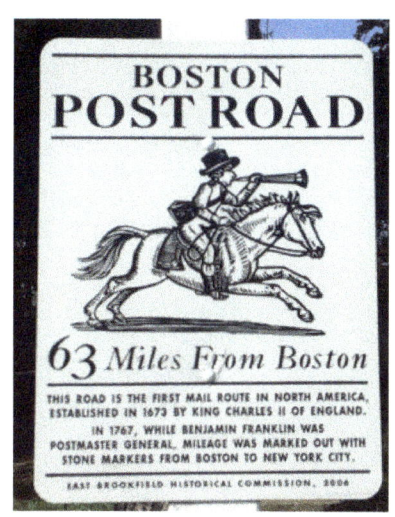

Historical Marker, North Brookfield Road, designed by Ron Couture, placed by EB Historical Commission.

Not only were the markers used for determining postage, they were also used to communicate during the Revolution about the location of troops. In addition, those who lived along the Post Road were able to boast of the variety of traffic that passed by them. People who were moving west, roaming pastors, traveling salesmen and tradesmen, and other types of nomadic people, as well as dignitaries and armies used the Post Road to get from Boston to points west. In the winter of 1775/1776, those living along the Post Road witnessed General Henry Knox pulling 60 tons of cannons and other munitions from Fort Ticonderoga along the shore of

Author Unknown. Hauling guns by ox teams from Fort Ticonderoga for the siege of Boston, 1775. Illustration. National Archives, Public Domain, 111-SC-100815.)

Lake Champlain to Boston to lay siege to the British. This ultimately led to the British evacuation of the city, which is still commemorated in the city today.

The town wasted no time building and improving upon the roads and bridges that would serve to connect residents to each other, to the mills, and to the meetinghouse. In 1720, a portion of rivers and adjoining land were set aside for building more mills, including the Seven Mile River from Hamilton's Mill to the town line. Also in 1720, two roads were built that residents still travel on a daily basis. The first was called "The New County Road" and corresponds with Route 9 from the Spencer town line, through the center of East Brookfield and along North Brookfield Road, then turning and reconnecting with Route 9 to continue into Brookfield and West Brookfield. Also built at this time was Matchock Road which connected the New Country Road to the mills on the Five Mile River and corresponds roughly to Harrington Street today. The bridge across the Five Mile River on the north side of Lake Lashaway was built in 1732; the bridge across the East Brookfield River on the northern shore of Lake Quaboag was built in 1730. The road we now call West Sturbridge Road was laid out in 1731. In 1737, Howe Street was built, running from Adams Road to what is today Young Road and connecting with the Post Road, approximately where Cove Street is today. (Louis Roy, History of East Brookfield...page 96-97) Prior to the creation of Lake Lashaway, the so-called "Cove District" was the town center. It wasn't until after 1870 that Howe Street connected with Podunk Road at the Seven Mile River, perhaps because the hill called Vizard's Hill or Los's Hill was too steep to easily traverse by horse and wagon. The building and maintenance of roads and bridges continued into the 1750s, attesting to the growing population and economy of not only the town of Brookfield, but the easterly section as well.

The roads were a key means of transporting soldiers and militia west when the French and Indian War broke out in 1754. The British were attempting to limit French influence in the area west of its North American colonies. This war eventually expanded to Europe where it was known as the Seven Years' War. Nathaniel Woolcot, Abraham Adams, and Joseph Walker, all of the village of East Brookfield fought in the war. Adams and Walker were injured in battle and each received pensions for their service. Woolcot served as an officer and also housed soldiers who were traveling to and from the frontier in his East Brookfield tavern. The settlement in the "Easterly Section" of Brookfield was soon to become a major industrial center of the region.

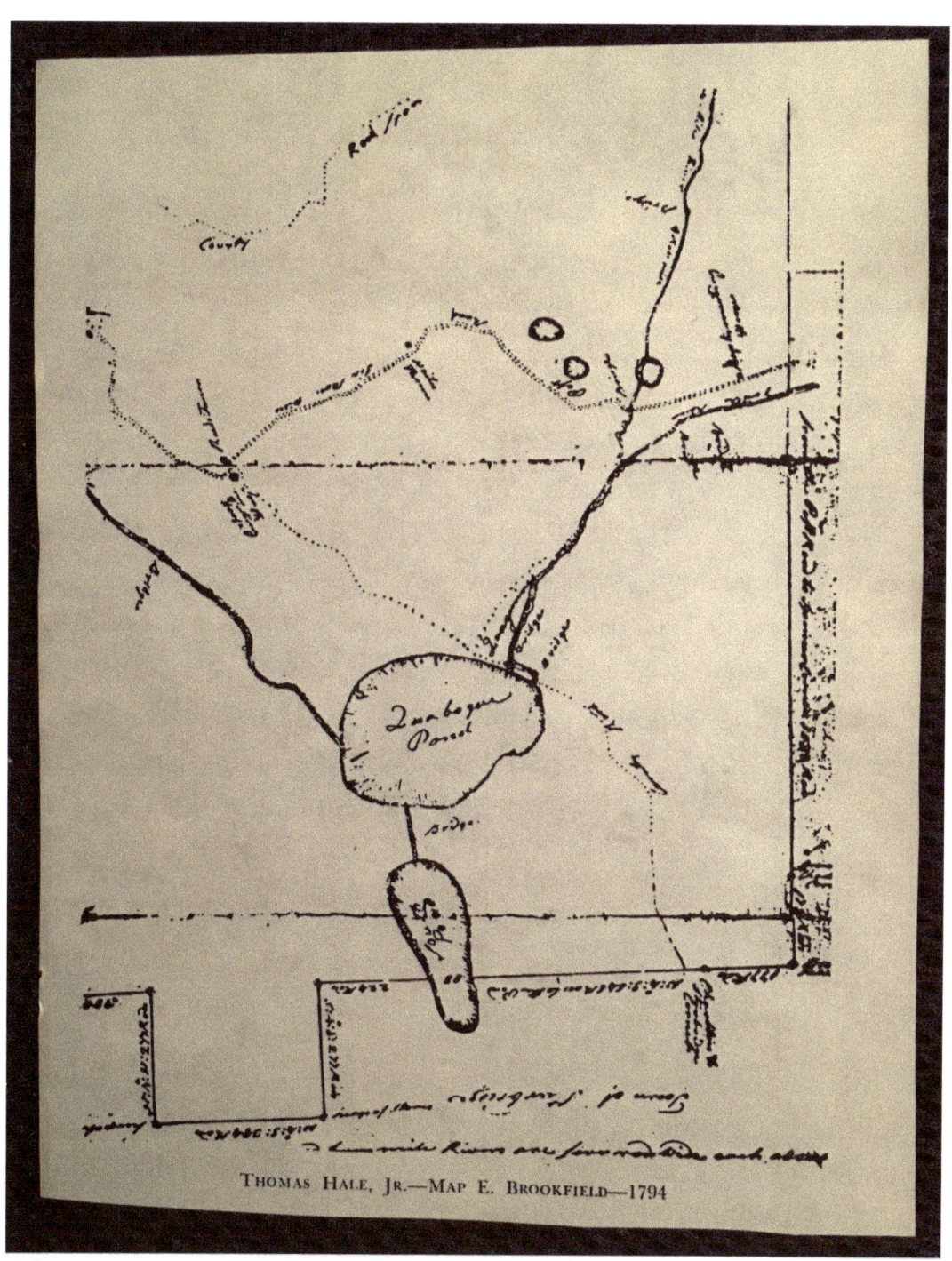

THOMAS HALE, JR.—MAP E. BROOKFIELD—1794

The 1794 Map of Brookfield was commissioned by the Selectmen of the Town of Brookfield and created by Thomas Hale, Jr, a certified surveyor. According to this map, the town contained 38,500 acres of land, including eight ponds. At the time of the survey, there was one iron works, seven corn mills, six saw mills, and three fulling mills located along streams. The Post Road is indicated on the map with a double row of dots. Photocopy of map that is part of the collection of East Brookfield Historical Commission.

Part 3

LIFE IN THE EASTERLY SECTION

As early as two years after Brookfield was incorporated as a town, there were distinct regions that were commonly referred to in town documents. The portion of the town that would become East Brookfield was referred to as the "Easterly Section." This portion of town grew quickly, eventually having its own industry, schools, and religious groups, perhaps due to its relative isolation from the rest of Brookfield. Land in the Easterly Section was more hilly and wet, and not as good for farming as land further west where agriculture was the main livelihood, so industry developed here instead. Farmers still grew crops such as hay, root vegetables, and grains and kept traditional farm animals, but farming on a large scale was not possible as it was in other areas of Brookfield.

Residents took advantage of the many streams to built grist mills, saw mills, and textile mills. There were several mills along the Five and Seven Mile Rivers. The mills allowed the Easterly Section to prosper during the American Revolution as manufacturers of goods for the Continental Army. A later factor in the growth of the Easterly Section as an economic center of the region was proximity to railroad tracks. It was relatively easy for materials to be transported into and out of town.

POTTERY

One of the major industries in the easterly section of Brookfield in the 18th and 19th centuries was the manufacture of bricks and ceramics. The first potter noted in historical records was Ezekiel Stevens, whose business was located on what would eventually be the northern shore of Lake Lashaway. At the time, it was located on the shore of the Five Mile River as Lake Lashaway would not exist until 1825. After Ezekiel's death, his nephew, Jeduthan, took over his business and began manufacturing bricks.

Amos Harrington learned the potter trade while living in what would become West Brookfield and relocated to the Easterly Section in the late 1770s. He built a shop at the corner of Harrington and Main Streets and began making brown earthenware. At the time, this was the main section of the village. After the creation of the lake, the village center shifted to southern shore of the lake and Harrington moved his shop here as well. He sold milk jugs, pie plates, pans, pots, pitchers, and other household goods to shops and customers in a 30-mile radius. ("Pottery in Brookfield: Prosperity Delights in Details." Spencer Sun, Jan 24, 1873) His major product, however, was malt roof tiles. These were considered preferable to English-made tiles and Harrington took orders from Boston, Providence, New York, Philadelphia, Baltimore, and Worcester. When not working in the fields, his sons, Thomas, Amos and Charles, worked at the shop and his son Charles took over and ran the pottery until 1836.

Advertisement for brick company. (Spencer Sun, August 18, 1880.)

Two other potters in the Easterly Section at this time were Nathan Porter and Justus Stevens. Nathan Porter arrived in 1793 and established a business that was run by two more generations of his family. Justus Stevens made sieves in town. Sieves were necessary to sift out the more course grains when making bread. Having someone in town who made these was a boon to the local residents since if they didn't have one, they must borrow this necessary tool from someone. Stevens peddled these from door to door, collecting hair from horse's tails (one of the materials used in making the sieves) while he was selling. Yet another pottery was run by Richard Linley and Abner Wight. This pottery was located just south of Route 9 and just east of the railroad spur that crossed Route 9 and followed Route 67 to North Brookfield. The business operated until 1888 when it was sold and the new owners moved the business to Southbridge. (Watkins, Lura Woodside. Early New England Potters and Their Wares. LaVergne, TN: Nabu Press, 2011.)

By the time of the Civil War, two brickyards in town produced 700,000 bricks annually. Brick and pottery making expanded and reached their peak in the 1880s and 1890s when three brickyards and a pottery were in operation. The largest was that of Twitchell and Brewster located on the southwest shore of Lake Quacumquasit. In the 1870s a steam boat by the name of "Dolly Hazzard" was used to carry finished bricks and workers between South Pond and Quaboag Pond along the Quaboag River to the railroad depot in the center of town. (Spencer Sun, August 13, 1874) This steamship was later replaced by a larger one, 60 feet long and 20 feet wide. This flat-bottomed boat could carry 40,000 bricks on its deck and another 40,000 on a scow towed behind it. Bricks were loaded on and off the barge with a derrick for the several daily trips between the factory and the railroad. In the 1880s the Quaboag Railroad was built to carry the bricks between the yards and to carry travelers between the village and the lakes.

The demand for bricks was so great that work sometimes continued through the winter and at night. The steamship had a searchlight that could be used to light the work area at night. Bricks from the Easterly Section were used in the construction of Trinity Church in Boston, Boston Latin School, dorms at Harvard University, and the Worcester State Hospital and Insane Asylum.

Both lakes were popular picnic spots for families and community groups. Work in mills, as opposed to work on farms, gave people set time off from work. Many spent this time at the nearby lakes. The same barge that transported bricks during the work week could carry up to three hundred people from the train depot in East Brookfield to the lakes on the weekends and holidays. The men who worked at the brick plant would supplement their paychecks by catching fish and making chowder to sell to vacationers.

The local production of wheels resulted in local businesses that sold carriages. (Spencer Sun, June 25, 1880)

The East Brookfield Pressed Brick Company had an extensive operation in order to produce an average of 20,000 bricks per day. First, they dug through the top soil to reach clay, transported it via a moveable railroad track to a tank where it was mixed with sand, and then poured into molds. It was then transported via rail to drying houses and then to kilns that held up to 350,000 bricks at a time. Bricks from this company were brought to the C.L. Moulton brickyard and used in the building of the Worcester sewer system as well as building projects in Newton, Massachusetts and Pawtuxet, Rhode Island. At one point, they were so busy they reopened the Twitchell and Brewster brick yard at South Pond in order to make two million bricks in one summer. ("The New Brick Yard." Brookfield Times, June 3, 1887)

The Parmenter Manufacturing Company, incorporated in 1890, was originally a pottery manufacturer but then transitioned to a brick maker, taking advantage of the readily available and high quality clay in town. Their operation was located over a five acre area at the end of what is today Connie Mack Drive. They produced high-quality bricks that were used in building projects within a one hundred mile radius. Their proximity to the railroad tracks was a benefit to their business. The body of water behind the Town Hall is called Clay Pit Pond as it was originally dug out during the manufacture of pottery and bricks.

Stevens, William X. *Improvement in Dominoes.* 17 June 1873.

MANUFACTURING

Manufacturing of cast iron was also plentiful in East Brookfield. After the dam was built across the Five Mile River, The Worcester and Brookfield Furnace Company was established and the former Jeduthan Stevens Pond became known as Furnace Pond. While it would eventually fail due to lack of raw materials, the company employed twenty-five men and produced 300 tons of castings for machinery, farm tools, and some stoves and was one of the main industries in the Easterly Section.

Charles Varney manufactured awl handles, pegging machines, and shoemaking appliances. In response to the variety of manufacturers in the area, the Woolcott Mills, operated by Charles W. Russell of North Brookfield Road worked to maintain and repair machinery, steam engines, sewing machines and guns. The George Forbes and Company Wheel Manufactory was the oldest wheel manufacturer in Massachusetts. It was founded in 1840 and purchased from the original owner in 1860 by George Forbes. The factory was located off Mechanic Street along the shore of the Seven Mile River. This factory was water-powered with a four-foot wheel generating about 60 horsepower. They averaged fifteen sets of wheels per day and during the Civil War produced eleven sets of cannon wheels for the government each day and became the largest carriage wheel manufacturer in New England. They had another factory in Springfield.

Other businesses were located in the Forbes Company's four-story building and the whole enterprise was a study in early U.S. trade. The wood used to make the wheels came from Ohio and Vermont and the hubs were made in Maine and New Hampshire. Another business, J.N. Vaughn and Company, produced all the spokes used in the manufacture of the wheels. The wood for the spokes was locally produced. Other businesses were M&J Hobbs, a machine shop which made "Curtis Shoe Leather Cutters," and Mordecai Carey's business, which made Carey Shingle Machines. The black birch and maple shingles made using this method were made from lumber from Vermont and sought-after in nearly every state for their superior quality.

In yet another room in this building was an inventor and patent attorney by the name of William X. Stevens. His inventions include such diverse items from improvements in breech loading fire arms, lathes, and vices, to alternate forms of the game of Dominoes using 8-sided blocks, and other "expedients for lessening labor for the lazy sons of men." (Spencer Sun, August 15, 1873)

During the mid to late 1800s, there were three woolen mills in town that employed nearly three hundred workers. Textile mills produced 900,000 yards of denim just before the Civil War, which cut off the cotton supply and stopped production. The Brookfield Manufacturing Company was a major industry in the Easterly Section. Established in 1850, they manufactured cotton goods until the Civil War and then they began producing flannel. At the height of production, they had forty-six looms, seventy employees, and produced approximately half a million yards of fabric each year. The water-powered factory building was 45 by 75 feet with an eighteen foot wheel that produced an estimated fifty horsepower.

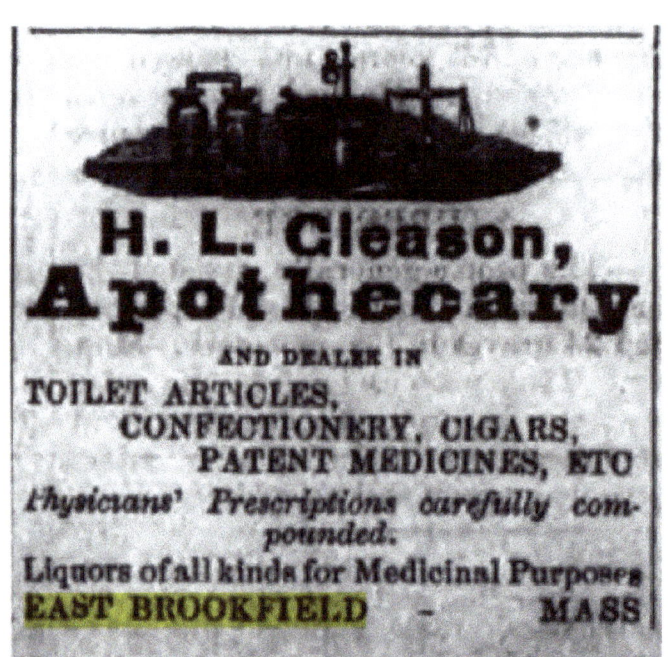

Businessmen had several interests as shown in this ad for Gleason's apothecary. Gleason also had a sawmill in town and built several houses on what would become Gleason Avenue. (Spencer Sun June 3, 1881)

A cloth mill was established in 1880 by Noah Sagendorph from Spencer. Sagendorph purchased an existing cotton mill and transformed it into East Brookfield Woolen Company in 1883. They became the largest producer of shoddy in the eastern United States. Shoddy is a low-quality fabric that was made from recycling rags and the byproducts of producing woolen cloth. It is also referred to as rag wool and was used to make low-cost clothing and other products, such as blankets. Some of the remnants from the process of shredding and grinding the material were sold to farmers for fertilizer or made into stuffing for mattresses. This business moved out of town in 1895.

The Mann and Stevens Woolen Company moved to East Brookfield in 1897 and employed about one hundred people to produce woolen and worsted cloth.

It had two factories: one located on the Seven Mile River at the junction of Podunk Road and Howe Street, and the other at the Lake Lashaway Dam on the Five Mile River, both taking advantage of the water power in its manufacture of satin and wool fabrics. The two factories were both four stories in height. When business declined, the company downsized to just the factory by the Seven Mile River. Some of the land at this location was sold to the Town of East Brookfield in 1937 and the Highway Department was located here for several decades.

The company was a casualty of the Great Depression and went out of business in 1939. The property was auctioned off in six separate parcels and included a mixture of brick and wooden buildings with over 40,000 square feet of space, various equipment, two tenement houses, and a 17.5 acre mill pond. (Pamphlet: "Liquidation Sale by Public Auction" February 1939, part of EB Historical Museum Collection). The factory was being operated as a shoddy mill in 1943 when it burned to

---

> A Day in the Life …
>
> *April 3, 1875: S cloudy and dull with drizzling rain. I did chores to the barn and worked on rug. Addie baked pies and cake and other housework and sewed on her dress. she went to the village p.m. and got some things for me….*
>
> *April 19, 1875: April 19 NW cold as winter, below freezing all day. Clara and I washed and washed the floors, the clothes froze before we could get them hung on the line. Did chores to the barn, sewed and mended in the afternoon …*
>
> *April 23, 1875: April 23 SW fair and pleasant Went to North Brookfield; Windsor and Addie went with me. Windsor fixed horse stable a.m. and did other work. Dr. Hodgkins called a.m. Bought grass seed to Warren's, took butter to Sibley's, 10 lbs got coffee and other things …*
>
> ---
>
> *Excerpts from diary of Mary Ann Harrington, Podunk (Howe Street) resident, age 61.*

the ground.

In 1916, Daniels Manufacturing Company purchased the land at the Lake Lashaway Dam from the Quaboag Manufacturing Company, which had previously leased it to the Mann and Stevens Mill. The Daniels Manufacturing Company ran a woolen mill in Connecticut and expanded that business in the village of East Brookfield, employing 300 workers. This was a great relief to residents as the mill complex here was a large employer in the town and had been empty for seven years.

The Greyhound Bicycle Company came to East Brookfield in 1894. It had been operating in Springfield as the Cole and Gerald Manufacturing Company. Unfortunately, the company went bankrupt in 1896 due to unpaid bills and alleged fraudulent transfer of property. Emerson H. Stoddard, a resident of East Brookfield and former president of the company, bought the property at a cost of $8,000. He planned to run the company under the same name, which caused a former investor in the company, E.L. Cole, to lease an unused building in town and begin his own bicycle manufacturing company. By the beginning of 1898, the Greyhound Bicycle Company appeared to have overcome its financial challenges and was in full production of their newest model which weighed twenty-three pounds and cost $50. However, by the end of that year, the company had closed due to lack of business. Several closings were eventually followed by a permanent closure of the company. ("The Wheel: Cycling Trade Review," New York and Chicago, 1896 & 1898 & 1899.) This appears to have been a pattern in the

Mann and Stevens Mill auction booklet, from collection of EB Historical Museum.

The 'lockup' was located in the basement of the fire department. Most arrests in town were related to public drunkenness or vagrancy. Subsequent articles note that in the first three months of the new jail being opened, 200 'tramps' spent the night. Common practice was to give them a meal in the morning before sending them on their way. This was determined to be costing the town too much money and tramps were no longer allowed to use the jail as free room and board. (The Brookfield Times, January 2, 1902.)

> The new lockup is now completed and East Brookfield can boast of the best institution of the kind to be found in this vicinity. The place is nicely finished, has a hard wood floor, and is well heated and lighted. The room to be used for those not criminals is large and contains two bunks. The criminal ward consists of two steel cages with a bunk in each. The place will be named after its first occupant.

industry throughout the country as many other bicycle companies were also closing plants or going out of business.

In June 1900, Stoddard sold the Greyhound bicycle factory to the Speedway Wheel Company, of Ware. The company produced "high class pneumatic speedway and road carriages" (Roy, <u>History of East Brookfield,</u> 187-189), pneumatic ball-bearing carriage wheels and controlled several patent rights for new products. They had about forty employees.

Many industries, factories and businesses came and went over the years for a variety of reasons. Some because there was a change in the economy, some due to a change in the demand for the items they produced, others due to a change in technology that made their product obsolete. Regardless of the reason, East Brookfield was a booming industrial center for a long period of time. Not including those already noted, the following is a partial listing of factories in East Brookfield in the 1800s and early 1900's.:

- Joseph Mullen - woolen goods manufacturer with 90 employees, produced 216,000 yards of fabric yearly.
- E.I. Cole and Co - 50 employees made insole and heeling leather goods.
- G.N Brown - 35 employees in the East Brookfield Pottery Works.
- J.G. Avery made anti-friction bearings for cars, carriages, bicycles and other vehicles.
- Green, Twitchell, and Company boot and shoe factory, employed 150 people and produced 10,000 cases of shoes and boots annually.
- Fred Seminster manufactured shoddy with about forty employees.
- C.T. Varney & Co had 25 employees making the Varney Pegging Machine.
- William Tucker made saw-filing machinery.
- E&J Hobbs made leather-splitting machines
- Jesse Moulton's Iron Foundry
- Amasa Stevens made all kinds of hammocks
- J.N. Vaughn & Son made wooden spokes
- C.P. Pettingill manufactured novelties and toys.
- F.L. Moreau's Carriage Ironing Shop,
- E.L. Drake's Bottling Establishment
- J.D. Randlett, Warren Corey, and H.L. Gleason' all ran lumber and saw mills
- EJ Nichols' Carriage Shop
- Linley, Wight, and Co, pottery
- Israel Wedge, boxes

A Day in the Life...

"The bowling alley craze has struck EB hard. A few weeks ago Henry Gleason installed two box ball alleys in one of Nathan Warren's buildings on Main St and has done a rushing business. Now W.J. Vizard is having two regulation alleys fitted up in the opera house building on Mechanic Street. ... Mr. Gleason has made arrangements to have the building that he occupies enlarged and when the addition is completed he will put in two of the latest improved slate alleys. The building will be 80 feet long and large windows will be put in the rear end. From the alleys can be had a full view of Lake Lashaway."

- *The Brookfield Times, August 12, 1904*

- C.A. Sable - awl halves
- John P. Day - wholesale western dressed beef
- CM Rand's Iron Works. (Brookfield Times, February 1, 1883)

In the early 1900's, when many across the country began working for fair labor practices, the factories in East Brookfield were notified that employing children under the legal age could not continue (The Brookfield Times, August 6, 1909.) and in 1910 when the 56-hour-a-week law was implemented for women and children, "the employees of the Mann and Stevens Woolen Co in the weave room are working shorter hours." (The Brookfield Times, January 7, 1910).

Clearly, East Brookfield was an industrial center at this time! In fact, in 1881, Brookfield town assessors noted that the decrease in property value in "Old Brookfield" was offset by the increase in East Brookfield. This was the same as in years past but it was noted that "*Even the prosperity of East Brookfield has not been able to overbalance the decrease caused by Old Brookfield's decay.*" (Spencer Sun, June 17, 1881) It is little wonder that agitation for separation continued.

The Easterly Section was not only an industrial center, but a tourist destination as well. Summer cottages were built around the lake, most owned by merchants and businessmen from nearby Spencer, and the population of the town nearly doubled every summer. A hotel where the 308 Lakeside Restaurant is currently located was a popular stopping place for travelers. Built in 1864, this hotel was named the Lakewood House. In 1885, the hotel was renamed the Crystal House. In 1909 a fire necessitated renovations and the name was changed back to the Lakewood House. The East Brookfield Literary Association met here for some time and had a reading room, a precursor to a town

Postcard showing the "New Crystal House," looking west on Route 9 towards the center of town. From collection of East Brookfield Historical Museum.

library since it was so far to the library in Brookfield. There was a boat dock in the rear, a public swimming area, and later, a billiard room was added. When the hotel was sold in 1915, it was assessed at $6800 and was described as a twenty room hotel with a cafe in the back, stables and one to two acres of land. (Brookfield Times, July 10, 1915) The stables would eventually be converted to a twelve-car garage. The hotel was destroyed by fire in the late 1950s and a smaller inn named the Lashaway Inn was built at the location.

Housing was in high demand due to the need for workers in the factories and mills. H.L. Gleason built several homes and boarding houses on his property, Gleason Hill. After he built seven houses, the local paper noted that the street should be renamed, "Gleason Avenue," (Spencer Sun, March 12, 1880.) which it eventually was. Tenements were built in town and most of the properties owned by factories also included housing for workers.

Along with the increase in residents, there was an increase in stores to sell provisions and provide services to residents and visitors. The stores along Main Street included a bakery in a building that was just to the east of the Trolley Stop, along with various lunchrooms and pool rooms, waiting rooms for the trolley, a barbershop, a hat store, and a branch of the library.

The East Brookfield of the late 1800s and early 1900s would not be familiar to the residents of today, particularly the area around Depot Square. L & N Warren General Store was on Pleasant Street where the Depot Square Deli is today. This building housed a general store and apartments for many years before becoming the offices of the American Express Company. It was purchased by Arthur LeDoux in 1915 and became, and has remained, a general store since that time. L. Doane and Company's general store was located in what is an empty space between the deli and post office today. The brick building on Mechanic Street was divided into four different shops, at different points in time housing a grocery store, tailer, cobbler, drug store, general store, the branch library, and the post office. The wooden house to the right of the brick building was also divided into multiple spaces and contained a barber shop, a hat shop, a general store, and the post office at various times.

The current Senior Center was originally called "Fay's Hall" and was a meeting house for town affairs. These included meetings regarding the desire for separation from Brookfield and in 1888, a meeting to "redeem the town of Brookfield from the reproach of being a rum community" (*The Brookfield Times*, March 30, 1888) by disallowing liquor licenses in town. According to the article, the supporters of liquor licenses far outnumbered those against it. The number of liquor licenses continued to be limited. In 1901, there were two licenses given out in Brookfield and two in East Brookfield; in previous years, two licenses were awarded in Brookfield and only one in East Brookfield. This regulation didn't stop several local establishments from continuing to sell alcohol. Raids at the time by the constable were plentiful, though it seems the fine imposed did little to stop them. At the end of the 1800s, Fay's Hall had a pool room and bar in the basement with office space and a drug store on the first floor. At the turn of the century, it became the home of the Improved Order of Red Men (I.O.R.M).

In 1887, construction began on the building commonly known today as "the Keith Block." Built by William G. Keith with the intention of moving his business here, the three story brick building would become an iconic sight in the village. Its location in Depot Square meant that residents visiting the stores

A view of Depot Square from railroad tracks. Keith Block on the upper right. Emerson, Paesiello. Keith's block. 07 Apr 1906. Web. 11 Oct 2017. <http://ark.digitalcommonwealth.org/ark:/50959/4t64hh66r>.

Ad for Keith and Hiscock store, Brookfield Times, Feb 8, 1895

in the area as well as those traveling through on trains would find their eye drawn to the building. The first and second floors were stores run by Keith and Hiscock where they had a hardware store, furniture store and undertaking business. In the basement was a workshop related to the hardware business. The third floor held a meeting hall. At the time of construction, the building incorporated all the modern conveniences including a steam heating system, elevator, paneled steel ceilings, Southern pine flooring and plastered walls. (Brookfield Times, Dec. 7, 1894) Later, one of the first telephones in town was installed in the store for the use of customers and residents. A first-of-its-kind telephone booth offered privacy for those using the phone and was quite the novelty in town. (Brookfield Times, May 31, 1895) Along with running this business, William Keith was on the fire department for fifteen years, led the East Brookfield Brass Band for ten years, and was a member of the Lassawa Tribe of Red Men.

Perhaps the biggest change in Depot Square was a large, four-story building adjacent to the train station. First used as a factory, it was renovated in 1894 by adding a concert hall and dance floor and was renamed "Vizard's Opera House." Basketball games were held here and in the basement was a four-lane bowling alley. Instead of machines, boys reset the pins. Vizard also ran Hotel Pilgrim in a brick building next to his Opera House for a short time but closed it when his wife became ill. In 1904 or 1905, the Opera House was converted to a factory and it was destroyed by fire in 1926.

> About 700 people saw the basket ball game, in the opera house, last Friday evening, between the teams from the Brookfield and North Brookfield high schools. It was an interesting game and the spectators were very enthusiastic, cheering their favorites from the start to the finish of the game. The game was the second of a series of three games, the first of which was won by North Brookfield. The third game will be played in the town hall, Spencer, March 10. There was a large attendance at the dance that followed the game.

The Brookfield Times, February 17, 1905

When William Vizard died in 1910 after becoming ill with rheumatic fever, he had been doing business in Brookfield and East Brookfield longer than any other man. He had emigrated from England and established a grocery store in Brookfield and then a hotel and livery stable on Central Street. He then sold the hotel and opened the drug store in East Brookfield. He also owned a

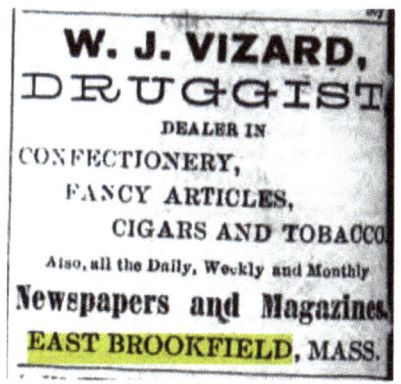

Advertisement for Vizard's Pharmacy, a popular store in town. (Spencer Sun, Nov. 4, 1881)

factory building adjacent to his drug store and Oakland Gardens, a park on Podunk Pond (Lake Quaboag). He was a Civil War veteran and great proponent of the town of East Brookfield, offering free space in his factory building for anyone wishing to do business in town. (Brookfield Times, March 18, 1910) He also served on several committees in town, including those that desired a separation from Brookfield.

His wife was equally accomplished, having been a partner with her husband for some time before she earned her pharmacy certificate and took over the drugstore on her own. She then purchased orange groves in San Diego and spent time managing her business there. After her husband's death, she sold the drugstore but then bought it back when the new owner became ill. (Brookfield Times, Oct. 13, 1911)

The East Brookfield of the 19th Century was one that was booming in terms of industry and manufacturing, which in turn attracted additional residents and the stores, services and entertainment that accompany such an increase. East Brookfield was noted for its brick and pottery companies, textile companies, and cast iron manufacturing.

TRANSPORTATION

Transportation during the 18th and 19th century consisted mainly of stage coach and railroad. Prior to the railroad, stage coaches traveled several times per week through Brookfield on the way to and from New York, Hartford, Boston, Northampton, and Springfield. (Lincoln, William and Charles Hersey; *History of Worcester, Massachusetts : from its earliest settlement to September 1836 ; with various notices relating to the history of Worcester County;* Worcester, MA, 1862 pp. 267-8.) The Brookfield area was a popular stopping point for travelers as it was a crossroads between Boston, Springfield, and Providence. With the improved condition of the roads, there was an increased need for rest stops for travelers.

Nathaniel Woolcot, George Harrington, and Jeduthan Stevens all operated small taverns in the Easterly Section of town.

The Stevens Tavern was the first built in the eastern portion of the village and was a popular stopping place for travelers between Springfield and Worcester. It was located at the corner of North Street and Main Street. The brick

Picture of root cellar on North Street, possibly from Stevens Tavern. Picture taken by author, 2008.

A Day in the Life...

"Peter Loungeway, who had his hands and feet badly frozen one cold night during the winter and was later reported to have died at a Worcester hospital, showed up in town, Wednesday. His reappearance in town was a surprise, as the general belief was that he was dead. Pete was also surprised when he was told that he wasn't supposed to be living."

- May 6, 1904, The Brookfield Times.

The Old Henshaw Tavern, Podunk. This is the only known photograph of the tavern. From the collection of the East Brookfield Historical Museum, donated by E. Stoddard.

house that stands on this spot today used some of the bricks from the original structure when it was built. A root cellar that may have been part of this tavern remains on the site. It was built into the ground to keep provisions cool and measures about six and a half feet in height, fifteen feet in length, and nine feet in width and has a vaulted stone ceiling.

Woolcot's tavern was located on what is today North Brookfield Road close to the North Brookfield town line on what is now called Slab City Road. There is a historical marker on the site of where the tavern once stood. A third tavern, run by the Harringtons, was located near the current center of town. While mentioned in the historical record, no maps show the exact location of this tavern.

A large tavern located between Draper Road and Adams Street in the Podunk section of town was operated by the Henshaw Family. Called "The Henshaw Tavern" or "Old Henshaw Tavern" or "Spring Hotel," it was built in 1721 on what was the major thoroughfare between Springfield and Providence. Several stage coaches stopped here daily and, according to Willis Gleason, who lived in Podunk his entire life, as many as forty teams of oxen per day would stop at the tavern as they carried goods between Springfield and Providence. While horses or oxen were switched for rested ones, travelers would eat, walk around the grounds, or trade news with villagers who would gather here. In addition to guest rooms, a large kitchen, and barns and pastures for horses and oxen, there was a dance hall, a barroom, a harness shop, and a cobbler's shop. Men from the area would gather at the barroom and after a few drinks would challenge each other to horse races. It was not an uncommon sight to see horses racing down the road, three or four abreast, at a full gallop.

A little known fact is that the region's first bowling alley was located in Podunk at the Henshaw Tavern. This had to be moved eventually as the noise from the game startled the livestock who were pulling coaches. Located

Henshaw Tavern, as depicted by Willis Gleason, 1892. From Collection of East Brookfield Historical Museum.

across the road from the tavern was a so-called "iron spring" which was used by natives and early settlers as well as travelers who stoped at the tavern. Alva Silliman, in his 1984 interview at the East Brookfield Historical Society referred to it as a seltzer spring and a notice on the sale of the property in 1883 referenced the "famous Podunk Springs." (Brookfield Times, Feb. 22, 1883) The water was said to be infused with sulfur and iron and to be good for healing many ailments.

With the coming of the railroad, the stages eventually ceased to run and taverns such as Henshaw's lost business in the 1840s. While there was still stagecoach traffic for freight and passengers between train depots and final destinations, the need for this type of transportation was greatly reduced. The advent of the trolley and then the automobile effectively ended coach service. The Henshaw Tavern was sold at auction in 1883 but the buildings were not dismantled until 1925. Much of the lumber was reused in other buildings but the bar and guest rooms were moved across the street and attached to an existing home at what is today 552 Podunk Road.

The railroad provided faster transportation that needed less frequent stops along its route. While the

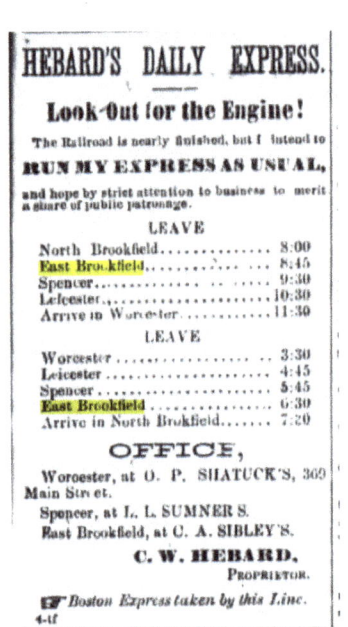

Clearly some of the men who made their business transporting people were nervous about the impact of the new branch line! (Spencer Sun, Nov. 19, 1875)

A Day in the Life...

"The factory whistle blew and blew and the first engine bell rang," Mrs. Lavigne recalled. *"We didn't know what was going on because we didn't have TV to tell us. We all went to the square, where we found out the war was over."*

-Jeannette Lavigne, as quoted in the Telegram and Gazette, November 12, 1990

railroad would usurp most of the stagecoach and wagon traffic, connections between the rail lines would keep horse-drawn transportation in common use for many years. For example, a stage line run by William Ayres transported residents between North Brookfield and the East Brookfield train depot and Charles Bush of North Brookfield operated a stage line that made three trips each day between North Brookfield and East Brookfield. (Roy, History of East Brookfield, p.168). Horses and oxen were used to bring freight to and from the railroad depots and surrounding stores and manufacturing businesses.

In the 1830s the railroad was beginning its slow creep across the state of Massachusetts. Originally used as a means of transporting coal throughout Worcester and to the Blackstone Canal, the railroad operated both passenger and freight service from Boston to Springfield by 1839. First called the "Western Railroad," it later became the Boston & Albany Railroad. The first trains to use the completed rail line through East Brookfield were powered by four locomotives built in Lowell. They were named "Worcester," "Middlesex," "Berkshire," and "Franklin." In the first year of operation, one freight train and two passenger trains passed through town each day. During the first year of operation, there was no depot in East Brookfield as there was disagreement over where it should be located. Passengers had to get on and off the train in South Spencer. (Hodgkins, Martha A.

Stage tickets for the trip between East and North Brookfield. From collection of East Brookfield Historical Commission.

This train schedule between East Brookfield and North Brookfield depicts the frequency with which the trains ran between the two towns. (Spencer Sun, June 27, 1879)

"Address to Quaboag Historical Society." East Brookfield, 3 June 1903.)

Once a location was agreed upon, there were a series of depots in East Brookfield. The original wooden structure was destroyed by fire in 1872. Another built shortly after this was used until 1893 when it was moved about sixty yards away to the opposite side of the Keith Building and converted to a lunch room. In the beginning of the 1900s the District Court was housed on the second floor of this building for several years before being torn down.

Early, undated, photos of the train depot. The stagecoaches in the photo above would carry passengers to and from the train and North Brookfield. This building was most likely the one destroyed by fire. The building to the right was moved to the opposite of the Keith Block when the stone depot was built. It held a lunchroom and the District Court before being torn down. Photos from collection of EB Historical Museum.

The granite and sandstone building that replaced the wooden depot was designed by Shepley, Rutan and Coolidge based on sketches by Henry Hobson Richardson, a prominent American architect of the 19th century whose style is known as Richardson Romanesque. The forty-foot by fifteen-foot building had a unique overhanging roof, included a ticket counter, waiting area, and telegraph office, and was a large part of the community center of the area.

Later, in 1876, the North Brookfield Railroad was established in order to build a track from the East Brookfield Depot to the town of North Brookfield. After constructing the four-mile railroad, it was leased to the Boston and Albany Railroad. The track ran from the depot, behind the current

Early photo of East Brookfield Depot, commissioned by Trahan's Market for postcard. From collection of East Brookfield Historical Museum.

A Day in the Life...

"John Houle...had the most exciting time of all last Saturday night. A man who was making a trip from Worcester to Springfield in an automobile stopped in East Brookfield for lunch. Houle picked up an acquaintance with the stranger who invited him to take a ride. John accepted the invitation and was soon seated in the auto. He says that the machine made the trip from East to West Brookfield in a very short time, just how long it took he is unable to tell, as he was too frightened to keep track of time. The machine stopped at West Brookfield and he boarded the first railcar he could for home. He says automobiles are all right for those who like them, but he could not be induced to take another ride."

- Brookfield Times, August 26, 1904

Town Hall on Connie Mack Drive towards Route 9, crossing at the junction of North Brookfield Road and running behind the houses on the eastern side of the road. This branch originally carried both passengers and freight but reverted to just freight in 1935 when car and bus transportation made the passenger service on the train less used. Over the course of its nearly one hundred years in operation, the train made over 50,000 trips carrying passengers and freight back and forth between the East Brookfield station and North Brookfield. (Spencer Leader, Dec 27, 1935) It stopped operation altogether in 1972. There was some talk of re-establishing the line in 2011 and again in 2015. This effort did not proceed, nor yet has a walking trail along the route of the rail line that was also proposed at approximately the same time.

A third line in the town connected the main line through East Brookfield to Lake Quaboag for the main purpose of transporting bricks from the brickyards and ice from the lake to Boston markets. In addition, this rail line transported residents from town to the lake and back again. Constructed in 1889, all that remains is a pathway and some random railroad ties where the tracks once were. (Spencer Sun, October 31, 1889)

In 1904, on a foggy and wet morning at the end of September, an event in East Brookfield made news around the world. George L. Merrill, the engineer of the regularly scheduled North Brookfield line, was just returning from his first trip and had dropped several cars onto the tracks on the opposite side of the depot before crossing back to the North Brookfield track with the passenger cars. He had just pushed the passenger cars onto the North Brookfield line and backed his engine onto the main line when when a Pullman train carrying its owner, financier John Pierpont Morgan and the Archbishop of Canterbury, who was on a tour of Canada and the United States, came through town traveling at approximately sixty miles per hour. The speeding train was not able to stop in time and slammed into the local engine, pushing it nearly one hundred yards down the track before coming to a stop. Miraculously, the engineer narrowly escaped with cuts and bruises and no one on the Pullman train was seriously injured. Two hours later, a replacement engine arrived and Morgan and the Archbishop continued on their journey to Washington, D.C. This story was reported in newspapers across the country and as far away as London and Australia.

The East Brookfield Depot was also the site where crowds of patriotic citizens bid farewell to those drafted to fight in World War I from the Brookfields, Spencer, Leicester, and Charlton as all who left for service departed from the East Brookfield train depot. The first group of eighty-nine men who left from East Brookfield for Fort Devens were seen off by a crowd of approximately 6,000. (Brookfield Times, Sept. 28, 1917)

Another means of transportation available to residents at the end of the 19th century was the electric trolley. Though used for a relatively short time since the automobile would soon trump it as an efficient mode of travel, the Warren, Brookfield, and Spencer Street Railway Company operated in town. This company began service in Spencer in 1891 and expanded west to Warren in 1896. Their office space was located near the Brookfield/East Brookfield town line between where Dunn Brook crosses Route 9, near the site of the former Carmella's restaurant. A large brick building housed the trolley cars when they were not in service. (Bill Jenkins report to Quaboag Historical Society, November 18, 2016) They offered trips between Spencer and Warren, eventually expanding to connecting East Brookfield and North Brookfield. During the week, passengers were mainly commuters traveling to and from their jobs at the mills. There were four cars dedicated just to the trip between North and East Brookfield. In order to create weekend business, the trolley company constructed and managed Lashaway Park, at the end of

Trolleys on Main Street in East Brookfield at the turn of the century. Source: Postcard, EB Historical Commission.

today's Lashaway Drive and Park Street.

In 1914 the trolley company was placed in receivership for unpaid debts. After six unsuccessful attempts to auction off the company, it was purchased in 1915 by Frank L. Palmer of Saco, Maine for $160,000. The property included a four-mile spur from East Brookfield to North Brookfield, an office building, car building, and a powerhouse. At the time of purchase, Mr. Palmer did not share what he planned for the sixteen miles of tracks that connected Spencer and Warren. Conjecture was that the line would be reorganized into a new company. The street cars continued to operate during this time. (Street Railway Bulletin, Volume 14, New England Street Railway Club, 1915)

The advent of the gas-powered engine brought with it both the personal mode of transportation afforded by the automobile, and buses as a means of public transportation. These two forms of transport would take the place of the stage coach, wagon and electric trolley beginning in the early 1900s. Charles Bugbee of North Brookfield ran regular routes between Spencer and North Brookfield using an 18-passenger bus. The bus ran seven times a day between the hours of 6:45 AM and 11:30 PM at a cost to passengers of fifteen cents for half the route, either Spencer to East Brookfield or North Brookfield to East Brookfield and twenty-five cents for the full route from Spencer to North Brookfield or the opposite. (Brookfield Times, May 3, 1918) The trolley wires and rails were removed beginning in 1918.

> The past weeek the number of automobiles that have gone through town has been a record breaker. One day a man who lives on Main street counted 25. Most of them were large machines carrying four or more persons.

As more people purchased their own automobiles, their reliance on trains and trolleys decreased. (The Brookfield Times, October 23, 1903.)

EDUCATION

In 1754, the first school in the Easterly Section (See map, page 51: #1) was located in the home of Abraham Adams to provide a place for children to learn to read and write. It was up to the people who sent children to the school to pay the teacher's salary. The Adams's house was located on Adams Road between Howe Street and Podunk Road. This school was only open for two weeks as the teacher who was available was not acceptable to parents and was removed.

In 1793, Brookfield was divided into six school districts. Schoolhouses in these districts were one-room buildings in which all children of the area attended multi-grade classrooms. Even the larger Hodgkins School combined two grades into one room. At some point in time, perhaps when there were more children than the school could hold, the second floor of the engine house was used as a school room as well.

Districts #3 and #4 were located in the Podunk section of town and provided a typical, colonial, one-room schoolhouse education. The District #3 Schoolhouse was located just south of where Adams Road meets Podunk Road (see map, page 51, #2) and students who lived between "east of the Great Brook" and north to what is now Pelletier Woods attended this school. When this school was closed in 1934, it was sold to a private owner, and moved about a mile east and added to a house currently located at 509 Podunk Road. At one point, each of the thirty students and the teacher had the last name of Adams. Alva Silliman, in an interview with the Historical Commission in the early 1980s noted that the doorstep of the school could still be seen as well as a path that led to a spring behind the school and supplied water for the students. Mr. Silliman, in recollections to his family, told of walking to and from school from his house on Howe Street, through the woods that are now Pelletier Woods, and out Draper Road to Podunk Road. In the winter, when the days were shorter, the walk was sometimes in the dark, particularly when he had the chore of bringing in the wood for the next school day. Elizabeth (Betty) Putnam Macia shared some of her recollections of attending one of the Podunk schools with Mrs. Eva Perron, who in turn wrote out the account. Betty shared that the Podunk school consisted of one large room and a small entry way for hanging coats. School began at nine o'clock with a prayer and the Pledge of Allegiance. There was no central heat, just a wood stove in the front of the room, no electricity or telephones, and no indoor plumbing, but two outhouses behind the main building. The older boys had the task of going to the spring to bring back water for the day while girls and younger boys sharpened pencils, clapped erasers and helped those younger than them. During recess, there were

Undated, unlabeled photo of District #3 School from Silliman Family Collection.

seesaws, a swing, and sledding in the winter along with the traditional games of jump rope, hide and seek, marbles and red rover. (Letter by Mrs. Eva Perron to author dated July 29, 2017)

The District #4 School, originally a wooden structure, was replaced by a brick one in 1848. The wooden schoolhouse was sold at auction for twenty-six dollars and seventy-five cents and land was "exchanged with Elihu Adams" on which to build the new school house. (Record of the 4th School District in the South Parish, Minutes of December 11, 1848.) The brick schoolhouse is still in its original location on West Sturbridge Road, (see map, page 51, #3) but is a private residence now. Children who lived "between the Ponds and Great Brook" and from Draper Road to the Sturbridge town line attended this school, which was known as the Podunk Brick School. This school was in operation intermittently after 1910 depending on the number of school-aged children who lived in the area. During some years, there were only three students enrolled! When there weren't enough children to warrant a full time teacher, the district paid for students who would have attended this school to attend the District #3 School.

According to the school accounts, school typically started after Thanksgiving, presumably so children were available to help with chores at home to prepare for winter. School was held in the summer depending on the availability of funds. A "women's school" was run in the summer months during the 1820s. (Record of the 4th School District in the South Parish, Minutes of May 25, 1824.)

In 1922, the School Committee voted to re-shingle the roof, put any remaining items into storage, and board up the windows. In 1923, it was rented out as a home.

District #4 School. Photo shared by Steve Londergan, current owner of building.

District #4 School, interior. Photo shared by Steve Londergan, current owner of building.

The following is a list of the bylaws instituted for the purpose of governing the newly built District #4 school, Nov. 1848.

Art. 1. If any schollar [sic] shall disfigure the seats or benches, break the windows or in any manner damage the school house, his parents, master, or gardian [sic] shall pay the damage accrued, thereby to the district for the public use. 2 If any schollar [sic] shall carry a knife into school the teacher is required to take possession of it and retain it as long as said school continues [Expunged]. 3 If any schollar [sic] shall willfully disobey the orders of the teacher said teacher is required for the second offense to expel said schollar from school by first giving notice to their parents or guardian or master. 4 If any schollar [sic] shall willfully neglect to inter [sic] the school at the appointed hour the teacher is required to send said schollar [sic] home and give notice to the parents master or guardian [sic] of the fact.   To be read once in two weeks by the teacher to the schollars [sic]

In 1800, District #7 was added to accommodate the needs of children in the "Spencer Corner" after residents of this area complained that they were paying taxes to fund schools, but were so far from a school that their children were not able to attend. "Spencer Corner" refers to the section of East Brookfield that is approximately from where Cove Street is today east to the Spencer town line and includes the Harrington Street area. The school was built near what is today the end of Young Road (see map, page 51, #4). It closed officially in 1901 though most certainly had no enrollment for several years prior to this as it doesn't appear in the 1891 Annual Town Report. According to Leo Fayard and the descendants of the Young Family, the wood from the schoolhouse was incorporated into the barn that stands on his property, which was formerly the Young Farm.

District #7 Schoolhouse. From Collection of Quaboag Historical Museum.

The District #8 Schoolhouse, built in 1849, served those children who lived in the center of town. Presumably, children attended school in

Brookfield prior to this time. This school was located on what is today Connie Mack Drive (see map, page 51, #5). In 1883, the Hodgkins Center School opened (see map, page 51, #6) and replaced the District #8 Schoolhouse, which was sold and converted to the original St. John the Baptist Catholic Church. In 1896, a two-story addition was added to the back of the building, increasing the school by two classrooms, one on the first floor and the other on the second floor. These rooms were occasionally closed depending on enrollment and the ability of the town to pay for heating (coal or wood) during the winter.

Having a centrally located school meant that communication was fairly easy. By ringing the school bell, it could be communicated to students and parents when school was cancelled for the day. Mostly school was cancelled for poor winter weather, as it is today, it was not unusual for school to be cancelled, or just a grade level cancelled, due to an outbreak of illness. For example, in 1918, schools were closed due to the influenza epidemic. Outbreaks of scarlet fever and measles would also result in schools being closed in an effort to curtail the illnesses in the early 20th century.

Hodgkins School, unknown date, but post-1913, when fire escapes were added to the school. Collection of East Brookfield Historical Museum.

Once, in 1906, the messenger who was sent to ring the 'no school bell' could not get into the building so rang the church bell instead. Apparently, the tones of the bells were different as the church bell was the means of sending the fire alarm. The firemen and other residents who left their jobs en masse to help fight the nonexistent fire were not impressed by the messenger's "Plan B." (Brookfield Times, Oct. 26, 1906). Later, the "no school" signal would be the whistle on the Daniels or Stevens Mill and then the siren at the fire department.

In 1894, a joint superintendency, or union, was appointed for the towns of Brookfield and North Brookfield. A joint school committee was organized as well as each town having their own School Committee. The purpose of this regionalization was to share resources in the relatively small towns. The positions that were shared included a music teacher, an art teacher, and a nurse. When East Brookfield became an independent town in 1920, they remained a part of this superintendency.

In 1896, the Annual Report of the Superintendent of the Town of Brookfield notes that *"The teacher of the grammar school at EB having resigned, the services of Mr. B.M. Avery were secured to fill the vacancy. The experiment of employing a male teacher for this school has been tried but eight weeks, yet the results secured fully justify the additional expense. It is not certain, however, that this arrangement will be continued."* (p.5). Clearly during this time, most school teachers were women, especially in the lower grades.

While the schools in Podunk remained open, there was much controversy over spending money on teachers and keepings the buildings open for a small number of children. In some years, there were less than five students attending one or the other of the schools in Podunk. In 1913 for example, the District #4 Schoolhouse, or the Lower Podunk School, had been closed for two years as a result of having too few school-aged students in the area. Those few students in the area were transported to the District #3 Schoolhouse, or the Upper Podunk School, which the superintendent and school committee agreed to keep open even though there was a growing movement towards single-grade classrooms and they were in favor of transporting all the Podunk students to the Hodgkins School. The next year, the District #4 School was reopened with students from Sturbridge attending to increase the enrollment to the level where it was feasible to hire a teacher for the school.

The cost of transportation and the time it would take to transport students to the center of town kept the rural schools open for many years. In 1901, when parents of school-aged children in the Podunk section of town refused to send their students to the center of town, the town took them to court and they were ordered to do so. (Brookfield Times, March 29, 1901.) This didn't last for long, though, and children from Podunk resumed attending the District #3 and #4 schoolhouses, perhaps because the unpaved roads made travel difficult for the twice daily trip to town. While parents had to send their children to school until they could read and write, they were not required to attend secondary school until much later. For example, of the approximately twenty students in the eighth grade class in 1900, only seven would continue their education at the high school level. Prior to separation in 1920, students from the East Village attended Brookfield High School.

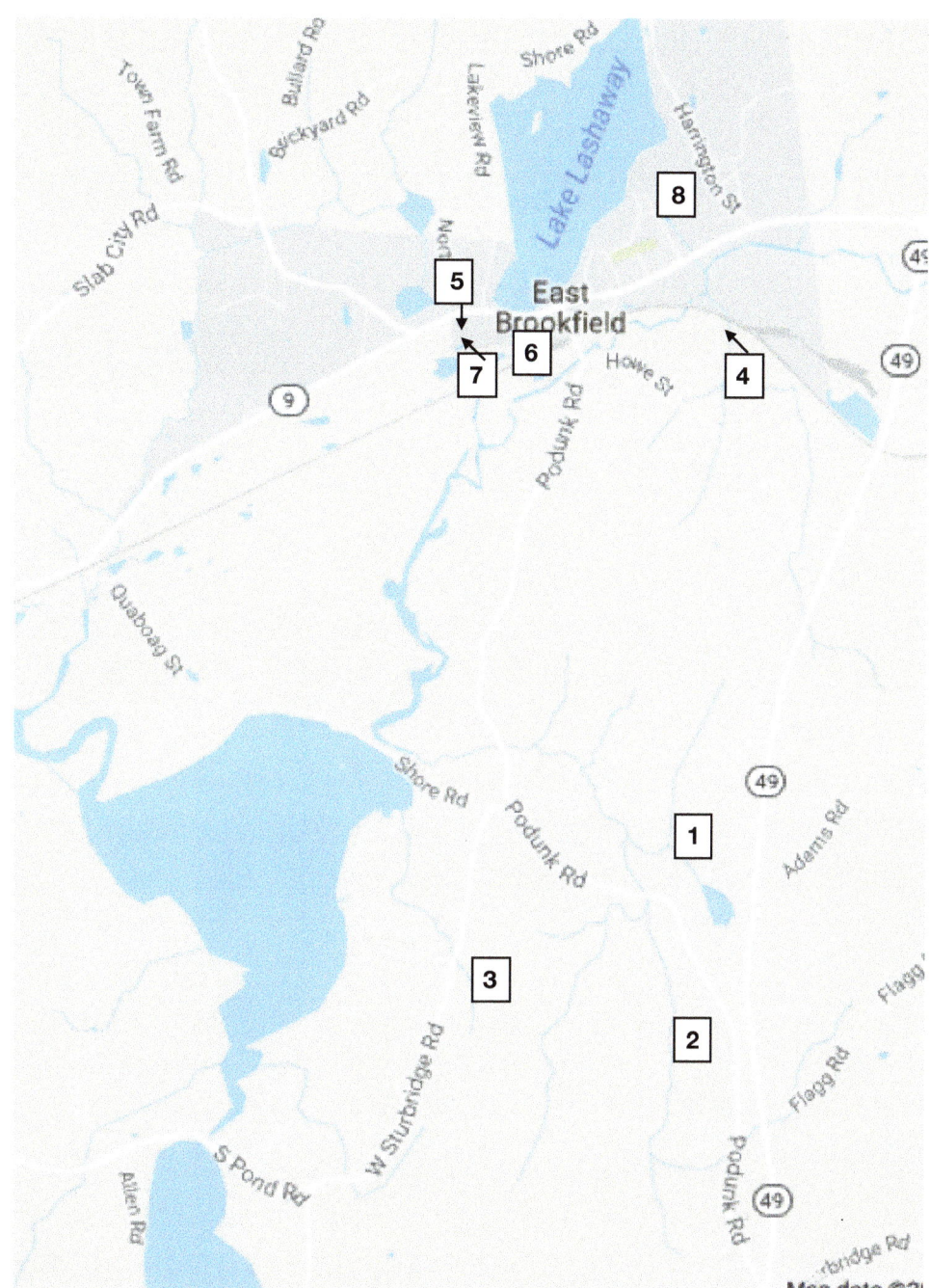

1: Abraham Adams Residence; first schoolhouse in East Brookfield
2: District #3 Schoolhouse or Upper Podunk School
3: District #4 Schoolhouse or Lower Podunk School
4: District #7 Schoolhouse or Cove District School
5: District #8 Schoolhouse
6: Hodgkins School / Lashaway Junior High School
7: Memorial School
8: East Brookfield Elementary School

RELIGION

Just as the Easterly Section of town was different from the rest of Brookfield economically, it also stood out as different in the area of religion. While the rest of Brookfield was firmly Congregationalist, by the middle of 1750 Baptists were holding regular meetings in this part of town, mainly led by traveling ministers in private homes and barns. Ephraim Harrington officially adopted the Baptist religion in 1783, when he was baptized in Woodstock, Connecticut, transitioning from the Congregationalist Church in Spencer. In 1786 a local Baptist organization was created and in 1788, eleven parishioners came together and hired Mr. Jeremiah Haskell as the Baptist minister ("Anniversary of the Baptist Church" Brookfield Times, 2 Nov 1900.) which caused quite an upset to the mainly Congregationalist area.

In 1795, the first Baptist church, a two-story building with no steeple that cost 381 pounds (over $45,000 in today's money), was built on a half acre plot of land on the corner of Harrington Street and the Old Country Road (Route 9). Baptisms were performed in the Seven Mile River at the bottom of so-called "Meetinghouse Hill." While there was negative response from some residents, in 1800 the Massachusetts General Court approved a 1797 petition sent to them by forty residents of the Brookfields and Spencer to establish the Baptist Society of Brookfield. Two factors led to the growth of the church. Some people joined in protest of compulsory taxes being paid to the established church. By joining the Baptist Church, residents did not have to pay this tax. The other was revivals held in 1818 and 1831, each of which resulted in more than fifty people being baptized into the church.

Those belonging to the church owned their pews and repairs were paid for by assessing a fee to the pew owners. Those who didn't pay this fee could have their pews taken back from them, though this only happened once. In the winter, parishioners brought portable stoves filled with charcoal and refilled them at noon during the dinner break to be prepared for the afternoon session of church. Church leaders later

East Brookfield Baptist Church, n.d., at the current location on Main Street. From the collection of the East Brookfield Historical Museum.

allowed people to install their own stoves in the meetinghouse and this became common practice.

In 1840, $3,500 was raised to build a new Baptist Church which was located a few miles west of the original building, on what is today the southern shore of Lake Lashaway on the corner of Route 9 and Maple Street. The half-acre of land had been donated to the church by Amos Harrington, after whom the Harrington Center, the building directly across the street from the church, is named. Harrington was a deacon in the church from 1818 until his death in 1856 at the age of 89. Beams and lumber from the original church were used. These were uncovered when the church was renovated in the 1960s. (EBBC 200th Anniversary pamphlet, 1986) As with most churches, there was originally a cemetery behind the Baptist Church. A map dated 1857 shows the cemetery located on Maple Street on the shore of Lake Lashaway. For undocumented reasons, this cemetery was closed, and those buried there moved to Evergreen Cemetery, which became the main cemetery in the town. This could have been because the water level of the lake was still rising or because the value of the land was increasing and a cemetery was not a good use of this potentially valuable real estate. There is anecdotal evidence of the move as well. At least one person who was buried in the cemetery was an ancestor of the Drake Family and when their remains were moved, a new stone marker was put in place. The former marker is now in private hands.

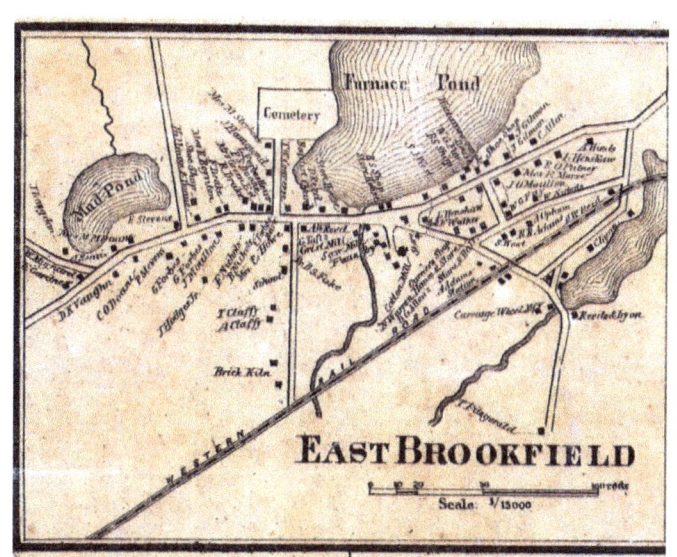

Map of East Brookfield showing cemetery on the shore of "Furnace Pond" (Lake Lashaway), 1837.

Two more markers were found being used as steps in a porch on Maple Street. When renovations were being made in 2006, the stone steps were removed and when turned over, they were discovered to be gravestones. The stones were that of Francis Hare, who died at the age of 70 in 1858 and his son Henry who was killed in 1862 while fighting in the Civil War. The Hare family has a large monument in Evergreen Cemetery that includes the names of Francis and Henry. Most likely, when the cemetery moved from behind the Baptist Church to Evergreen Cemetery, the old stones were replaced with the monument and the stones were repurposed as good, frugal Yankees are prone to do. The stones were donated to the Quaboag Historical Society.

Repairs made to the Baptist Church in 1874, costing $1500, were paid for by the continued practice of selling pews following a tradition in early churches of families paying for specific seats within the church. (Spencer Sun, May 1, 1874) This practice continued until 1873, when pews were rented out instead of sold. Pew rents ranged from $3 to $20 a year. In 1885, the means of raising money was changed from renting pews to taking a weekly offering to encourage church attendance by those who may not be able to afford the rent for a pew. The church was rented out for a variety of gatherings and town meetings for the village were held here for several years. In 1870, a parsonage was built and the church continued to grow until 1900 when disagreement on church policies caused some members to split from the church and start the First Baptist Society of Brookfield. The groups could not agree on the use of the church building, so the Baptist Society dubbed the brick building on the corner of Main Street and North Street the "Brick Chapel" and held services there while the other group held services in Red Men's Hall. In 1921, the groups resolved their differences and reunited, services again being held in the church.

The Second Universalist Society established a group in the Podunk section of town in 1819. The church, located in front of the Podunk Cemetery was built in 1820 on land owned by Moses Hobbs. In 1827, the church purchased the land. The church was led by the Reverend John Bisbee, Jr., formerly of the First Universalist Society of Brookfield from 1821 to 1824. The position was then filled by ministers from nearby churches who would travel to the church to preach on Sundays. The Universalist Church became known as the Old Podunk Church. Iron rings are still in the stone wall at the edge of the cemetery that allowed people to tie their horses and oxen while they socialized in the two-story wooden building.

Over the years, the building became more of a social hall than a religious meeting place. In 1870 the church was renovated, the pews were sold and the building was renamed Union Hall and church services and social functions for all denominations

Union Hall, artist rendering, with Podunk Cemetery in background. Source: EB Historical Museum.

were held here. On September 4, 1881, a fire broke out in the hall and burned it beyond repair. A letter to the newspaper from C.E. Stebbins summed up the feelings of the community: *"The ties which bind the people of such a community to such a building, in the course of years, become many and exceeding strong and to see this center of so many hopes and aspirations reduced to ashes in an hour must have been to many a sore trial."* (Spencer Sun, Sept. 16, 1881)

After Union Hall was destroyed, the residents of Podunk raised funds to build another meeting place and Union Chapel opened in 1882. This chapel was built approximately a mile closer to the center of East Brookfield, on land donated by Henry Trask, to make travel there by residents of Podunk a bit quicker. It was described as "very attractive in appearance, convenient in all its arrangements, substantially built and handsomely furnished." (Brookfield Weekly Times, November 9, 1882)

Today it is named the Union Chapel at Podunk and is privately owned. When built, the chapel was overseen by trustees of five area churches. Services of different denominations and a Sunday School were held along with bean dinners, whist parties, holiday parties for Christmas and New Years, religious services, Old Home Day gatherings, plays, and concerts. Another popular event was Farmer's Institutes, at which speakers from area colleges would discuss such topics as the best methods for raising high-producing chickens, haymaking, the use of silos, and other topics of interest to the mostly agrarian society around the church. But the most popular events were socials for young people, card parties, and plays, put on by local residents. These special events were organized by a "Social Committee" of five men and women and were held to raise money to pay for the Sunday services. While collections from a religious service might bring in less than $10.00 each week, each social event typically added between $20 and $40 to the treasury as they brought in many people from East Brookfield, Charlton, and Sturbridge. (Secretary's Reports, Podunk Chapel, 1896-1908.) A comedic play in January of 1899 called, "The District School of Blueberry Commons" raised an astounding $44 and brought in a crowd of three hundred. How they all fit in the Chapel is amazing in and of itself! This play went on to be

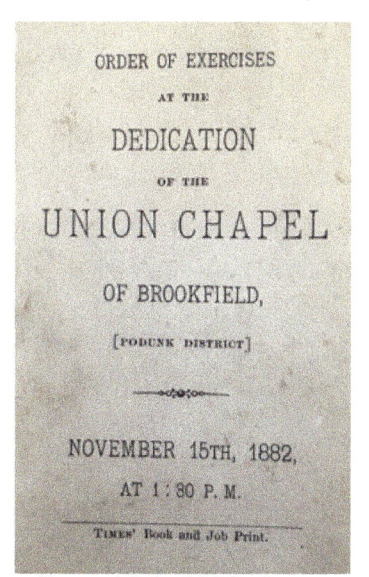

Pamphlet, 1882, from collection of East Brookfield Historical Museum.

A Day in the Life...

March 15, 1883: SW fair most all day windy ....freezing at 9 p.m. worked about the house did part of the churning worked on rags and colore [sic] some rags Clara did the work and worked some on her dress Leander went to the woods Mary Harrington came up a.m. and Leander [Morse} took her home before night L[eander] and C[lara] went to Podunk in the evening to a party at the Chapel...

Excerpts from diary of Mary Ann Harrington, Podunk (Howe Street) resident, age 69.

Podunk Chapel, 1920, EB Historical Museum collection.

presented at the Baptist Church in Spencer and the Methodist Church in Brookfield. (Secretary's Report, Podunk Chapel, January 1, 1898 to April 1, 1899.)

When repairs or supplies were needed for the Chapel, members of the church who were part of the "Local Committee" went door-to-door soliciting any amount of money people could pledge or any materials they could donate. For example, in 1895 when the chapel needed to be painted, the "Local Committee" collected $27.75 from the residents of Podunk, $47.50 from church members in Brookfield, and $25.00 from those in Spencer. In addition, Dr. Hodgkins donated seven gallons of oil. The job was completed with $12.00 left over in the treasury! (Secretary's Report, Podunk Chapel, July 1895.)

The congregation was relatively small, with the Secretary's report of 1896 noting that an average attendance of twenty-eight at Sunday services was "very good." Services could be called off due to bad weather or lack of ministers, who traveled from surrounding towns to preach at the Chapel and were paid $2.00 per sermon.

Attendance at services began to decline as the automobile allowed residents to travel to churches further away and older church members passed away. By 1908, the "Local Committee" was no longer elected annually, but was a standing committee of the remaining active members of the Chapel. Sunday services were cancelled from January through March 1908 due to the small attendance being "discouraging to the ministers" and the annual Children's Day service was not held, due to too few children attending Sunday School. (Secretary's Report, Podunk Chapel, 1907-1908). The Secretary's Reports of this time period end with the statement, *"The Sunday School is not in that flourishing condition in which we would like to see it, but trusting in Him who doeth all things well we hope and pray for better things. Financially the Chapel is in the most flourishing condition for years. Spiritually let us pray for an awakening of the Spirit."*

Methodist services were held as early as 1810 in the Podunk section of town, using barns as meeting places and traveling ministers as preachers. Both Methodist and Congregationalist services were held in a variety of halls around town at the end of the 1800's and beginning of the 1900s. Ministers from surrounding towns served as preachers and residents of East Brookfield and neighboring towns attended the services. There was some talk of approaching the Baptist Church to share space or perhaps join together, but this was not done.

As Massachusetts was settled by Puritans, the original settlers were mainly Protestants. Just as there was upset when those of the Baptist denomination begin to hold regular meetings in town, there was some anti-Catholic sentiment in the primarily Protestant region. Many of the first Catholics in this area were immigrants, who worked on the railroad or in the many mills in town. According to the "Souvenir History of the Catholic Churches of Brookfield, West Brookfield, and East Brookfield, 1885-1901," when the railroad was built in 1839, a Father Fitton reported that while stopping at the station, he heard confession and offered a mass to area Catholics. There are no other records of practicing Catholics until 1852, when the same pamphlet reported that twenty people gathered in a private home near the depot to attend a Mass officiated by Reverend Father Bouvier. When a Catholic Church was built in Spencer, Catholics from the Easterly Section traveled to that town for Mass. Priests from nearby towns, including Spencer, Millbury, Ware, and Webster, traveled to East Brookfield and offered mass in private homes. Jean Robichard, in her personal account titled, *"The Early History of the Catholic Church in Our Area"* wrote that there was resistance to Catholicism at first, including a traveling priest being threatened with tarring and feathering and protesting against a Catholic cemetery and church being built. The priest was rescued by a group of Irish mill workers who saw what was happening. Open-minded Protestants stepped in and helped promote freedom of religion when Amasa Walker, a Protestant, purchased land for a Catholic Cemetery and another Protestant resident bought land for St. Joseph's Church in North Brookfield in 1867.

A Day in the Life...

"You never missed Mass unless you were on your death-bed, never went into a Protestant Church, you were pretty daring if you had a friend that belonged to another church, seldom married outside the Catholic church. Everyone had tremendous loyalty to their Parish, supporting the church financially even if it meant sacrifices for the family."

- Historical Account, Jean Robichaud, collection of EB Historical Museum.

St. Joseph's Church was the first Catholic Church in the Brookfields and for almost thirty years, all Catholics in East Brookfield either made the eight mile round trip to North Brookfield to attend Mass there or attended in private homes or halls. The latter mostly in the winter when travel was more difficult.

Catholics from the Brookfields attended St. Joseph's until 1885, when a rift in the church caused by the hiring of a French priest who would only minister to French Catholics caused some parishioners from Brookfield, East Brookfield and West Brookfield to leave St. Josephs. St. John's Catholic Church in East Brookfield was established as a mission of the St. Mary's Church in Brookfield in 1889. By the turn of the century, the population of Catholics in the Brookfields increased to more than 1,500. Services in East Brookfield were held in public halls in the town, including Fay's Hall, what is today the Senior Center, until 1891, when the former District #8 schoolhouse was sold and renovated to serve as a church. A belfry, vestibule and sanctuary was added to this building, located on what is today Connie Mack Drive. The building was torn down in the 1970s.

St. John the Baptist Catholic Church, located on what is today Connie Mack Drive. Note the Hodgkins Building in the background. Source: Old Sturbridge Village Photo by Henry Peach. Used with permission.

Many buildings in town which are familiar to us once served very different purposes than they do today. Maps from the 18th, 19th, and 20th centuries provide information on the uses of these buildings. Sources are numbered as follows:

1. 1794 Map by Thomas Hale, Jr.
2. "Brookfield" Map by H.S. Stebbins, 1828
3. "Brookfield" Map by Walling, 1857
4. "Brookfield" and "East Brookfield" in Atlas of Worcester County, F.W. Beers & Co, 1870
5. "The Village of East Brookfield" and "Town of Brookfield" in Atlas by George Walker & Co, 1885
6. "Brookfield, May 1893" Sanborn Insurance Map 2c, Sheet 2 and Sheet 3
7. "Part of the Town of Brookfield" and "Towns of Brookfield, North Brookfield, West Brookfield, and Warren" in Atlas of Worcester County, 1898
8. "Brookfield, October 1898" Sanborn Insurance Co., 2c, Sheet 3 and Sheet 4
9. "Brookfield, January 1904" Sanborn Insurance Co, 2c, Sheet 6

In 1870 (Source 4), the building at this site was simply labeled, "Hotel." By 1885, (Source 5) it had been renamed the Crystal House, and E.N. Adams was included on the map as the occupant and J. Moulton the owner. Maps in 1893 (Source 6) and 1898 (Source 7) continue to label the building Crystal House, but in 1904 (Source 9) it is named the New Crystal House. By 1911 (Source 10) it is renamed the Lakewood House, which changes slightly in 1928 (Source 11) to the Lakewood Inn. In 1948, the new owner called the establishment "The Lashaway Inn," (locals called it 'The Lash") a name it kept until 2013 when it became "The 308 Lakeside."

Photo by author, 2019.

Photo by author, 2019.

This local breakfast favorite got its name from the late 1800s when it was literally where the trolley stopped. In 1904 (Source 9), it is titled, "D.G. News and Stationary." Around 1910, this became the Trahan Store, a general store with a soda fountain where people could wait for the trolley. It was first owned by Domathilee and Isidore Trahan and then Aldai and Ida Trahan. Ida continued to run the store after her husband's death, getting into some trouble during prohibition for selling liquor! The empty lot to the west of the Trolley Stop once had a shop built on it. In 1904 (Source 9), it was a bakery with a waiting room for the trolley.

This building, currently a realty office, was a variety of stores over the years. In 1898 (Source 8) it had a bakery and a pool room. By 1904 (Source 9), the bakery was gone, but the pool room remained. In 1911 (Source 10) a barber shop joined the pool room and all were replaced by a "Mission" in 1928 (Source 11.) Later, it would be "King's Variety" where you could get the paper, sit at the counter for lunch, and buy penny candy. Both Trahan's and King's allowed children to come in with their ice skates on to buy hot chocolate after skating on the lake!

Today a music shop and an antique store, this building was home to a lunch room in 1898 (Source 8) which most likely catered to those waiting to catch the trolley. In 1904 (Source 9), it is labelled "Milly" which is a hat store and "Drugs." In 1928 (Source 11), it is labeled with an "S" for store and is also home to the East Brookfield branch of the public library. The building just to the west was home to the post office at one time.

Photo by author, 2019.

Photo by author, 2019.

Dunny's Tavern hasn't changed too much over the course of the last hundred years or so. It is first labeled on a map in 1893 (Source 6) as a pool room and in 1898 (Source 8) a waiting room was added for the trolley. By 1911 (Source 10), it is labeled, "vacant," though how long it stayed that way is unclear. At this time, the building next door was a lunch room.

Photo by author, 2019.

This building has certainly seen its share of change! In 1893 (Source 6), it is listed as a cobbler. In 1898 (Source 7), it is owned by the town. Much later, in the 1960s, it will house the town library. And in the 1980's was a TV repair shop, a fish store, and a video rental store. Today it is the home of East Brookfield Pizza.

Photo by author, 2019.

This was the site of several potteries and brick kilns over the years. In 1857 (Source 3) it is simply labeled, "Brick Yard." In 1870 (Source 4) it is "J Moulton Brick Yard." The 1885 map (Source 5) lists the area as "C.L. Moulton's Kiln and Residence." By 1893 (Source 6) it has changed names to Parmenter Manufacturing Company Brick Yard. There are several buildings drawn on the map including a pottery in the process of being built, a work room, a painting room, and two kilns. In 1904 (Source 9), it has again changed hands and is the New England Brick Company. In 1928 (Source 11) it is only called the warehouse for this company with many of the buildings listed as vacant. It would be the site of the town dump from 1964 to 1988. The Independence Day fireworks are set off from this location today.

Photo by author, 2019.

This location at the Lake Lashaway Dam was prime industrial real estate for hundreds of years. This currently empty mill building served many purposes over the years. The Five Mile River was the source of many mills in the earliest settlements in the area. On this location in 1828 (Source 2) was the J. Stevens' Mill. In 1870 (Source 4), there were several mills at this location including a grist mill, saw mill, and cotton mill. At this time, Jesse Moulton had a furnace here to process ore found in the area. In 1885 (Source 5), it was a Shoddy Mill, processing woolen products. In 1893 (Source 6), it was Brookfield Woolen Company which comprised several buildings for sorting, washing, picking and carding wool. In 1898 (Source 7), it was owned by the Quaboag Manufacturing Company who leased it to the Mann and Stevens Woolen Company, who also had a factory along the Seven Mile River. In 1928 (Source 11), it became Daniels Manufacturing Company, which processed wool and had seven buildings on the site. Later it would be home to the Maclan Hat Company, Brookfield Athletic Company, and Saucony Shoe Company.

The area around what is today Depot Square was a thriving area for shops as people would get on and off trains at the depot station.

This brick building on Mechanic Street is first labeled on an 1893 map (Source 6) as having a tailor, a general store, and the post office in the first floor rooms. In 1898 (Source 8), it was a drug store and a grocery store. In 1904 (Source 9), it was vacant and then in 1911 (Source 10) it was a cobbler, a grocery store again, and housed the town library. It would continue to have stores in it through the 1960's. Today, it is an apartment building.

This building, with its close proximity to the railroad tracks allowing for easy deliveries was the location of A.A. Putney's Hay, Grain, and Coal store in 1898 (Source 8). It is listed as vacant in 1911 (Source 10) but becomes a grain warehouse again in 1928 (Source 11) through the 1940s when it was owned by the Checkerboard Grain Company.

Photo by author, 2019.

Photo by author, 2019.

In 1893, with the mills in full operation, housing was needed for workers. This building included tenements and a grocery store with a feed warehouse in the yard (Source 6). In 1898 (Source 8), it was a barbershop, a hat store, a general store, and had the post office in one room. In 1904 (Source 9) and 1911 (Source 10), these businesses remained with the exception of the hat store. By 1928 (Source 11), there were three small stores and the post office still in this building. Today it is an apartment building.

Photo by author, 2019.

Today's Depot Square Deli enjoyed a long history as a market. In 1870 (Source 4) and 1885 (Source 5), it was the N. Warren Store. In 1893 (Source 6) and 1898 (Source 8) it is simply listed as "General Store." In 1904 (Source 9) it is home to the American Express Office and by 1928 (Source 11), is a store again. It has had several names over the years including LeDoux's Market, Ahearn's, Podunk Deli, and The General Store.

Originally, there was also a building in the lot between the deli and where the post office is now. In 1870 (Source 4), this was "Currier's Store" and in 1893 (Source 6), 1898 (Source 8, and 1904 (Source 9), it is a "General Store." By 1928, the lot is listed as vacant.

Photo by author, 2016.

This building has been a meeting hall for over a century. In 1870 (Source 4) it is simply titled "Hall." In 1893 (Source 6), and 1898 (Source 8) it apparently enjoyed a short stint as a pool room and drug store with office space in the basement. In 1904 (Source 9), it is home to the Improved Order of Red Men, who were a very active community group in town. This building has been used as a gathering space for town meetings, a venue for wedding receptions and held meetings calling for independence from Brookfield. Today it is home to the Senior Center but community groups continue to meet here.

Photo by author, 2019.

This building was a warehouse in 1898 (Source 8) and 1904 (Source 9) and a movie theater in 1928 (Source 11). Today it is the office of a financial advising company.

Photo by author, 2019.

This 1962 photo shows a little of what the area behind the depot looked like. Photo from collection of EB Historical Museum.

During the height of train travel, this area was often the first visitors saw when arriving in town. In 1885 (Source 5) it had four freight buildings, the passenger depot, a water tank, and G.H. Hammond & Company who sold beef imported via train and had a refrigerated building on the site. In 1893 (Source 6), the buildings surrounding Depot Square included a Shoe Counter Manufacturer in the large wooden building, a saloon and drug store in a smaller brick building. Along the tracks was an ice house, bottling house, two freight storage buildings and a coal shed. In 1898 (Source 8), the Keith Block is shown with a hardware and furniture store with a tin shop in the basement. A dining room and bakery is adjacent to the Keith Block. Along the railroad tracks is still G.H. Hammond Company Meats and a blacksmith on the opposite side of the bridge. In 1904 (Source 9), the area where the veterans memorial is today is labeled "park" and the building adjacent to the Keith Block is home to the district court. The large wooden building is labeled with "Opera House" on the second and third floors and a market in the basement. The adjacent brick building continues to house a pharmacy and a lunch room. G.H. Hammond Meat Company is still in operation across the train tracks.

The 1911 (Source 10) map shows limited changes except for the opera house labeled "Vacant factory," and the second and third floors of the Keith Block labeled as vacant. The 1928 map (Source 11) tells a story of an area in decline. The Keith Block is no longer a store, but woolen storage with the remaining buildings 'vacant" including Hammond's Meat Company. The district court has moved into a small brick building.

CHAPTER 3

Separation

Governor Calvin Coolidge and Senator Warren Tarbell at the signing of the bill establishing East Brookfield as an independent town.

Between 1718 and 1920, the residents of the "Easterly Section" of the town of Brookfield would petition for separation several times, but were not successful as other portions of Brookfield had been. "Western" became the town of Warren in 1742; New Braintree separated in 1751, North Brookfield's petition for separation was successful in 1812, Ware's in 1823, and West Brookfield's in 1848.

The earliest attempt at separation from Brookfield of the "Easterly Section," came in 1753 when tavern owner George Harrington petitioned the General Court to join with the newly established "Western District" of Leicester, named Spencer. Harrington asserted that that meetinghouse in Spencer was closer than the meetinghouse in Brookfield. His petition was met with pushback not only from Brookfield proper, but from the Podunk section of town as well. Allowing the easterly portion of Brookfield to join with Spencer would mean that many of the best mill streams would be lost to Brookfield. In addition, many residents of the region did not wish to leave Brookfield, including every inhabitant of the Podunk section of town. These men were closer to the meetinghouse in Brookfield than the one in Spencer and thus the same hardship Harrington cited in his petition would impact them. In spite of the opposition to Harrington's petition, the Massachusetts General Court and the governor of Massachusetts approved the petition and the "Spencer Corner" was annexed to the town of Spencer, though it was eventually returned to Brookfield. "The Spencer Corner" correlates roughly to the Harrington Street section of town today.

In 1764, sentiment in Podunk seems to have changed as several residents petitioned for separation from Brookfield to join Spencer, citing again as reason the closer proximity of the meetinghouse there. Previously, they had felt that the size of Brookfield would lead to the establishment of a separate town, but perhaps in the years since their opposition to leaving Brookfield to join Spencer with George Harrington, they had become disillusioned of this belief. Instead of approving the petition, the town of Brookfield approved the building of a road that would provide a more direct route to the Brookfield meetinghouse. This road corresponds to today's Podunk Road from Draper Road to Bridge Street where the intersection with Howe Street is today.

In 1793, Josiah Hobbs added an article on the town meeting agenda asking for "consent that the Petitioners with the lands described be set off from said town" (Town of Brookfield, *Town Meeting Minutes*, 29 October, 1793). This article was not approved, but Josiah Hobbs was a leading citizen of Podunk. It seems the building of the road enabling these residents to reach the Brookfield Meetinghouse faster did not entirely mediate the desire for separation from Brookfield.

In 1868, members of the "Easterly Section" were angered by the actions of Brookfield, as they were not in support of funding to build a new town hall in the center of Brookfield. Their anger was not great enough to cause them to push for independence but perhaps this perceived ignoring of the desires of the residents of the eastern portion of town fueled discontent in the years to come. An article in the local paper in 1874 speaks to the continued tensions between the residents of the Easterly Section and Brookfield Proper. The article predicted a "storm" as the residents of East Brookfield felt they were "deserving of a branch library and other good things which the other village does not see fit to grant." (Spencer Sun, December 25, 1874)

In 1888, this discontent arose again due to a perceived higher rate of taxpayers' funds spent on public works projects, including roads and schools, in Brookfield. Those in the Easterly Section felt that they were not the equal beneficiaries to these projects even though, as the industrial center of the town, they contributed more to the tax base. In January, a meeting was held at Fay's Hall, currently the Senior Center, and a committee of twenty men was chosen to investigate separation of the village from the mother town. A follow-up meeting was held in December to report on the committee's findings and all voters of "Precinct 2," the village of East Brookfield and the Podunk section of town, were encouraged to attend. (Brookfield Times, Dec. 21, 1888) Two petitions for separation were submitted in this year, and both were rejected; the first was submitted late and the second was put on hold by the state legislature and eventually denied. However, the creation of a committee in Brookfield to oppose separation served to anger East Brookfield residents and further sour relations between the two groups.

The residents of what would become East Brookfield complained again and again over the course of the next twenty years that they saw little return on the taxes they paid. Any projects or expenditures that would benefit their area of town were consistently voted down at town meeting. Residents of Brookfield declared that they were only looking out for the interests of the whole town, but tensions were continuing to rise as residents of the smaller village felt their wants and needs were ignored, even though they were contributing to the town coffers. This was especially true in 1899, when Brookfield reduced the number of selectmen from five to three and the subsequent town election resulted in no representative from East Brookfield on the Board of Selectmen. In previous elections, at least one of the selectmen was from the village as there were more seats available. That spring, two East Brookfield men were running, Leander Morse and Warren Tarbell. Tarbell stepped aside in an unsuccessful effort to ensure that the East Brookfield vote would not be split and at least one East Brookfield man would be on the board. The injustice of no representation on the board when the village of East Brookfield contributed a large percentage of the tax base did not sit well with residents, who petitioned for a return to a five-member board as there were insufficient voters in East Brookfield to elect a candidate from their section of town. The Brookfield Times warned that "If the present state of affairs is to be continued, the old question of a separation, which has been asleep for a long time, will be revived and pushed with more vigor than ever before." (Brookfield Times, Feb. 23, 1900)

When the Brookfield Town Hall burned in 1902, many residents of the east village wanted it rebuilt in East Brookfield. Their rationale was that this section of town had significantly more businesses and therefore was paying more in taxes, so it made sense to move the town hall to where the center of the economy was located. They also felt they had been inconvenienced for many years by having to travel west for town meetings and it was only fair that others would now have to travel east. (Brookfield Times, Sept. 12, 1902) So great was the desire for the town hall to be in the Easterly Section, that one resident volunteered to donate a building for the new town hall and another resident offered to donate land to the town if they would build the new town hall on it. (Brookfield Times, Sept 19, 1902) After much heated debate, the town hall was rebuilt in Brookfield center, further solidifying the beliefs of residents of the village that they would always be treated as secondary to the larger population of Brookfield proper.

It must have truly felt this way when, in 1905, the voters at the town meeting did not allocate funds for the street lights in the easterly village. Not only did they not light them, the lights were taken down for safe-keeping. The incensed residents were angered by their now-dark streets, especially since their allocation of taxes was not lowered when this service was removed. Many claimed that "East Brookfield has for years paid a good share for the improvements that have been made in Brookfield center which this end of the town has received no benefit" and that " less attention was paid to the wants of East Brookfield at the annual town meeting than ever." (Brookfield Times, May 12, 1905). It is a wonder after all this upset that it took another fourteen years for serious movement towards separation. This could be because in the next year's election, the ire of the voters was such that a large number of East Brookfield residents ran for public office. After the election, two of the three members of the board of selectmen were from East Brookfield, and other East Brookfield residents were elected to the Board of Health, school committee, assessors office and as constables.

Another topic of contention was the water supply to the east village. Brookfield had built a water works, paid for by taxpayer funds, which did not benefit the residents of East Brookfield at all. At times of low rain, residents were forced to cart water to their homes by bucket and felt that a water supply system should be supplied for the center of the village. (Brookfield Times, March 15, 1907) At the 1908 town meeting, a standpipe with a pumping system on Corliss Hill, on the west side of Lake Lashaway, was built to provide water for the center of East Brookfield was approved. The project cost $25,000 and was completed in January 1909.

The issue of separation seems to have fallen silent until the summer of 1919. Citizens met in Leon Boutin's barber shop on Mechanic Street to again discuss separation from Brookfield. Senator Warren Tarbell was in attendance and agreed to help in any way as long as most of the citizens of East Brookfield were in favor of separation. It was decided to canvas the town to gather public opinion on the topic and to meet again in November.

On November 15, 1919, the Worcester Telegram and Gazette ran a story about renewed efforts at separation. It was titled: "East Brookfield to Seek a Divorce from Old Brookfield: Citizens to meet Monday night to demand separation, alleging incompatibility, cruel and abusive treatment and nonsupport, and claim they are fit for home rule." Two hundred registered voters met at Red Men's Hall and voted unanimously to create a committee to investigate the legal and financial implications of separation and move for separation from Brookfield. The committee was made up of leading citizens of town including George J. Daniels, owner of the large Daniels Manufacturing Mill in town, Emerson H. Stoddard, A. Howard Drake, Leander C. Bodge, Fremont N Turgeon, Leander Morse, and Arthur Ledoux. George Putney served as clerk and Frank E. Holden as treasurer. State Senator Warren Tarbell was also in attendance at the meeting and declared, *"the American Colonies had no more reason for demanding separation from England in 1775 than East Brookfield has from Brookfield at this time."* A similar article published in the Brookfield Times cited anger over East Brookfield paying a significant portion of the taxes, especially since most of the industry was located in the village, and still not being able to get a "sidewalk or street repaired" and also that since the voters of the main village outnumbered those of the east village nearly two to one, there was no democratic means for getting their needs met. (Brookfield Times, Nov. 14, 1919)

On November 19, about 200 citizens again gathered at Red Men's Hall to continue their call for independence. Respected citizens who had served on the Board of Assessors, the School Committee, and other town boards shared several examples of what they believed to be evidence of unfair practices and "extravagances" in the town of Brookfield while East Brookfield went without basic upgrades to infrastructure. There were no dissenters in the crowd and from the vitriolic description of the newspaper reports, it is unlikely they would have been received well!

Unlike in previous years, there was no fight from their mother town, and in fact, there was little discussion at all. The town leaders of Brookfield took "no action on the matter" (Spencer Leader, Jan.9, 1919) and willingly let the village go out on their own and become, "The Baby Town of Massachusetts." House Bill 152 was introduced to the Massachusetts House of Representatives and a hearing was held on February 5, 1920 regarding the partition of the town of Brookfield.

> *"In 1920, tired and disappointed in being a disregarded and forgotten section of the town of Brookfield, the residents of this area took a bold and daring step. They announced their desire for independence. This example of strong willpower and determination was not reflected alone in cases like this, but was an example of true American spirit, the spirit which began in the Revolutionary War and continues through this day." David Mullett, jr. high essay for 1970 Anniversary of EB*

During the separation process, there were two land areas under dispute. Both of these were along the north and northwest shores of Lake Quaboag to which both Brookfield and East Brookfield laid claim. In addition, there was $30,000 worth of shared debt between the two entities. A compromise was made with Brookfield assuming the debt but also taking the land on Lake Quaboag. A bill for the incorporation of East Brookfield was submitted to the House and Senate for approval. On March 24, 1920, East Brookfield officially became an independent town with a population of eight hundred. The town celebrated with an impromptu parade led by a brass band and heralded by the ringing of the church bell for thirty minutes. The first town meeting was held on January 3, 1921 in Red Man's Hall.

The first meetings of the General Committee who governed the town between the time of separation and the first elections were held in the Engine House.

A celebration was held on July 4, 1920 with a picnic and baseball game. About five hundred people attended, watching a baseball game between the teams of the Improved Order of Red Men and Daniels Manufacturing Company and then enjoying a picnic lunch. Speakers included the Speaker of the Massachusetts House of Representatives, Joseph Warner, Senator Warren Tarbell, Emerson Stoddard, and Reverend Doyle of St. John's Church. There was a patriotic sing along, performances by local children, and games. That evening, the party continued in Red Men's Hall with a dance.

Children in East Brookfield continued in the pre-established schoolhouses with the exception that students attended North Brookfield High School for grades 9-12 instead of Brookfield High School, where they had previously attended. (Spencer New Leader, August 6, 1920) East Brookfield joined a "superintendency" with Brookfield and North Brookfield, sharing a superintendent and other staff - including a nurse, music teacher, and drawing teacher - with those towns.

East Brookfield students' attendance at North Brookfield High was short-lived as in 1921 students began attending David Prouty High School in Spencer. Families complained about the time it took to travel to North Brookfield. Upon investigation, the School Committee saw that considerable savings could be had by sending high school students to Spencer High School. The cost of transporting pupils to North Brookfield was $5.00 per day as opposed to $2.00 a day if students took the train from Depot Square to the Spencer station. In addition North Brookfield charged $80.00 per year for tuition and Spencer agreed to tuition of $70.00 per student per year. (East Brookfield School Committee Minutes, September 1, 1921.) East Brookfield sent fourteen students to David Prouty that year but continued to pay tuition for students whose parents decided to keep sending them to North Brookfield High. Other students attended the trade school in Worcester.

The School Committee also decided in the first two years of separation to install indoor bathrooms and electricity in the Hodgkins School. This resulted in the building being used more for community meetings. The ever-frugal town reused the wood from the outhouses to build a new fence around the school yard.

In the first years after separation, the economy of town was strong. There was a hotel on Main Street, The Lakewood Hotel, two gas stations, a barbershop, two grocery stores, one on Main Street, the newly open Ledoux's market in Depot Square, and a variety of other stores and businesses.

First officials of the Town of East Brookfield **(Town of East Brookfield, Meeting Minutes, January 3, 1921)**	
Dr. Hayward	Moderator
George J. Daniels	Selectman
A. Howard Drake	Selectman
Warren Tarbell	Selectman
George A. Putney	Town Clerk
Theodore E. Davidson	Town Treasurer & Collector of Taxes
Francis H. Drake	Assessor
Leander Morse	Assessor
J. Matthew Walsh	Assessor

CHAPTER 4

Our Town: Then and Now

Driving through East Brookfield today, a visitor would be surprised to know that this town was once an industrial center of Central Massachusetts as the mills and other evidence of this activity is mostly gone. Only a few rental properties remain to tell the story of Lake Lashaway as a tourist attraction. To those who live here, the town has three distinct sections: the center, including Lake Lashaway; the Flats; and Podunk. While the center of town has changed from mills and workers' housing to small businesses and shops, the Flats has transitioned from a mainly agricultural area to one of more businesses and residential houses and Podunk has remained relatively unchanged with much open space and wooded areas though new homes are built fairly frequently in this area of town.

Part 1
TOWN CENTER

As East Brookfield was originally part of Brookfield, it did not have its own common, as other colonial towns and villages did. The center of town became the businesses along Route 9 at the southern shore of Lake Lashaway and the area to the east where Pleasant and Mechanic Streets merge. Even before becoming an independent town, this area was a bustling community center with a train depot, court house, restaurant, shops, and meeting halls.

One could argue that the train depot was one of the most important buildings in town. People gathered here to greet visitors and to send off those who were traveling. The mail arrived here along with grain, lumber, coal, and everything else the town needed to survive and prosper. Messages could be sent via the Western Union Telegraph inside the building before phones were prevalent in private homes.

There can be no argument that the location of the train tracks helped East Brookfield become an industrial center and economically prosperous. Train service after East Brookfield became a town continued much as it had before, with East Brookfield a central hub of the area for travelers. Linda Ciejka remembers "the beautiful depot, where many times, we, as children, used to get off at after trips with mom from Connecticut, where we then lived. I so looked forward to those trips! (Linda Ciejka, written account, April 2019.) Over time, passenger service was cut due to lack of passengers. In 1948, service was decreased to two west bound trains and one east bound train per day. Twelve years later, in 1960, lack of

Passenger and commercial trains stopped at East Brookfield, approximately 1950s. Photo from Quaboag Valley Railroaders.

East Brookfield Depot, approximately 1950s. Photo from Quaboag Valley Railroaders.

passengers caused the railroad to cancel the commuter train stop in East Brookfield. The waiting room in the depot had already closed by this time. The last train left from East Brookfield's depot for Worcester on March 31, 1960 carrying Joan Bedard and her class of pre-school students from Happy Day Nursery School. ("18 Youngsters Ride Last Train," Mel Singer, Worcester Gazette, March 31, 1960.)

In 1999, CSX Corporation bought the depot from Conrail, and a year later, selectmen and members of the Historical Commission, with the assistance of Senator Stephen Brewer, met with CSX officials in what would be an unsuccessful attempt for the town to acquire the depot. The major roadblock in acquiring the building was CSX's requirement that the building would need to be moved at least fifty feet from the railroad tracks. CSX felt that it was too close to the tracks to be safe. This would require moving the granite and wood building about thirty-five feet, which would require a herculean effort, and perhaps up to $500,000. This was insurmountable and no further action was taken by the town.

Tragically to many town residents, at 10:30 P.M. on September 18, 2010, an arsonist set fire to the historic depot. Firefighters' efforts were hampered as the building was boarded up and flames were mostly coming from the side of the building nearest the tracks. In order for them to safely fight the fire, they first had to stop all trains so firefighters would not be struck. The wooden roof collapsed before the flames could be put out. An effort by hundreds of people to save the depot was firmly rebuffed by CSX, who would not allow anyone near the site to salvage any remains and declared that the granite blocks were contaminated. The building was razed and remains a much missed icon of the town.

East Brookfield Firefighters attempt to douse the already engulfed building. Photo from EB Fire Department FaceBook page, 2010.

In December of 2011, David W. Hays of Oxford was arrested and charged with arson in the case.

One staple of Pleasant Street has been a market, which is currently Depot Square Deli. In 1916, Arthur LeDoux first leased and then purchased the building from Senator Warren Tarbell and opened Ledoux's Market. The property consisted of the store on the first floor, living quarters on the second floor, and an adjoining storehouse to the left of the main building, which has since been removed. In 1986 Paul and Diane Mitchell purchased the business from Pat and Chris Ahearn. The store was called Ahearn's Market at the time. The Mitchells renamed it "The Meat and Spirit Shoppe" and ran it until 1992 when they sold it to Steve and Karen Brennan. Retirement was not to be for the Mitchells yet, and they purchased the store back in 1998. At this time, they renamed it The General Store. It was the Podunk Deli for a short time under the operation of Mike and Amy Bosse, and then Depot Square Deli, which it is called today. In January of 2019, Paul and Diane Mitchell sold the store to Trikal Darshi Bhaila.

Another of Arthur LeDoux's business ventures was a movie house. In early 1926, a moving picture house opened in the building that is currently between Depot Square Deli and the Senior Center. The Swan Theater had a seating capacity of 150. Joan Leger Bedard, in her memoir, All Ya' Need is Love remembers attending shows here as a child, noting that local pianists would play along with the films until "talkies" came into being in 1930. The theater was the American Legion headquarters during World War II and they continued to show movies on Saturday afternoons and held minstrel shows until the late 1950s or early 1960s.

This turn-of-the-century postcard shows Pleasant Street. On the left you can see the building that was on the vacant lot between today's Post Office and the Depot Square Deli, followed by the general store. The Senior Center appears green in this hand-colored photo. (Postcard from collection of EB Historical Museum.)

A Day in the Life...

"Most of this time was during the Depression and my dad was a bricklayer and stone mason, but no one was having this work done, as no one had any money. So during the Depression he worked for P.D. Bousquet, carrying ice and shoveling coal. I remember him wearing a heavy rubber sheet on his back, carrying a block of ice and of course he'd always chip off some little pieces for his little girls."

Account of Pauline Dilling, April 21, 1994.

A fire destroyed the former Vizard's Opera House as well as the district court house, a barn, a blacksmith shop, and a paint shop on January 22, 1926. The Opera House had been sold ten years prior and was operating as Default Brothers Counter Factory at the time. The 15 degree weather impeded the ability of firemen to fight the fire. Hoses were run from the fire to Lake Lashaway where holes had to be chopped in foot-thick ice to provide water to the those fighting the fire. The fire was believed to have started in the boiler room of the factory. Joseph Dufault, owner of the factory when it burned, built the two small brick buildings that now occupy the location on Mechanic Street. These buildings were his new shop, and then a barbershop, the District Court, and were rented by the town as town offices.

Other businesses that have operated in Depot Square include a bakery run by Mr. and Mrs. John Beebe, a beauty salon, a bookstore, a candy store and several others. Depot Square was also the location of the first Western Worcester County Courthouse. It

Vizard's Opera House is the large white building, Vizard's Pharmacy and the Hotel Pilgrim were located in the brick building. Photo from EB Historical Museum.

Before it was an Opera House, the building was a factory, as pictured here. It was converted to a factory again about ten years before being destroyed by a fire. Photo from EB Historical Museum. No date.

was first located in the former depot building that had been moved to the north of the Keith Block and then in a small brick building leased from a private citizen. Locating it near the train station made it readily accessible. Since the efforts of East Brookfield resident and State Senator Warren Tarbell were essential in the creation of this courthouse, it made sense to locate it in East Brookfield.

The 100,000+ square foot mill building at the corner of Mechanic Street and Route 9 continued to be used as a manufacturing plant in the twentieth century. The Daniels Manufacturing Company, which made woolen products, purchased it in 1915, employing hundreds of workers. In 1929, at the start of the Great Depression, they, along with the Stevens Mills, closed indefinitely, leaving 450 people out of work. In 1935, The Daniels Manufacturing Company moved out of town, relocating to a larger factory in Indiana.

> *"They called them the good old days - and I agree. We didn't have much, but we appreciated what we had, and I personally thank God that I was part of it." - Pauline Dilling, April 21, 1994 account to Historical Commission*

In 1936 the Maclan Hat Company purchased and renovated the buildings to meet the demand of their parent company, the H. McLachlan and Company Inc. of Danbury, Connecticut. They manufactured felt hats in what was publicized as "the finest and most modern factory of its kind in the industry." (Spencer Leader, July 30, 1937). The plant was designed to produce 1500 dozen hats per day but averaged 500 dozen per day. Each hat required five gallons of water in its production so the waters of Lake Lashaway were essential to the operation of the plant. The hats were made of rabbit fur that was imported from Australia and France. The company was known for fair treatment and concern for their employees. They prided themselves on maintaining a clean work environment, and as healthy a one as could be that used mercury and acid in production. Uniquely for the time, they gave their workers turkeys for Christmas. The safety features of their plant were copied by other factories who used the same materials because the ventilation system they used was thought to have remedied the health concerns for workers. An article in the Spencer New Leader in December 30, 1938 noted that "the modern industry gives many of its employees more comfort in the factory than they enjoy in their own homes." The Maclan Hat Company operated in East Brookfield until 1941 when a scarcity of raw materials forced their closure.

The building remained vacant until 1946 when Brookfield Plastic and Rubber Corporation purchased it. They changed their name to Brookfield Mills in 1947 and continued to manufacture plastic products until 1949. In that year, it was purchased by an affiliate of Holliston Mills, named the Brookfield Mills of East Brookfield and manufactured fabrics. It became home to Brookfield Athletic Shoe Company in 1956. The company made baseball shoes and roller skates and had a store attached to the plant where many, if not all, people in town purchased their roller skates, basketball shoes, and jogging shoes, one of their most popular items. Founded by Brad Hause, Charles Daniels, and Edward Urban, the company also manufactured football and basketball shoes, including purple basketball sneakers for the Holy Cross team. Ed Urban left the company in 1959 and founded American Athletic Shoe Company in Ware. This company still makes ice skates. Their website states that they are the leading supplier of ice skates in the country today. ("About Us." American Athletic Shoe, 24 Feb. 2019, americanathleticshoe.com/pages/about-us.).

Alvin Wolfe and David Landay bought the company and expanded production to include ice skates. Brookfield Athletic Shoe Company was the largest manufacturer of ice skates in the world in the 1960s, producing 750,000 pairs a year. The company partnered with athletes, including Bobby Orr and Lee Travino, whose names were then attached to products. Saucony, once named Hyde Athletic Industries, purchased the facility in 1985. At the time, canvas shoes were quite popular and Brookfield Athletics held the patent to PF Flyers. After purchasing the company, Saucony re-released PF Flyers in 1988 to compete with Keds and Converse. They used the facility as a warehouse and distribution center instead of manufacturing products there. They employed about fifteen people at their 109,000 square foot facility. They later sold the company to Stride Rite.

The years of manufacturing that took place at this site, particularly that of the Maclan Hat Company, resulted in contamination of the soil and sediment in the East Brookfield River. Before anyone knew of its damaging effects, on both the health of workers and the environment, mercury was used to soften fur pelts that were made into hats. In 2010, due to a build up of metals, including mercury, coal, and fuel residue, then owner Saucony cleaned up the site by removing sediment from the river bottom and some soil, a process that cost between $3 and $4 million. Luckily, no elevated levels of contaminants were found in the water, just in the soil.

East Brookfield, even before it was an independent town, was always lucky enough to have strong fire and police departments.

The fire station, or Old Engine House, was originally located behind the current fire station on School Street. This building was used for a variety of purposes throughout the years. The police department was once located on the second floor; the town lockup was in the basement; school committee meetings and meetings of the first town officers were held here in the first year after separation from Brookfield; during the Depression there was a shop on the second floor, where Joan Bedard remembers her mother sewing pajamas. The Civil Defense Department used the building as their headquarters and communications center. Eventually the recreation department used it to store equipment. The building fell into disrepair and was torn down in 2018.

The Old Engine House, as it looked in 2017, before being torn down in 2018. Photo by author.

At the time of the separation from Brookfield, the fire department was made up of volunteers. Arthur LeDoux served as the first fire chief. When the mills were operating, each had its own fire fighting company to ensure the fastest response possible to a fire that could easily destroy an entire business, especially in the mainly wooden structures and the pottery and brick factories in town. In the days before motor vehicles, the town fire department would respond to alarms with a "steamer," which had a hose attached to it to pump water from a close water source like a lake, pond, or river. Whichever fireman arrived first at the station

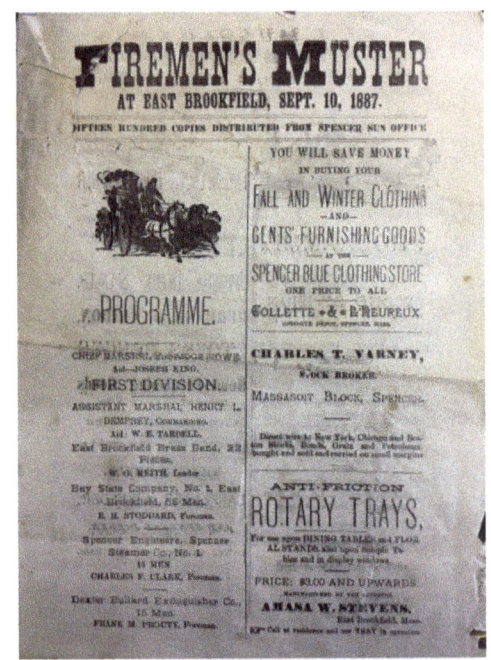

Flyer for Firemen's Muster held in East Brookfield. From collection of EB Historical Museum.

would use his own horses to pull the steamer. Those who arrived to the engine house later would also use their horses to bring a supply wagon to the fire. Firemen were compensated when they had to use their own horses.

Initially, there was no siren on the engine house. A report from the Fire Engineers in 1908 expressed concern that using the bell at the Baptist Church as the fire alarm caused confusion as it was also rung for other purposes. The engineers were in support of asking a nearby mill building to install a whistle that would be used by the fire department to signal an emergency. The situation had not improved by 1917 when the bell on the church was not functioning so there was no way to alert firemen to a fire. (Report of the Fire Engineers, Annual Report of the Town of East Brookfield, 1908 and 1917.) It was not until 1925 that a siren was installed.

Firemen's musters were a popular event in the 1800s and 1900s. The East Brookfield department won their share of trophies in these competitions. Fire departments from all over the area competed with each other and showed off their new equipment, particularly in the late 1800s when new technologies were used. The town purchased a new fire truck in 1925 and another in 1929.

In 1953, the town authorized $20,000 to build a new fire house. The one story, cinder block building was completed in October of 1954. It was the first town building that was built and owned by East Brookfield since its incorporation in 1920. A second story was added in 1980.

Today's fire department is comprised of a fire chief, David Messier, a deputy fire chief, Jim Bain, a captain, and four lieutenants. In 2006, the fire department added its first full-time paramedic. Today, Joshua McCrillis and Tricia Durand are the two full-time employees on the fire department. Both are firefighters. Mr. McCrillis holds the rank of lieutenant and is also a paramedic. Ms. Durand is also an EMT. They serve as fire inspectors for the town and work with the SAFE program to educate children on fire safety.

The second story being added to the fire department. Photo from collection of EB Historical Museum.

The East Brookfield Fire Association is one of the most active groups in town. They have taken on the town's tradition of hosting an Independence Day

East Brookfield Fire Department, Photo 2011, courtesy of the Fire Department.

Celebration, in partnership with the Friends of the Community Group. This is one of the events for which East Brookfield has become known. In 1956, a committee was formed to plan this annual celebration. The 1958 parade included sixty separate groups, encompassing all branches of the military, drum and bugle corps, floats, marching bands, and fire departments from area towns. Another tradition, a bicycle and baby carriage parade was held, along with midway rides on the field near the school. According to the Worcester Daily Telegram, 20,000 people came out to watch the parade and participate in the other festivities of the day. (Worcester Daily Telegram, July 5, 1958). The East Brookfield Fire Association raises over $12,000 a year for this day-long event through donations and volunteer their time for the event. The town is quite lucky to have these dedicated men and women who help not only keep us safe, but work to make this a fun town in which to live.

The Police Department was once made up of constables, who were elected town officials. They served on a one year basis. The first police station was in the Old Engine House and George Bolac was the first chief. Eventually, a police department was created and their ranks were supplemented with officers from the Civil Defense. The police chief earned a small salary of $500 per year and had to use his own vehicle, for which he received a stipend. Much of the police work, including booking and holding those arrested, was done out of their own home. Larry Gordon remembers when his grandfather, Howard Green, was police chief and there was a button on the wall in his house that would set off the alarm at the fire department. The grandchildren were always warned not to press the button, though what a temptation it must have been! It was not until 1978 that a full-time police officer was added to the town. The first to serve on a full-time basis was then Chief Eric Hunderup. Later, in 1987, a second full-time patrolman was added. The town currently has four full-time officers. Over the years, the Police Association has hosted Bicycle Safety program for children, pizza parties on Halloween, and has been an integral part of every event in town. We appreciate all these officers do to keep our town safe.

Varney's Garage was originally located where Parsons Auto is today, on the corner of Route 9 and Mechanic Street. It was the area's first Authorized Ford Dealer. In addition to selling cars, there was a lunch room located on the second floor. Lionel Lamoureux purchased the Ford dealership and the building in 1977 and Varney's moved to the Flats. In 1981, Lamoureux Ford moved to its current location on Main Street near Evergreen Cemetery and Parsons Auto Incorporated started their auto body business here. Parsons Auto was originally founded by William Parsons, Sr, a veteran who also was head of the local American Legion. Today, Parsons Auto Inc. continues to be run by members of the Parsons family.

William Parsons, owner of Parsons Auto Body, Post Commander of the American Legion, and EB Fire Chief for 20 years. Photo by Tracy Holt.

> *"While the 'baby town of MA has a few specks of industry, it is mainly a peaceful and truly old-fashioned town, a breath of fresh air compared to the present day urban America. Its people are as hospitable as if they had just stepped out of the mid-nineteenth century. To supplement this, EB has a beauty and charm often lost in today's world."*
>
> *Richard Jones, junior high essay for 1970 Anniversary of EB.*

During the early 1900's, there was a large portion of the town that wanted the town to be alcohol-free. A question on the first ballot of the newly independent town asked residents to decide if they wanted to allow liquor to be sold in town. In response to the question of whether "intoxicating liquors" should be licensed in town, fifty-nine residents voted no and thirty-nine voted yes. However, just a year later, in 1922, the vote was in favor of selling these drinks, with 106 residents approving the sale of liquor and 104 opposing; still a controversial issue! One of the most common reasons for arrests during this time was being drunk in public, which probably influenced public opinion. Mrs. Jeanne LeBeau recalls her grandfather, Alphonse Gaudette, owned the building where Dunny's Tavern is today. This building was a luncheonette and also their home. Prohibition and a lack of a liquor license didn't stop Mr.

Gaudette and others in town from selling alcohol and resulted in frequent raids by the police. Mrs. LeBeau shared that her grandfather's store included hiding places for liquor in the event of a raid. She remembers her grandfather showing her hiding places in the floor and described another method for hiding liquor through the use of a dumbwaiter to send the liquor to the living area on the second floor which was not searched during raids. This could be because the carpenter who built these hiding spaces was also the chief of police! In 1933, at the end of Prohibition in the United States, three East Brookfield residents were arrested after raids on their businesses. Constables and State Troopers found one person in possession of 300 bottles of beer. (Spencer Leader, February 2, 1933.) He escaped fines or jail time as it could not be proved that he sold any of the beer. Apparently, possessing the beer was not illegal, just selling it without a license.

The current Senior Center has served as a meeting place for town government, church groups, scouting groups, other community groups over the years. As early as 1860 it was used as a type of town hall and from 1921 until Memorial School was built in 1957, it held graduation ceremonies. Private events such as fundraising events, wedding receptions, anniversary parties, and baby showers were frequently held in this building. It was the home of the Improved Order of Red Men from 1900 to the 1970s. The Red Men purchased the building from W.G. Keith in 1913 and donated it to the town when it disbanded. Today, it houses the very active East Brookfield Senior Center and serves as a meeting place for cub scouts, the Lashaway Quilt Guild, the Spencer Garden Club, and is a reception hall after Memorial Day and Veterans' Day ceremonies at the nearby Depot Square Memorial.

East Brookfield Senior Center today. Formerly Red Man's Hall, Fay's Hall, and Doane and Spellman Building, photo by author 2016.

The Improved Order of Red Men was a national fraternal society whose motto was "Freedom, Friendship, and Charity." Officially begun in 1813 in Pennsylvania, as the "Society of Red Men," the organization spread into surrounding states and was reorganized in 1834 as the "Improved Order of Red

A Day in the Life...

"I will always remember skating on the lake. I will always remember the old ice house and the men cutting the ice. I will always remember crunching through the snow for 5 AM Mass on holy days at the old church. I will always remember my grandmother frying eggs and salt pork and making toast on the stove for my grandfather and Great Uncle Joe before they went to cut wood at the wood lot for the day. I will always remember the rows and rows of wood in the backyard stacked so neatly they weren't an inch out of line."

Account of Pauline Dilling,

The Keith Building, 2018. Photo by author.

Men." Membership in the society grew and in 1847 a Grand Council of the United States was established to oversee the many local groups. Even though the society officially began in 1813, they trace their roots back to the many patriotic societies that existed in the American colonies and were the driving forces behind the American Revolution. As evidence of this connection, in "The Official History of the Improved Order of the Red Men," the authors cite the fact that the Sons of Liberty dressed as Native Americans during the Boston Tea Party as well as similar traditions and ceremonies between these early groups and their own. The organization was established in East Brookfield in 1900. In 1964, there were 476,000 members of the society across the country. The group was very active in East Brookfield, holding meetings as well as dances and other events.

The Keith Block has perhaps had the most varied use of any building in town. As described previously, it was built in 1887 by W.G. Keith and used as a combination furniture store and undertaker's office. In 1936, the Keith Block was donated to the town by Bertha Turner. The town then sold the building and used the proceeds to purchase land for the highway department near the Seven Mile River. This land is still used by the town for sand and salt storage and the recycling center and housed the highway department prior to their move to Main Street. At this point, the Keith Block was purchased by Joseph Benoit, who rented it out to the state guardsmen during World War II before selling it to the railroad. In 1944, the railroad renovated the building into a dormitory for workers by adding showers in the basement, a kitchen, laundry, and cafeteria on the first floor, sleeping quarters on the second floor, and a recreation room on the third floor. The railroad used it as a dorm for workers for several years; approximately seventy workers were housed in the building while they worked on rails in Central Massachusetts. In 1956, A&W Machine Company of Charlton purchased Keith Block from the Railroad.

The rear of the Keith Block and the main entrance to the town library when it was housed here. Photo by author, 2018.

Between 1920 and 1975, there was no town hall in East Brookfield. The town held their weekly meetings in rented space in Roger Archambeault's Barbershop near Depot Square and the annual town meeting was held in Red Men's Hall. The town clerk and the library operated out of private homes, and, while the police department was located above the fire barn, you were more likely to reach the police chief at his home. In 1975, the barbershop would no longer be available for meetings. In the same year, the A & W Machine Tool Company declared bankruptcy and put the Keith Building up for auction due to bankruptcy. This seemed like a good opportunity to finally have all town offices under the same roof. Since a town bylaw did not allow the town to make a purchase without knowing the price, a group of five residents bought the building themselves at auction and then sold it to the town. In a true example of Yankee frugality, the revised building plan was completed for free by students of David Prouty High School, the Highway Department removed any remaining equipment and library trustees held a green stamp drive to purchase furnishings. The building was ready within five weeks and cost the town a total of $77,000. ("They Did It Their Way," Jeff Hunter, Yankee Magazine, March 1980) A dedication ceremony was held on June 13, 1976 and the town government of East Brookfield finally had a home to call its own.

The Keith Block was used as the town hall until 2005, housing the police department in the basement, town offices on the first floor, the library on the second floor, and a meeting hall on the third floor. The third floor meeting hall was used by the Boy Scouts for many years. Eventually, air quality issues caused by years of drainage issues mandated a move out of the building. In addition, the tiny police department in the basement was not sufficient for the needs of the growing department. There were no holding cells (detainees were handcuffed to the wall), it flooded on every rainy day, and it was accessible only by descending a flight of stairs under the fire escape, making it not handicap accessible. A committee established in the late 1990s tried to purchase or build a new police station. Potential sites were the old courthouse at 104 Mechanic Street and land that would be donated by Lionel Lamoureux on Drake Street for the purpose of building a police station. Neither of these were accepted and at the same time plans were being made to build a new elementary school which would leave the former school available for a town complex.

By 2008, the move to the new Memorial Town Complex was complete. The Town Offices had moved in first with the library and police department following several months later. While waiting to move to the new location, the police department relocated from the basement to the first floor of the building. At this time, the historic Keith Building remains empty.

During World War II, the first conflict since East Brookfield became independent, the entire town supported the war effort. Various recycling drives were held, an armory was established in one of the buildings of the Maclan Hat Company, and citizens volunteered to man the air-raid warning system 24 hours a day. At one time, sixty-three women volunteered for this task. Frank E. Gaudette served as chairman of the East Brookfield Committee on Public Safety. Auxiliary police and fire and highway departments were established to be put to work in the event of an emergency. The post office sold bonds and stamps to support the war. A Civilian Defense Club, established in April 1942, sent items to men and women from East Brookfield who were stationed overseas or on U.S. bases. In 1942, this included twenty-eight men and one woman with more enlisting each year. By the end of 1942, sixty-two men and women from East Brookfield were in the armed forces and were serving in Trinidad, Italy, New Guinea, Hawaii, Australia, North Africa, England, the Pacific, and bases throughout the U.S. By the end of 1944, the number of enlisted men and women increased to one hundred twenty three.

Many East Brookfield men and women served with distinction during the war. A few are noted here: Special Sergeant Fred Walker, Jr. was stationed at Pearl Harbor during the attack. Another East Brookfield native, Raymond Bialobrezewski, was on the aircraft carrier U.S.S. Princeton when it was sunk in battle. He reported jumping eight-five feet into the water and spending four hours in the water before being rescued (Spencer Leader, Dec, 22, 1944). Corporal Gregory Walsh received the Purple Heart after being wounded in France. Sergeant Howard Green earned a Purple Heart as part of the 3rd Armored

Division at the Battle of the Bulge. When he returned home he became Chief of Police. Frederick Fish, a twenty-one year old resident of East Brookfield and a Seaman, First Class in the U.S. Navy, was stationed on board the U.S.S. Albert W. Grant. This destroyer assisted in the landing of troops in the South Pacific before sinking a Japanese battleship near the end of the war. Corporal Wilrose Goodro of East Brookfield was awarded a Good Conduct Medal during his time with the 359th Fighter Group as an Ordnance Expert. Corporal Michilina Ficociello was a member of the European Division of the U.S. Air Force's Transport Command which carried troops and supplies back and forth between the United States and Europe. Radioman Arthur Beaudette was stationed on the U.S.S. Hyman in 1945 when the Japanese commander of the region surrendered and Ernest Zalatores served on the U.S.S. Denver as it traveled over 150,000 miles in the South Pacific over the course of the war. This ship had previously supported the attacks on Iwo Jima and Okinawa by shooting down Japanese planes during the battles. After the war, Sergeant Charles J. Fitzpatrick, Jr. served as a special guard with the U.S. Army at the Palace of Justice in Nuremberg. Ralph E. McCoy received the Bronze Star Medal for exemplary conduct against the enemy in 1944 when he was part of General Patton's Third Army during the Normandy Invasion. McCoy also served in Canada and England and was on the Susan B. Anthony when it was sunk in the English Channel. After serving four years in the Army, Mr. McCoy returned to East Brookfield and worked for the Post Office. Major Sergeant Wallace Grimes served as Section Sergeant of H Company in the 259th Infantry, 65th Division. This division was tasked with defending France from invading German forces. The 65th Division was the spearhead of General Patton's 3rd Army in Germany and drove the Germans back from France to Austria. Mr. Grimes returned to his farm on Adams Street in East Brookfield after the war ended.

In November 1942, John Brooks Williams, who lived on Mechanic Street with his sister, Hazel Card, was listed as missing in action by the Navy. His ship, the S.S. West Chetac had been torpedoed two months earlier. He was twenty years old when killed in service, having enlisting in the Navy at age eighteen. Prior to enlisting, he worked at the Maclan Hat Company. In 1944, his sister was given a Mariner's Award in recognition of his service during the war.

Private First Class Carl Skyten was eighteen was he was killed in a plane crash at Davis Montham Army Air Base in Tucson, Arizona. Private Skyten was a nose gunner. He was one of six men killed in the crash; five others were wounded. He and his family lived on Cove Street. After attending David Prouty High School and Worcester Boys Trade School, he joined the army in January of the same year he was killed. He was buried with full military honors in Evergreen Cemetery.

Army Corporal Mitchell H. Boulette, age 27, was on the front lines in France when he was killed by a German blast that exploded the gas tanks of his tank. He had lived on Putney Court in East Brookfield for thirteen years and worked at the Maclan hat Factory when war was declared. He enlisted the next day. Three of his brothers were also in the military, one in Italy, one in France, and a third training in Georgia at the time of his death. Two other brothers served with the Massachusetts State Guard.

Another man, H. Jacques Von Rosendael, is listed in the Town of East Brookfield's Annual Report of 1945 as killed in action in the war. His name is not mentioned in other reports, though it is noted that he was not serving in the U.S. Forces at the time of his death. Von Rosendael was a sergeant in the Number 10 Commando 2 troop in the Dutch Army when when he was killed by a German rocket in Princenhage. He is listed in research by Frans Kluiters as a secret agent who infiltrated Amsterdam on behalf of the Allied forces. ("Dutch Agents, 1940-1945," September 2008, www.nisa-intelligence.nl/PDF-bestanden/KluitersDAG2foto.pdf). It is unclear what his connection to the town of East Brookfield might have been, perhaps he worked in town or his family lived here.

During the war, many of those who were not enlisted, or who were retired from military service, prepared to protect the town. Members of the State Guard's Company 6 of Brookfield and Company 7 of East Brookfield held an overnight training exercise on Vizard's Hill and Teneriffe Hill on Howe Street. In charge was Captain Frank Gaudette of East Brookfield and Captain Herman Wright of Brookfield. They drilled in scouting, patrolling, and maneuvers of guerrilla warfare. The guardsmen rented the Keith Block in Depot Square, which at the time was owned by Joseph Benoit, and used it as a headquarters. The newspaper articles of the time show how residents all joined in the effort to support those fighting in the war. There were book drives, metal drives, and stamps that were sold to raise money. Volunteers manned the whistle at the Maclan Hat Factory twenty-four hours a day to warn the town in the event of an air raid.

American Legion Officers, 1948. Back row: Wilrose Goodro, Joseph Perry, Julian Fedler, Ray Chapin. Front row: Dave Gagne, Lawrence Gordon, Richard Young, Jimmy Hebert, Emil LeBlanc. From collection of EB Historical Museum.

American Legion, Women's Auxiliary, 1948. Back row: Eve Donnelly, Lora Young, Pauline Dilling, Vida Moynaugh, Ruth Green, Mary Grenier. Front Rom: Mary Gordon, Elizabeth Goodro, Lena St. Germain, Rita Chapin, Bea Gagne. From collection of EB Historical Museum.

After the war ended, the Boulette-Skyten Post of the American Legion was established in 1946. A committee made up of Joseph Perry, Wallace Boulette, Anthony Kowalski, and Ephraim Manning were tasked with raising funds and finding a meeting place for the newly formed post. The post was highly active for many years, earning commendations for high membership.

On May 20, 1947, an airplane carrying East Brookfield resident Ernest R. Young, a twenty-five-year-old Lieutenant in the army, crashed in a thunderstorm in Champagne, Illinois. Lieutenant Young enlisted in the army in October of 1942. After graduating from radio school, gunnery school, and the Air Corps Cadet School, he spent six months in Korea before returning to the United States. He had been married six days before the crash.

After World War II, tensions and fears did not disappear and the Cold War had an impact on the town. At the end of 1950, citizens gathered in the school to organize a civil defense program. Led by James Herbert, the Commander of the American Legion, the group sent pamphlets to residents offering tips for protecting themselves from an atomic attack. They also created plans

Ernest Young, photo from his personal collection, donated to EB Historical Museum.

for potential evacuations, shelters, and fires. The Cold War continued through the 1970s and many East Brookfield residents served in the wars in Korea and Vietnam.

Army Captain Paul D. Berthiaume was killed in action on December 23, 1965 during the Vietnam War by small arms fire in the Quang Ngai province of South Vietnam. He was twenty-seven years old and had graduated from Norwich University in 1959. His name is inscribed on the Vietnam Veteran's Memorial in Washington D.C. on Panel 04e, Line 35.

Army Captain Paul D. Berthiaume. https://www.honorstates.org/index.php?id=262194

To date, those on the East Brookfield Honor Roll are: Army Corporal Mitchell H. Boulette, killed in action during World War II, Army Air Force Private First Class Carl F. Skyten, died in service during World War II, Merchant Marine Able Seaman John B. Williams, missing in action during World War II, Army Air Corp Second Lieutenant Ernest R. Young, died in service after World War II and Army Captain Paul D. Berthiaume, killed in action during the Vietnam War. The two bridges nearest to the Depot Square Memorial were dedicated to the men killed in World War II. The bridge over the railroad tracks is named in memory of Mitchell Boulette and Carl Skyten; the bridge over the Seven Mile River in memory of John Williams and Ernest Young.

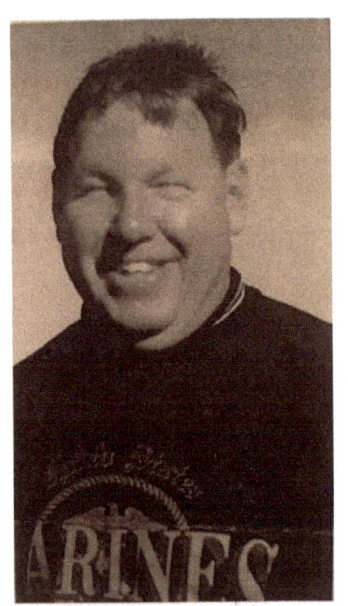

Colonel Jim Terry, U.S. Marine Corp, Ret. Dec. 2014, www.fairfaxmemorialfuneralhome.com/obituaries/Col-James-Philip-Terry?obId=2418003#/obituaryInfo.

Men and women from East Brookfield have served their country in many capacities and with great honor over the years. One example is James Terry, a Podunk resident, 1964 graduate of David Prouty High School, and U.S. Marine Colonel, who became one of the top military lawyers in the United States. Born in East Brookfield in 1946, Colonel Terry was the son of Philip Terry, a World War II Navy pilot. He graduated from the University of Virginia in 1968 and became a lieutenant in the United States Marine Corps. He volunteered for service in Vietnam and sustained multiple gunshot wounds as an infantry platoon leader during Operation Virginia Ridge in 1969. As a result of his injuries, he was paralyzed from the waist down.

After spending over a year in the hospital, he attended George Washington University School of Law and earned multiple doctorates. He served forty-two years in various federal government various posts. In 1992, he became legal counsel to then Chairman of the Joint Chiefs of Staff Colin Powell and retired in 2011 as Chairman of the Board of Veterans' Appeals. He then became a Senior Fellow at the University of Virginia's Center for National Security Law and wrote several books on constitutional and international law. Over the course of his career, he earned a Purple Heart, a Bronze Star with Merit, the Legion of Merit and the Navy's Commendation Medal as well as The State Department Superior Honor Medal, the Defense Superior Service Medal, and numerous other commendation medals. Colonel Terry died in 2014 at the age of 68 and is buried in Arlington National Cemetery. ("Col. James Philip Terry Obituary - Visitation & Funeral Information." Fairfax, VA Funeral Services - Fairfax Memorial Funeral Home, Dec. 2014, www.fairfaxmemorialfuneralhome.com/obituaries/Col-James-Philip-Terry?obId=2418003#/obituaryInfo.)

East Brookfield resident Captain Glenn A. Fletcher United States Navy Special Operations is the highest ranking member of the military in the history of East Brookfield. Captain Fletcher enlisted in the Navy in 1965 as a Seaman Recruit and, after a 38-year career, retired with a rank of Captain. He attributes his impressive career to the help and guidance of several outstanding Chief Petty Officers and Naval Officers. His duties included serving on three ships, three tours as an Executive Officer and two tours as a Commanding Officer. Additionally, he served as a liaison officer (LNO) to the Navy Special Warfare Group 2 (SEAL) during Operation Earnest Will in the Northern Persian Gulf; as a combat veteran in Desert Storm; four tours of duty in the Middle East; Inspector General for the U.S. Southern Command; and participated in counter-drug operations in Central and South America and the Caribbean. At the time of his retirement, he

Captain Glenn A. Fletcher, U.S. Navy, Ret. at Podunk Cemetery leading the Honor Guard, 2018. Photo by Tracy Holt.

held the distinction of being the senior and longest continuously qualified diver in the U.S. Navy. In the Diving Navy, the person who holds this position is oft times referred to as "The Gray Shark." Captain Fletcher held the title of "The Gray Shark" for his last three years in the Navy. He attended college on the GI

Bill and earned a degree in Natural Science/Marine BioPhysics, graduating Summa Cum Laude from Worcester State College. In addition, Captain Fletcher was a police officer in the town of Brookfield and a Massachusetts Environmental Police Officer. He served as a constable for the Town of East Brookfield for many years and has been a member of the East Brookfield Honor Guard on Memorial Day since 1991.

Military service is embedded in Captain Fletcher's family. His father served under General Patton at the Battle of the Bulge. He was wounded, captured and became a prisoner of war in a Nazi concentration camp during World War II. His children both have careers in the military. His son Tristan is a Naval Special Warfare Special Boat Team Chief Petty Officer (SWCC - Special Warfare Combatant Crewman) with multiple combat tours in the Middle East and South and Central American Counter Drug Operations. His daughter, Aldebaran Kari, is a Navy Pilot and Combat Veteran, who served in the Persian Gulf as a Senior Pilot and Mission Commander on multi aircraft combat operations in the Middle East. She was the first female shooter on the USS Harry S Truman on a Persian Gulf Combat deployment and qualified as the 174th OOD Underway on the USS Truman. His son-in-law is an F-18 fighter pilot with multiple combat tours in the Middle East. Clearly patriotism and pride run deep in his family. In Captain Fletcher's words, he has "had the honor and privilege to serve with the finest and bravest people on the face of the Earth." (Gablaski, Heather. "Interview of Captain Glenn A. Fletcher." 5 May 2014.)

The current Depot Square War Memorial was formerly known as "Vizard's Common." It was donated to the town by Joseph Default in 1933 to be used as a war memorial to the twenty-eight East Brookfield residents who were veterans of World War I. Later, during World War II, Charles E. Worthington made a donation to the town to improve Depot Square. As part of the Memorial Day services in 1949, an eight-foot tall granite memorial to veterans of all wars was dedicated. The memorial is inscribed with the words, "The memory of a great name and the inheritance of a great example is the legacy of

Depot Square War Memorial. Photo by author, 2016.

heroes." Symbols inscribed on the memorial include a shield, an eagle, a cross, and a sword. In 2000, the Depot Square Reconstruction Committee, led by Tim McNeaney, added two more monuments to the site, one with the names of East Brookfield residents who fought in World War II, and another for veterans of the Korean and Vietnam Wars. Part of the project was the addition of an an iron fence, brick pavers, some inscribed, and landscaping.

Each Memorial Day and Veterans' Day veterans and residents gather here to pay their respects to the men and women from East Brookfield who have served in the armed forces and in particular those who were killed in service to our country. The Memorial Day commemoration has followed a similar schedule and series of events since the 1800s. A small ceremony is held at Podunk Cemetery early in the day. Then, a parade leaves from Connie Mack Drive, to a ceremony at Evergreen Cemetery and regroups to march to a final ceremony at Depot Square. The first Veterans' Day Ceremony was held in 1990, sponsored by the Depot Square Reconstruction Committee, to honor veterans and bring attention to the group's plans to enhance the memorial. Mr. McNeaney continues to facilitate the Veterans' Day program to this day.

Located just west of the veterans' memorial, today's post office was completed and dedicated on September 11, 1958. This building was the first in the town that had been specifically built as a post office. The first post office in the town was commissioned in 1833 inside one of the general stores in town that was located on the site of what is Parsons Auto today. The post office later moved to the Neish Block on Mechanic Street. The Neish Block is now the wooden apartment building between the current post office and the brick building, which was the former location of Thibeault's Market. In this location, the post office had a whole room to itself rather than sharing space inside a store. In August 1948, the post office moved to Main Street, near where the Trolley Stop is today. As time went by, this location proved to be too small to accommodate the business done at the post office and the new building, the current building, was commissioned.

Current East Brookfield Post Office on Pleasant Street. Built in 1958. Photo by author, 2016.

Prior to the establishment of rural mail

delivery, people had to travel to the post office to pick up their mail. Frank Gaudette delivered mail to those living in the Podunk section of town for over forty years. His route extended into Sturbridge and Charlton and covered fifty-six miles. he delivered mail to almost four hundred families a day. Before the roads were paved in the 1930s, if the roads were too muddy, he had to use a horse and buggy or his car would get stuck. He had to rely on farmers to pull his car or buggy out of snow or mud at times. Using the horse and buggy extended the time it took to deliver the mail by twelve hours. ("Rural Mail Carrier Retiring at EB," Singer, Mel; Sunday Telegram, 5/24/1964). He was probably pretty happy when the roads were all paved!

Another staple of East Brookfield that may have been forgotten since it closed in 1985 was the blacksmith shop on Bridge Street. Run by the Benoit Family for two generations, it was located in the stone house that is now on Water Street. Ernest Benoit's father started the business in 1892 and Ernest, nicknamed Pet, worked with him and ran the business after his father died. Glen Silliman, in his junior high essay for the 50th Anniversary of the town shared: *"We have a blacksmith shop whose owner and worker is Ernest (Pet)*

The Benoit Blacksmith Shop on Bridge Street. Today, it has been converted to a home. Photo from EB Historical Museum Collection.

Benoit. Pet doesn't shoe horses any more. He mostly welds and if you have a broken runner on your sled he is the one to see about getting it fixed." A common sight was Mr. Benoit working in the door of his shop as before the new bridges were built the building was right on Bridge Street. Ernest Benoit retired in 1985 at the age of 79, sold the shop and the house behind it, and moved to Florida.

Before curbside pickup began in 1988, the town dump was located at the end of Connie Mack Drive. Formerly the location of a succession of brick yards, first Moulton's, then Parmenter's, and finally the New England Brickworks, the town purchased the land in 1945. They had plans to tear down the remaining house to build a new school. Before they could, it was destroyed by a fire, thought to be set by young people celebrating V-J Day. The town dump finally opened in 1964. If you wanted to hear the gossip of the day, you would head to the dump and invariably meet up with many others who were engaged in conversation after disposing of their trash. Those who were running for office could be found here campaigning for votes in the weeks leading up to election day. This area is now vacant except during the Independence Day Celebration when the fireworks display is set off from here.

The strength of the community in the mid-twentieth century is clear through the sheer number of community organizations. In the year 1950, all of the following organizations are mentioned at least once in the local papers: the Connie Mack League, Quaboag Button Club, East Brookfield Civic Club, St. Ann's Sodality [Guild] of St. John's Church, Ladies Benevolent Society of the East Brookfield Baptist Church, the Parent Teacher Association, Lashaway Rod and Gun Club, Lassawa Tribe No 139 of the Improved Order of Red Men, the American Legion and Ladies Auxiliary, Youth Fellowship of the East Brookfield Baptist Church, the Podunk Community Club, and the Civil Defense Department. Nearly every weekend, there was at least one and many times multiple community events. Examples of events include whist parties, pitch tournaments, costume parties for Halloween, strawberry shortcake parties, Old Home Day in Podunk, trap shoots at the Lashaway Rod and Gun Club, dances, suppers, plays, minstrel shows, Christmas parties, and performances by the students at the school.

The East Brookfield Baptist Church has stood in the center of town since 1840 and provides a bucolic backdrop to many lake views. The church was renamed East Brookfield Baptist Church in the 1930s and was aligned with the Spencer Baptist Church until 1935, when that group disbanded and remaining members were invited to officially join the East Brookfield fellowship. The hurricane of 1938 severely damaged the church, causing the steeple and the bell to crash into the roof and causing structural damage. Services were held in Red Men's Hall while repairs were conducted.

In 1964, an addition was added to the back of the building for classroom space.

Pastor John Lindsay came to the East Brookfield Baptist Church in 1974 and led the church in a time of prosperity and growth. Over the course

East Brookfield Baptist Church, post-1938. Note the missing steeple which was damaged by the 1938 Hurricane.

East Brookfield Baptist Church, 2016. Photo by author.

of his thirty-two years of leadership, not only did the church membership triple to over three hundred, but the physical building grew as well. In 1977, the church purchased the property across Main Street and renamed it the Deacon Amos Harrington Center. The building has been used as a counseling center, youth group meeting house, Sunday School classroom space, and as a meeting place for Alcoholics Anonymous. The upstairs apartments are rented.

In 1981, the church was renovated and an addition was added. The main platform in the sanctuary was extended and a second seating area for the choir was added. The two aisles were raised to eliminate a small step into the pews and a sound control room was added and a 175-seat balcony was added. Men from the church built the pews for the balcony and used wood from the original church doors to build the dividers between the organ and the piano, the hymnal racks in the balcony and temporary shelving in the kitchen. The mahogany railings in the balcony were made from bannisters salvaged from the Immanuel (Dewey Street) Church in Worcester. The wooden front steps of the church were replaced with brick. A brick home which was located on the Maple Street side of the church was relocated to near the junction of

View of the sanctuary after the last worship service before the renovation. Source: Dedication book, p.6, April 26, 1981.

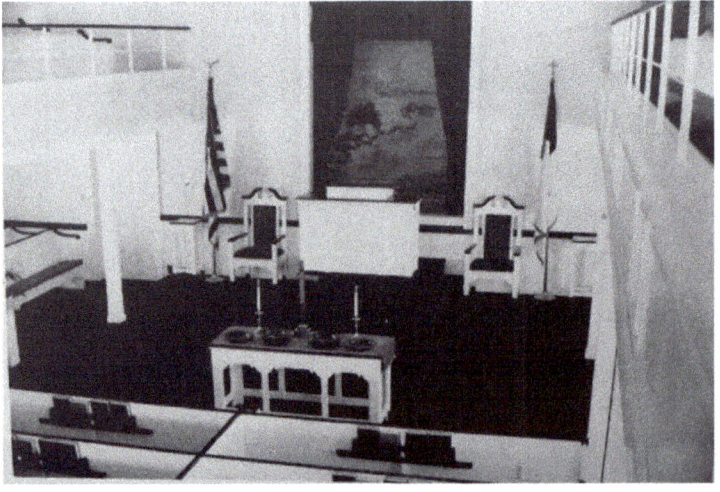

View of the sanctuary from the new balcony. Source: Dedication book, p.6, April 26, 1981.

Town Farm Road and Donovan Road in North Brookfield to provide room for "The Elder Memorial Building," named in honor of Charles and Grace Elder. The addition included classroom space, a library, a narthex, an area to display art work, and the Franklin Drake Chapel, named after a long-time member and prominent citizen. Trees that had been planted in memory of a former paster, the Reverend Charles L. Hoffman, had to be removed for the addition and log benches were made from these blue spruces. They were painted and etched by church member and local artist, Mildred Terry. A small table in the library was made from planks from the original sanctuary.

The classroom space in the new addition was used in the 1980s for public school classes when West Main Street School in Spencer was closed and when repairs needed to be done to Lashaway Junior High. Some elementary classes were held here when the roof of Memorial School needed repairs.

After the separation from Brookfield, a new library was formed with trustees meeting for the first time in January of 1921. The first librarian was Belle Howe Hayward. The new town's library received a lot of support in the form of donations of money, books, and magazines both from residents and other libraries. The Massachusetts Free Library in Boston helped to jumpstart the collection of the fledgling library with a donation of $100 worth of books. They continued to send books and supplies throughout the year. In his junior high essay for the 1970 Anniversary of the town, James Dilling wrote, *"In the first library...were about $100 worth of books from the Massachusetts Branch, plus books people donated or loaned...In those days if people borrowed a book, they paid two cents for that privilege."*

The main library was first located in the Tarbell building on Main Street, which was the next building to the east of where the Trolley Stop is today. In 1943 it moved next door after a fire damaged the building in which it was located. The fire damaged some books and the librarian's desk. Later, it moved across the street to where East Brookfield Pizza is located at 289 East Main Street and still later, in 1976, to the second floor of the Keith Block when the town purchased it as a town hall. This move to a 3,000 square foot single room tripled the size of the library. It took two days to move the collection from Main Street to the new library which officially opened on December 4, 1976.

On April 1, 1950, native East Brookfield resident, Doris Lavigne, was hired as town librarian. She continued in this role for forty-one years until her death in November of 1992. There are few people who grew up in East Brookfield who do not remember Mrs. Lavigne in her role as librarian. Eva Perron recalls that

Author's Memories...

"I remember volunteering at the library after school when I was in junior high. Along with re-shelving and checking out books, this included walking to the General Store and bringing back a Moxie soda for Mrs. Lavigne."

- Heather Gablaski, 2018

she was "a favorite with townspeople and children" and "made every visit a special occasion." (Eva Perron, written account, April 2019.)

Students and their teachers would walk from the school to the library every other week to check out books beginning in 1971 and continuing through the 1980s.

When the Town Hall moved to the newly renovated Memorial Town Complex on Connie Mack Drive, the library moved as well. Its grand re-opening was held on February 25, 2008.

There was also a branch library serving the Podunk section of town that had been established since 1910. This library was located in a private home, most likely that of Mary Putnam, the teacher at the District #3 Schoolhouse, although it could have been in different homes depending on who was serving as librarian at the time. This branch of the library depended on the main branch for its collection, but when first opened, averaged one hundred books checked out to patrons each month. It closed in 1951 due to a decrease in use.

At the time of separation from Brookfield, East Brookfield children attended three schools, two in Podunk and one in the center of town. The two Podunk schools were one-room schoolhouses which at different times had anywhere between two and twenty students enrolled. They have been described in more detail in a previous chapter.

The Hodgkins School, built in 1883, housed students in grades one through eight, and was the oldest operating wooden school in Massachusetts when it closed in 2002. The original three story building had two rooms added onto the

Hodgkins School, unknown date, but post-1913, when fire escapes were added to the school. Collection of East Brookfield Historical Museum.

Author's Memories...

"I remember wearing a coat and gloves in the winter when the heat didn't really work that well. Walking in all kinds of weather to the school next door to eat lunch, having art class in the basement, and one bathroom on each floor; boys on the first floor and girls on the second. I also remember teachers knowing everyone's name, my teacher also being my neighbor or my father's teacher, and a sense of community that larger schools just don't have."

- Heather Gablaski, 2018; student at Lashaway Jr. High late 1980s.

back in 1896. After the separation from Brookfield, improvements were made to the building including installing indoor bathroom facilities and electric lights in the basement and some of the classrooms in 1922. In true Yankee fashion, the lumber from the outhouses was repurposed to build a wooden fence on the west side of the school grounds. (Annual Report of the School Committee, Town of East Brookfield, Year Ending December 31, 1922.)

In 1932, the school was restructured to create a junior high school model; though both elementary and junior high 'schools' were in the same building. Students in grades one through six attended Hodgkins Elementary School, whose classrooms were located on the first floor of the building. Mrs. Jeanne LeBeau recalls starting at the elementary school at the age of five and only speaking French. The principal, Franklin Leeds, allowed her to bring her dog to school to help her adjust, but then suggested to her parents that she stay home for another year to give her time to learn English.

The second floor of the building housed Lashaway Junior High for students who were in grades seven through nine. During this time, classrooms were still multi-age to a certain extent, depending on the size of each class and the space available in the building. This new structure alleviated the overcrowding at the District #3 Schoolhouse in Podunk as once students reached seventh grade, they would attend the school in the center of town.

In 1932, the District #4 Schoolhouse on West Sturbridge Road was permanently closed due to lack of enrollment. It had not been opened for several years prior to this; students were driven to the District #3 Schoolhouse. In 1934, a combination of faster transportation over paved roads and lack of funds due to the Depression resulted in the decision to close the District #3 School house. Students in Podunk would now attend school in the center of town at the Hodgkins Center School. The month before the District #3 School was to close, a fire broke out and the teacher, Miss Mary Downey, and the older students helped to contain the fire until the firemen arrived. (Spencer Leader, May 11, 1934)   At the time, it was the last one-room schoolhouse in operation in Brookfield, East Brookfield, and North Brookfield. In 1937, John Plimpton purchased the building from the town, but sold it in 1945 to Mr. and Mrs. James Rio, who moved it to an already built foundation less than a mile east on Podunk Road and made their home out of it.

One of the first decisions made by the new School Committee of the Town of East Brookfield was to join the Superintendency Union with Brookfield and North Brookfield. The schools had been part of this Union before 1920 and this decision officially continued the relationship. The schools in these towns shared a superintendent, music teacher, art teacher, and eventually a nurse. Students who wished to continue their education at the high school level, which was not required, attended North Brookfield High School in this first year. However, due to an increase in tuition and difficulty finding transportation for students, in 1922, these students were sent to Spencer High School. They took the train from the East Brookfield Depot to the stop in South Spencer and then walked to school from there until 1925 when the School Committee negotiated with the Conlin Bus Company to change their schedule in order for students to take the bus and be dropped off right at the school. Some students opted to go to the Worcester Trade School. The town paid for the same amount of tuition and transportation costs as they would if they attended school in Spencer and parents paid the remainder.

The growing population of East Brookfield led to overcrowding in the school. Enrollment averaged about 150 students but the number of students in each grade fluctuated. Due to the space available, grades were combined into one room with one teacher. Grades 3 and 4 were grouped together as were Grades 5 and 6. Class size for these combined grades totaled 38. Other grades had between 17 and 19 students. In 1945, there were few students in the ninth grade class and the need for more space for younger grades. The decision was made to send ninth graders to David Prouty High School for the school year beginning in September 1945. Mrs. Jeanne LeBeau remembers being the first freshman class to start at David Prouty and also that some students from Lashaway Junior High chose to attend North Brookfield High instead of Prouty.

While there was talk in 1947 about creating a large regional district with Brookfield, North Brookfield, East Brookfield, New Braintree, and West Brookfield with a shared high school, eventually Brookfield joined with Sturbridge, Wales, Holland, and Brimfield to form the Tantasqua Regional School District and the plan for a regional high school went by the wayside. In 1980, East Brookfield left the Superintendency with North Brookfield and had its own superintendent for several years.

The aging Hodgkins School needed renovations and upkeep each year. In 1950, an exit from the basement was added, allowing the space in the basement to be used as a cafeteria and shop class. Later, an exit from the basement at the rear of the building was added. Then, in 1952, discussions began regarding how to enlarge the school to accommodate the growing enrollment. Over the next few years, the crowded conditions worsened. In his Annual Report, the principal noted that were were two water fountains and two bathrooms for the over two hundred twenty students in the six room building. Discussions quickly turned from building an addition to the Hodgkins School to building a new school.

Memorial School, 1957, from collection of East Brookfield Historical Museum.

Memorial Elementary School was opened in 1957, at a cost of $217,359 and included six classrooms, a faculty work room, combination gymnasium, auditorium, cafeteria (cafe-a-gym-a-torium!), and office space. Teachers carried desks and chairs from the Hodgkins School to the new school. On February 25, students from grades one through four moved from the Hodgkins School to the new building. The combination cafeteria, auditorium and gymnasium was a welcome addition for students who had been eating their lunch in their classrooms since the basement lunchroom in the Hodgkins Building had been used as classroom space for the past several years. The once overcrowded Hodgkins School now had space to spare and three classrooms were rented to the town of Brookfield, who moved a second grade and two fifth grade classrooms into the first floor of the school.

Even a new building didn't alleviate overcrowding for long. As early as 1964, the School Committee was warning of the need for an addition. By the early 1970s, classrooms had to share space. In 1973, when the state mandated each town needed to provide public kindergarten, this class was held on the stage at Memorial School. The first Kindergarten teacher in the town of East Brookfield was Louise Meyerdierks, though she was Louise Dilling at that time. The Kindergarten later moved into the Hodgkins School, and then in rented space at the privately-owned Happy Day Nursery School. In 1977, a four room addition to Memorial School, named the Franklin Leeds Wing (after the long-time principal) was added.

Students in Kindergarten through grade five attended Memorial School while Lashaway Junior High was home to students in grades six through eight. This configuration would change over the years as East Brookfield regionalized with the town of Spencer and formed the Spencer-East Brookfield Regional School District in the 1980s. The district agreement was originally for students in grades 9-12 who attended David Prouty High School on Main Street in Spencer, but in 1984 was expanded to include students in Kindergarten through high school. This district-wide regionalization was one that had been investigated since the late 1960s. Voters in Spencer opposed regionalization several times until it finally passed in 1984. On July 1, 1985, the new Spencer-East Brookfield Regional School District was officially formed.

Students in East Brookfield continued to attend school in East Brookfield through 8th grade until the 1994-1995 school year when Knox Trail Junior High in Spencer opened and students in grades 7 and 8 from both towns attended this school and then transitioned to the David Prouty High School. At that time, Lashaway Junior High School became home to students in grades 4, 5, and 6 while students in Kindergarten through grade 3 continued to attend Memorial School.

School space continued to be an issue and a 1996 attempt to put another addition on Memorial School to house all elementary school students under one roof was defeated by voters. The main issue was the cost of renovating and putting an addition on the building as it would need to be brought up to new building codes. An attempt to revise the plans by reducing the size was also rejected as was a regional intermediate school in Spencer, and plans to build a new school were developed.

Eventually, East Brookfield Elementary School was built on twenty-three acres of land between Lashaway Drive and Harrington Street, purchased for

$160,000 from the Antell family. At the time of this book's publishing, it educates students from pre-school to grade six.

East Brookfield Elementary School, photo by author, 2016.

When Lashaway Junior High closed in 2004, it was the end of a one hundred twenty year-era that was truly unique. Not many schools of that age were still in use. It had no intercom or bell system and no cafeteria, requiring students to walk daily across the field to Memorial School for lunch. It still used the original bell, rung by pulling a rope in the secretary's office, to announce the beginning of the school day and the end of recess. Generations of East Brookfield residents had attended this school, including parents and grandparents of students; many of the teachers were graduates of this school as well.

When the K-12 Regional District was in the planning stages, there was considerable disagreement over the configuration of the School Committee. East Brookfield wanted three Spencer representatives and two East Brookfield representatives on the committee. Spencer argued for an eight to two split since the finances of the district would be split 80-20. The School Committee was established with five to two representation. Funding of the regional school district would begin to cause strife between the towns of Spencer and East Brookfield in the second decade of the new millennium. A budget crisis brought on by the recession of 2008 and alleged mismanagement of funds by the superintendent as well as a sometimes contentious relationship between the School Committee and the town led to deep cuts in educational funding and rising class sizes. Voters of the town of East Brookfield appeared to be willing to shoulder tax increases to provide additional funds for teachers and technology, but the voters of Spencer defeated several override requests.

    This declining situation led to a majority of East Brookfield students attending private school or opting to attend school through school choice programs at surrounding towns, including North Brookfield, Auburn, and Leicester, and schools in the Tantasqua and Quabbin districts. In the midst of rising discontent with the administration of the district, a School Advisory Committee was formed in 2016 to investigate options related to whether or not East Brookfield should remain in the district at all. Several options were investigated including pulling out from the district entirely and joining with another district, forming an independent district, or amending the existing district agreement to one that included only high school as had been the case in the past. In the end, East Brookfield decided to remain a part of the Spencer-East Brookfield Regional School District and continued the work to ensure a quality education for the children of East Brookfield. During this challenging time, our town was lucky to have the leadership of Heather Messier and Mike Ethier as our representatives on the school committee. It was not easy work to be in the minority on this board and they did so with skill and always with the best interest of the children of our town in mind.

LAKES

Lake Lashaway, located in the center of town, is a 293-acre lake seen by all who travel through East Brookfield and enjoyed by many residents and visitors. This lake, however, is man-made and was originally just a stream. As early as the 1730s, there were four mills along the Five Mile River that were located in what is today the town of East Brookfield.

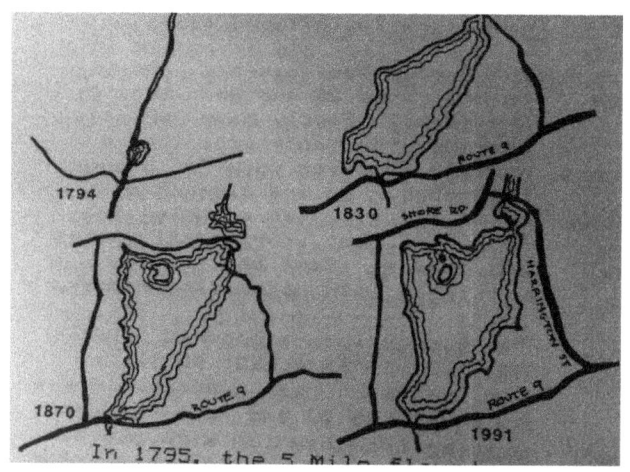

Different sizes of Lake Lashaway. Source: Lake Lashaway Community Association Newsletter, March 1991.

Jeduthan Stevens was a Revolutionary War veteran who moved to Brookfield from Connecticut in 1790. He built a grist mill on the Five Mile River, approximately where the the river flows into Lake Lashaway today. Stevens also ran the first tavern in the village of East Brookfield, a brick building called Stevens Tavern on the corner of North Street and Main Street. Stevens felt a dam on the Five Mile River would be of great use to the community and in 1795 purchased, from the Haire Family for three pounds, the right to build a dam on the river and raise the water level in the meadow. The original dam, completed on April 8, 1825, was a simple pile of logs. Depending on the amount of water needed for the mills, logs would be added or removed. The first mills were a grist mill and a saw mill and Stevens eventually moved his home to the southern shore of the lake. Much of the lumber used in buildings in Spencer and the Brookfields came from the Stevens lumber mill powered by this dam.

Several accounts note that the creation of this dam resulted in the village center being moved from the "Cove District" to where it is now, at the southern shore of Lake Lashaway. The Cove District was located near Cove Street, which formerly extended to connect to Howe Street along today's Young Road. There were several establishments in the area including a saw mill, grist mill, carding mill, fulling mill and dye house on the Seven Mile River, and a blacksmith shop on the Post Road, where Cove Street meets Route 9 today. Even the Baptist Church was located in this area, on the corner of Harrington Street and Route

9. The Baptist Church moved to its current location in 1840 and all the mills and shops in this area were closed by 1853. The District #7, or Cove District School, was located on what is today Young Road, and was attended by children from the eastern portion of town and along the Harrington Street area. Its closing at the end of the 1800s could have been a result of a population decline in this area of town, or the availability of faster transportation to the school in the center of town.

The lake first appears on a map in 1828, as the "J. Stevens Mill Pond." This body of water was then simplified to Stevens Pond, and then changed to Furnace Pond on an 1868 map. On a map from 1885, it is labeled, "Furnace Pond or Lashua Lake," and its present name was first seen on a map in 1898. At some point in the first decades of the 1900s the lake was labeled Crystal Lake, perhaps in a failed attempt to link the lake to the hotel on its southern shore, the Crystal House, now the 308 Lakeside.

Photo of the southern shore of Lake Lashaway, circa 1850. Many mills took advantage of the water power provided by the dam. Note the steeple of the Baptist Church in the background. Photo from collection of East Brookfield Historical Museum.

The different names of the lake were directly related to the history of the town. First, it was named after the man who created it, Jeduthan Stevens. When deposits of ore were discovered in the Podunk section of town, at the foot of High Rocks and on the western shore of Podunk Pond, a blast furnace was built where the former shoe factory is located on the corner of Main Street and Mechanic Street. This furnace produced charcoal needed to process the ore, and this is when Stevens Pond became known as Furnace Pond. The foundry did not last for long as raw materials were not as plentiful as was first thought.

Lashaway was a term used by Native Americans to describe a place where two rivers met. At the time of the first English settlements at Quaboag Plantation, it meant the point where the stream at the southern end of Lake Wickaboag flows into the Quaboag River. For example, in the Cooper deed, there is reference to "Naltaug Lashaway" which is understood to be the place where the Naltaug Brook entered the Quaboag River. Another "lashaway," was located where the Five Mile Brook entered the East Brookfield River. This is most likely how the lake got its current name.

Regardless of the name of the body of water, the dam that created it caused the stream to swell, and trees that were growing on the now flooding land needed to be removed. Stevens and other men waited until the water froze and then cut down the trees. Some of the pine trees were used in the construction of the North Brookfield Congregational Church. A drought in 1910 caused stumps of trees to be three to four feet above the surface of the ice and townspeople took advantage of this to cut them to create a safer boating route among the camps on the lake. Previously, a longer route was taken to avoid potential damage from the submerged stumps. (Brookfield Times, Jan. 14, 1910) In the 1920s, as more summer cottages were built around the lake, more of the remaining stumps were removed.

A stump in Lake Lashaway, n.d. from a postcard in collection of EB Historical Museum.

A view of the root system attached to a stump that rose to the surface of the lake in 2015. Photo by author, 2015.

In late 2015, a remnant of one of these trees floated to the surface of the lake. The enormous size of the stump and root system of the tree, which predates English settlement in North America, was impressive. While there was some discussion on possible ways to display the stump as an interesting piece of East Brookfield's history, the size of the stump made it impossible to move it in one piece. Eventually, the stump was cut into pieces and removed. It took eight dump truck loads to remove all the pieces of the stump.

Over the course of the 1800s, textiles became a larger part of the industries in the Brookfields. Along with the textile industry, the plentiful supply of water and clay allowed for a thriving brick and pottery industry to develop. A more in-depth description of the mills and other industry in town can be found in a previous chapter.

Before electricity, the lakes in town provided a necessary staple: ice. Ice was needed to help preserve perishable foods and was harvested from all the lakes in town in the winter months as soon as the ice reached eleven inches thick. It was stored in sawdust and hay in icehouses on the shore and sold to residents of town and also businesses in nearby cities throughout the rest of the year. In her memoir, All Ya' Need is Love, Joan Leger Bedard recalls the ice man visiting her home on Main Street in the summer. Her mother would post a sign in the window with an amount of money that would

If you wanted to buy ice, a sign like this one would be placed in your window. Depending on the size of the block of ice you wanted, you would pace that number at the top. Donated to EB Historical Museum by Bain Family.

correspond to the size of the block of ice she needed. The ice man, then P.D. Bousquet, would have a piece of rubber on his back to protect it from the cold as he carted the requested ice into the house. He would kindly chip off pieces of the ice for the children to eat. Mr. Bousquet served on the Board of Selectmen for several years after the incorporation of the town, was on the fire department and served as a constable.

The island in the northern portion of Lake Lashaway is named Sheep Island. Though this name seems to be an unofficial one and most likely wasn't on any maps, Jean Bain remembers that sheep were put on the island to keep the brush trimmed.

Sheep Island as shown on an early 1900s postcard. From Collection of East Brookfield Historical Museum.

The lake provided a source of entertainment for residents and visitors.

A Day in the Life...

"*My summers on Lake Lashaway began in 1896 when my father had a cottage built on the east shore, known as "The Bluff". Harrington Street was a narrow country road, hot and dusty in the summer and black as pitch at night. ..For many years there were no motorboats on the lake. It was very restful and life seemed to go at a much slower pace. As changes came it seemed that much of the freedom and the friendliness was lost.*"

Helen Pickup, as quoted in the New Leader on the occasion of her 100th birthday. November 21, 1991

During the summer, an average of 1,000 vacationers would stay in camps on the shores of Lake Lashaway. In addition to swimming and personal boating, there was a club on the lake and cruises offered.

An 1880 article advertised for steamship cruises on the lake on Wednesday and Saturday afternoons and other days by reservation. The boat, named, "Wide Awake" was originally the "Elid" from Brookfield but was repaired and refitted to provide "pleasure parties" on Lake Lashaway. ("East Brookfield: Special Correspondence." Spencer Sun [Spencer] 2 July 1880: 8. Print.) While most appeared to be enjoying the excursions on the lake, in the fall of 1880, the captain of the "Wide Awake" let the water in the boiler run low and fearing an explosion, let the steam escape, stranding all on board in the middle of the lake. In an attempt to get to shore, two passengers boarded a smaller boat, which promptly capsized and a woman had to be rescued from the water. (Spencer Sun, 10 September 1880: 8. Print.)

Postcards from the early 1900s include messages to friends from those vacationing on the lake. One, from a Mrs. Fetties to friends in Jamaica Plain, reads in part, "This is some fine place and I am having the time of my life." (Postcard, "Lake Lashaway, East Brookfield, MA, mailed August 8, 1919, from collection of East Brookfield Historical Museum.). Another, from "Grace" to a friend in New Haven, Connecticut, notes, "The lakes are beautiful. The house overlooks two. We have been to two dances and had [a] fine time." (Postcard, "Bird's Eye View, East Brookfield," mailed 1918, from collection of East Brookfield Historical Museum.)

A humorous incident occurred in 1881, when a man, perhaps thinking he was actually at Niagara Falls, went over the dam at the southern end of Lake Lashaway in a tub. He fell out once while using a dipper to bail water from his "boat" but then continued on his ill-advised journey over the dam, to the delight of onlookers. (Spencer Sun, July 29, 1881)

A popular lake excursion was steamboat rides. In June of 1888, George Forbes finished a new dock and celebrated by offering free rides on his boat to residents. Approximately one hundred people took advantage of his offer. (Brookfield Times, June 17, 1888) The new dock was possibly named "Harper's Ferry" as there are several references to boats that served as pleasure cruises loading and unloading at "Harper's Ferry" on Main Street, including Mattie Sullivan's fleet of six boats which launched in 1899. One of the steamships sunk and the hull can still be seen in the lake. A piece of the wooden hull was retrieved by Theodore and Tanya Schubert and Chris Batzer when they were teenagers. This remnant can be seen in the East Brookfield Historical Museum.

In 1987, another pleasure boat sailed on Lashaway when a group of residents purchased the "African Queen." The boat was a 25-foot 'liberty' boat built in 1926 that was used on Webster Lake for decades before being donated to the Boy Scouts of America, who decided to auction it off to raise funds. Seventeen friends got together and purchased and restored the boat and enjoyed time together on the boat on major holidays. The members of the "African Queen Society" were Neal and Linda Labaire, Ray and Ann Auger, Harry and Anne Blaisdell, Bob and Jean Bain, Bill and Jill Compton, Alan and Diane Dion, Duke and Candace Richard, Louise and Gerry Ryan, and Michael Meyerdierks.

Another, perhaps surprising, attraction on the lake in winter was horse races. Teams of horses would scrape the snow from the ice and people would come from surrounding towns to compete against each other on this flat surface. An article in 1879 reports that the first Horse Trot of the season resulted in an audience of nearly 10,000 people. (Spencer Sun, January 10, 1879). Horse races on the lake were still being held in 1934, as an article in the Spencer Leader tells of the cars of 2,000 spectators lined up on both sides of Main Street through the center of town.

Large crowds from the surrounding towns enjoyed the excellent skating on Lake Lashaway last week.

Brookfield Times, June 5, 1900.

—Horse trot No. 1 came off on Lake Lashaway Monday last—9999 spectators in attendance.

The Spencer Sun, January 10, 1879.

Ice skating was also popular in the winter and would invariably result in youngsters trying out the ice before it was thick enough to support their weight. At times, an estimated five hundred skaters could be seen enjoying the lake in winter. In 1917, hockey teams from East Brookfield, Brookfield, North Brookfield, and Spencer formed the Quaboag Valley Hockey League and held all their games on Lake Lashaway. (Brookfield Times, Jan. 12, 1917)

Lake Lashaway Park was a popular destination for those looking for a night out and a variety of entertainment options. When the Warren, Brookfield, and Spencer Street Railway first came to town, the company leased the property near the far end of Lashaway Drive and built a track there along with a theatre, to bring business to their rail line. Additions to the park over the years allowed the railway to enjoy the profits of a thriving entertainment area. The many social groups in the region, including church groups from surrounding towns, held their annual picnics at Lashaway Park and enjoyed the onsite restaurant, stage for performances, a dance pavilion, roller skating rink, sports fields, merry-go-round, and overnight accommodations. Electric lights were added in 1897. Performers came from as far away as New York and as close as Spencer to perform for the crowds who gathered on warm summer evenings. A steamer called "The Lashaway" made daily trips from the park to the center of town and boats could be rented for personal use. The annual opening of the park was looked forward to with excitement and often marked with a "Dawn Dance" where there was dancing from 9:00 P.M. until sunrise. Newspaper accounts of the day assert that a good crowd on a weekend night at the park was about 4,000 people. The trolleys had to run extra trips to North Brookfield and Spencer to get everyone home on the weekend. The advent of the motor car

Entrance to Lake Lashaway Park, photo from collection of EB Historical Museum.

Base Ball Challenge.

Brookfield, April 27, 1882.
A selected team of nine Brookfield base ball players, hereby challenge the East Brookfield professionals to a match game of Base Ball, to take place at Lake-side Park grounds on Saturday, May 6, at 2 o'clock P. M. Address acceptance of challenge, to
William Murphy, Brookfield.

A ball field at Lakeside Park allowed for games among area towns. (Brookfield Times, April 27, 1882)

and the end of the trolley resulted in the end of the park as well. In 1915, the property was sold to a developer who built cottages on the site.

Camps around Lake Lashaway were popular summer destinations for families to gather, much as Cape Cod is today. These camps had charming names such as "The BandBox," "Lakeview," "Hilltop Lodge," "Parkview," "Comfort Camp," "Overlook Villa," and "Whitewood Lodge" to name but a few. The local papers would publish the names of those staying in each camp as well as any who visited for a few weeks during the summer. After the 1920s these summer cottages slowly began to be renovated into the year-round residences they are today.

The company that owned the factory on the southern shore of Lake Lashaway had great power over the lake. Since the lake was man-made, they controlled water rights that included Lake Lashaway, the Five-Mile River, and Brooks Pond. These rights extended into New Braintree and Oakham where

> *"The lake [Lashaway] is very good for all kinds of fishing....There is water skiing, sailing, boating and swimming. Every Sunday the Sailing Club has sailboat races....In the winter the lake is buzzing with action,,,snowmobiles...also skating, hockey, or just walking around the lake for pleasure. Once in a while in the winter an airplane will land on the ice to get coffee at King's Variety."* -Robert Ramsey, jr. high essay for 1970 anniversary of EB.

streams feed into Brooks Pond. This water in turn flows through the Five-Mile River into Lake Lashaway and in the days of the mills, provided the power for the operation. The activities at the lake were in jeopardy in 1906 when, for some reason, Quaboag Manufacturing, the owners of the factory at the time, decided to ban all fishing on the lake and planned to put a fence around the water. They offered a $100 reward for information regarding anyone fishing in the lake from a boat, from shore, or through the ice. (*The Brookfield Times,* August 10, 1906) When the company began installing post holes for a fence, the residents of the lake formed a committee, including Senator Warren Tarbell, who successfully opposed this action. In 1963, new owners of the property, Brookfield Athletic Shoe Company, gave the water rights to the town.

Camp Atwater is the country's oldest African-American camp and is listed on the National Register of Historic Places. While located on Shore Road in North Brookfield, Camp Atwater had a closer relationship with the town of East Brookfield than North Brookfield. Campers attended church at the Baptist Church and the organization participated in many East Brookfield celebrations. The camp was established in 1921 by Dr. William N. DeBerry during a time when camps for children were segregated by race. First called Saint John's Camp, the name changed in 1926 when Mary Atwater donated $25,000 with the stipulation that the camp be renamed for her father, Dr. David Fisher Atwater. With little opportunity for the children of African Africans, Camp Atwater was filled each summer with campers. Most came from the Springfield area though it was not unusual for children to come from further away. Attendees included those from states along the eastern coast of the United States as well as from several foreign countries. During the 1960s the number of campers declined as more camps were desegregated and children attended camps closer to their homes. (https://www.blackpast.org/african-american-history/camp-atwater-1921/.)

The camp encompasses seventy-two acres of land, including the three-acre 'Sheep Island' just off their shoreline. There are forty buildings on site including cabins and the "Lodge," a 4,000 square foot conference center that can accommodate up to one hundred people in its meeting space. Also on site is White Cabin, built in 1760. It is located on the north side of Shore Road and is where the first campers were housed.

Today, Camp Atwater is owned and operated by the Urban League of Springfield. and continues to operate its summer overnight camps for children aged eight to fifteen. Campers can engage in a variety of outdoor skills such as boating, canoeing, archery, hiking, and swimming. They can play basketball, volleyball, softball, soccer, golf, or volleyball. Or, they can build their leadership skills, participate in STEM (science, technology, engineering and mathematics) activities, and learn about environmental science or career awareness. (https://www.campatwater.org/, July 2019.)

Planes on Lake Lashaway. Source: undated photo, post 1980s, from the collection of EB Historical Museum.

The Lakewood House, a twenty-room hotel on the southern shore of Lake Lashaway was a popular spot for visitors as well as the meeting place for local clubs. When the Lashaway Rod and Gun Club was established in 1946, they held their meetings at the Lakewood. During the summer, the beach at the hotel was the site for Red Cross sponsored swimming lessons for young people. In 1948, the hotel was sold to George Rusecki, who renovated the building, adding a bar on the first level so patrons could relax near the water. He also changed the name of the hotel to the Lashaway Inn, which it was known as until 2014, along with its nickname, "The Lash." The original three-story building was destroyed by fire in the late 1950s and was replaced by a smaller structure. In 2013, the cost of installing an up-to-date sprinkler system forced the owners to sell the property. It was nearly completely demolished, with the exception of one wall, and renamed the "308 Lakeside," a reference to their address on Main Street. The 308 includes two large rooms, one with a three-sided bar, and an outside dining area. It is common during the warmer months to see boats docked at the rear of the restaurant as lake residents enjoy a relaxing dinner close to home.

The Lakewood House. photo from collection of EB Historical Museum.

Life on the lake continued to be a focal point of the center of town. Beginning in 1949, the Lashaway Boat Club began to sponsor regattas that were very well attended. These events included water skiing, canoe races, and inboard and outboard races. A race course was marked from the beach at the Lashaway Inn to the northern end of the lake and back again. In 1951, over 5,000 people came to watch the finals of a boat race sponsored by the New England Outboard Racing Association. Contestants came from all over New England and New York. The winners of the various races would compete in the National Championships. (Spencer New Leader, September 21, 1951) Races the following year brought in a smaller crowd of 3,000 spectators but were not less exciting. (Spencer Leader, August 29, 1952)

In 1968, a conflict over the land under the waters of Lake Lashaway resulted in a court case between the towns of East Brookfield and North Brookfield. The factories that had been located at the southern end of the lake near the dam had always had rights to the lake and were the owners of the land beneath the lake. These companies had paid taxes to the town of North Brookfield on this land until 1963, when it gave the title to East Brookfield.

North Brookfield then sent the tax bill to East Brookfield. An Appellate Court ruled that this was illegal as the land was no longer private property.

While the owners of the Lashaway Inn were very accommodating in allowing the town to use the beach behind the hotel for swimming lessons, many in town wanted a public beach. In 1975, the town had a swimming hole constructed near the Seven Mile River at the site of the town barn, today the recycling center. Swimming lessons were taught here but the water tended to stagnate and become muddy. Susan G, who grew up on Podunk, reminisced on Facebook about being excited to go to the swimming hole in town. Her excitement didn't last long as there were snakes and leeches in the swimming hole. Needless to say, she didn't return! (Facebook post, East Brookfield Historical Commission Page, January 28, 2019). The swimming hole was officially closed in July 1982, when the Town Beach on the western shore of Lake Lashaway was opened. Near the spot of the former swimming hole, which is just a muddy hole today, a canoe launch was constructed in 2016 as part of the Chicopee River Watershed's "blue trails" project.

Town Beach, photo courtesy of Aubrey Messier, 2019.

The public beach on Lake Lashaway was a joint effort between East Brookfield and North Brookfield. Town officials had been looking for land to make into a beach for town residents for many years but the cost of land around the lake was too high for the town to purchase. When the town well was moved to the Podunk section of town, a piece of land that the town already owned became available for a public beach. The highway departments of both East and North Brookfield worked to construct a parking lot and install an L-shaped dock built by local carpenter David Snay. Picnic tables were donated by the North Brookfield Recreation Committee. The East Brookfield Fire Department burned brush. The first of many years of swimming lessons were held here. Volunteers and the recreation committees of both towns continue to make improvements to the town beach, adding grills, maintaining a changing house, and keeping the area clean. The town beach is only open to residents of the towns of East Brookfield and North Brookfield.

In 1985, a culvert was built under Route 9 to allow for an annual drawdown of the lake in the late fall. The Lake Association raised more than

$30,000 to help pay the cost of this project to lower the level of the lake approximately eight feet as a natural means of weed control. After the first drawdown, members of the Lake Association worked to remove nearly one thousand stumps, exposed for the first time in one hundred fifty years. Also during this time period, the Boards of Health in both East and North Brookfield required an upgraded septic system for all cottages that were converted to year-round residences to further protect the lake from pollution.

The Lake Lashaway Dam underwent repairs in 1992 for the first time since it was rebuilt after being washed out by the Hurricane of 1938. The concrete dam is U-shaped and between twenty-four and twenty-seven inches thick. In 2010, the Board of Selectmen partnered with the Massachusetts Department of Transportation to renovate the area around the Route 9 dam. During this four-year project, the entire spillway under the bridge was repaired and upgraded and the weir was replaced, the earthen dam was repaired and improved, and an observation platform was constructed with docks for people to moor their boats while they visit the downtown area. The entire project cost almost $2,000,000; the town of East Brookfield had to pay only $70,000 of the total cost. In 2014, an opening ceremony was held on the completed observation platform.

Representative Gobi, Senator Brewer, members of the Lake Association and Board of Selectmen at the ribbon cutting ceremony of the Lake Lashaway Overlook. Photo by author, 2015.

Today, the lake continues to be enjoyed by swimmers, boaters, and fishermen alike. Currently, Lake Lashaway has a maximum depth of eighteen feet, with most parts averaging about ten feet in depth. The town line between East Brookfield and North Brookfield cuts the lake almost in half and the two towns share the Town Beach area as well as responsibility for maintaining the lake itself. In addition to town oversight, the Lake Lashaway Community Association, made up of residents with homes on the lake from both towns, is active in monitoring lake and dam conditions and running events on the lake. There are over one hundred fifty houses on the shores of the lake, with the majority of them serving as year-round residences.

In addition to Lake Lashaway, there are many ponds and streams that run through the town. According to MassGIS, 10% of the area of East Brookfield is either wetlands or open water. Major water features in addition to Lake Lashaway include Quaboag and Quacumquasit (South) Ponds, the East Brookfield and Seven Mile Rivers, Dunn and Great Brooks, Great Swamp, Allen Swamp and Podunk Marsh. (United States. Department of Conservation and Recreation. CMRPC. Upper Quaboag Watershed and North Quabbin Region Landscape Inventory: Massachusetts Heritage Landscape Inventory Program. Boston, MA: Massachusetts Department of Conservation and Recreation, 2008, p. 18 Print.) All the lakes in town were heavily used in the past for recreation, including fishing, hunting, camping, and entertainment.

Both Quaboag Pond, at various times in the past called North Pond and Podunk Pond, and Lake Quacumquasit, also known as South Pond, fall into the category of "Great Ponds." "Great Ponds" are those larger than ten acres in size in their natural state. Lake Lashaway, as a man-made lake, is not considered a "Great Pond." The status of "Great Pond" means that the water is available for public use. Over time, people used these bodies of water for a variety of purposes, both commercial and recreational, even before the Great Ponds Law.

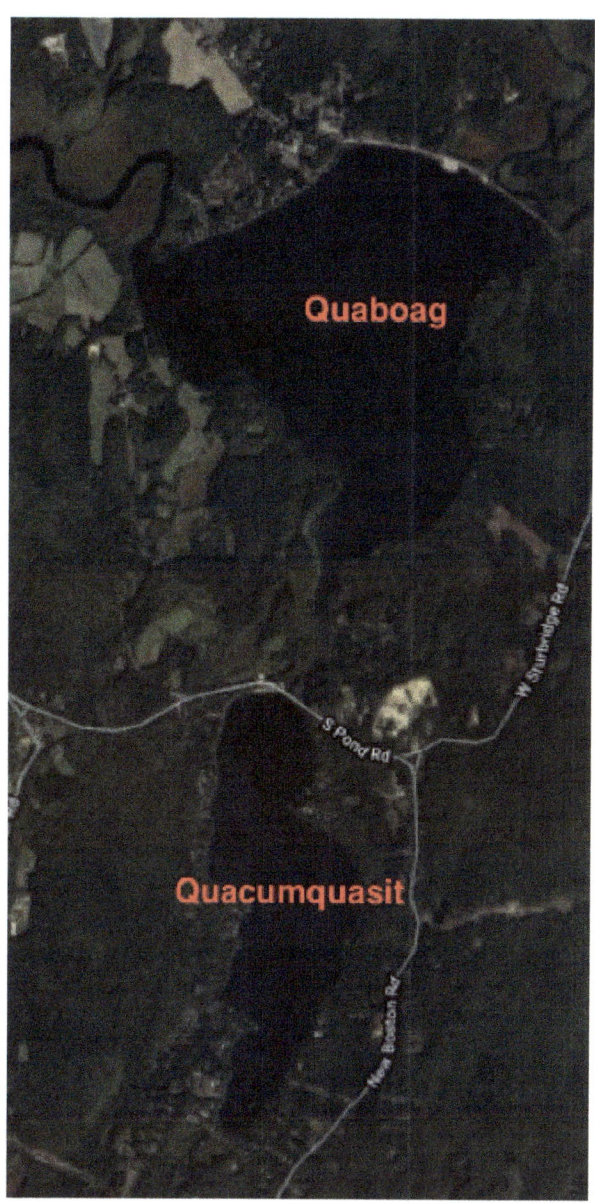

Even though it has a larger surface area, Lake Quaboag has about half the capacity as Quacumquasit, due to the differences in depths of the two bodies of water. Lakes Quaboag and Quacumquasit. Google Maps, December 26, 2018.

While only the towns of East Brookfield, Brookfield, and Sturbridge physically border the lakes, the Quaboag Watershed, which includes both lakes, encompasses 50,688 acres and includes the towns of North Brookfield, New Braintree, Oakham, Rutland, Paxton, Leicester, and Spencer. Most of the water in the watershed eventually flows into Quaboag Pond.

Both Quaboag and Quacumquasit were formed by glaciers as they slowly advanced and receded across the land. The lakes are connected by an area of muck and peat moss that forms a natural filtering system. In 1887, Brookfield Selectmen allowed the Quaboag Steamship Company to build a drawbridge to allow a steamboat and barge to access Quacumquasit's brickyards and recreational areas. This allowed water, for the first time, to change direction and flow into Lake Quacumquasit from Quaboag during heavy rains or snow melt. Typically, Quacumquasit is a spring-fed lake and its water flows north into Lake Quaboag. The "back flow" during wet times has become a major ecological concern between the two bodies of water.

This 'back flow' became the major impetus for the creation of the Quacumquasit Lake Association, which organized in response to a proposed campground and trailer park on the southern shore of the lake and a housing development on the northern shore. The builders of the proposed housing development wanted to build a dock and swimming area and, in 1965, dredged the channel between Lakes Quaboag and Quacumquasit. This removed the gravel, silt, and weeds which served as filtration for when water flowed in the opposite direction as it usually did and entered the spring-fed Quacumquasit. This pond, being one of the deepest in Massachusetts and without a large outlet, retains water for a very long time. Thus, pollutants from Quaboag, including nutrient-rich runoff from the Spencer Waste Water Treatment Plant, entered the clear waters of Quacumquasit more easily without the natural filters in the channel. In 1991, after decades of grant-writing, fundraising, scientific studies and legal fights, the Quacumquasit Lake Association was successful in installing a flow barrier along the channel so that in times of heavy rain, water from Quaboag cannot enter Quacumquasit. Initial hard feelings over the amount of state funding awarded to the Quacumquasit Lake Association led to a partnership between this association and the Quaboag Lake Association, which was founded in 1990. Today, the QQLA, or Quaboag Quacumquasit Lake Association, works to preserve and protect both lakes.

http://qqla.org/

Quaboag Pond is a 558-acre, relatively shallow body of water on the Brookfield/East Brookfield town line. Quaboag means "red water place," its descriptive name coming from the iron-stained, reddish gravel on the bottom. It has an average depth of only six feet. The pond is fed by the East Brookfield River, which flows south from from Lake Lashaway, and connects with the Seven Mile River before flowing into Lake Quaboag. Water from Lake Quaboag then flows out of the lake and into the Quaboag River.

Lake Quaboag, or Podunk Pond as it was commonly known in the past, was a popular destination with summer campers. Initially, wealthy residents of nearby towns owned cottages on the shore but changes in the economy resulted in many others enjoying the area. The schedule of factory workers, with set hours and weekends free, was different from the schedules of farmers who worked every day, and had especially longer hours in the summer. As industry developed in town, workers in the mills and factories valued the fresh air and free time that could be enjoyed just south of the center of town. New technology, such as electric trolleys as well as spur lines on the Boston and Albany Railroad and a steamship that ran down the East Brookfield River, allowed for faster transportation to the formerly out-of-the-way areas around the lakes in the southern part of town. Just like Lashaway Park, the annual opening in May of Oakland Gardens on the northwest shore and Comfort Cove on the western shore of Lake Quaboag were highly anticipated events during the 1880s and 1890s. Track meets and baseball games were held here and local church groups and others enjoyed picnics on the shore of the lake. In 1870, a group formed to bring horse racing to the area. A half-mile track along with stables, tack rooms, a grandstand, and housing for jockeys was constructed on the north shore of Lake Quaboag

It was at Oakland Gardens near Lake Quaboag in 1883, that a baseball game that is still talked about today was played. This game led to a rivalry

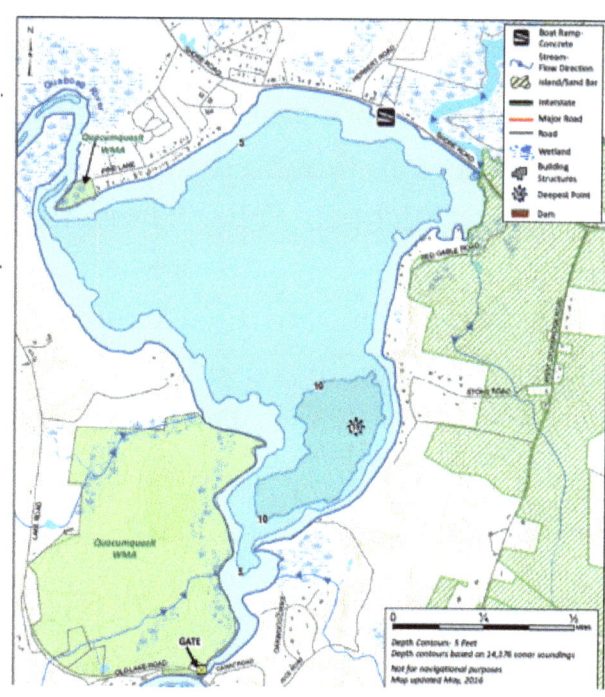

Massachusetts Division of Fisheries and Wildlife, MassWildlife. "Quaboag (North) Pond,"<www.mass.gov/eea/docs/dfg/dfw/habitat/maps-ponds/dfwquabo.pdf> 2016.

between North Brookfield and East Brookfield that has lasted for over a century. During the late 1800s and into the 1900s, local baseball leagues were run similar to professional baseball today. Players were traded and drafted and their careers highlighted in the local papers. In the league in 1883 were the towns of Chicopee Falls, Thorndike, the Ware Firemen, the Ware Clippers, North Brookfield, East Brookfield, and West Warren. By the end of the season, North Brookfield and East Brookfield were tied. Each team had only lost one game in the whole season and it was to each other. They played one final game to determine who would be the winner of the Silver Bat. The games were attended by thousands of spectators as well as sports writers from as far away as Boston. Connie Mack was catcher for the East Brookfield team, which won the game. At a ceremony in Fay's Hall, the president of the league presented the East Brookfield team with the Silver Bat.

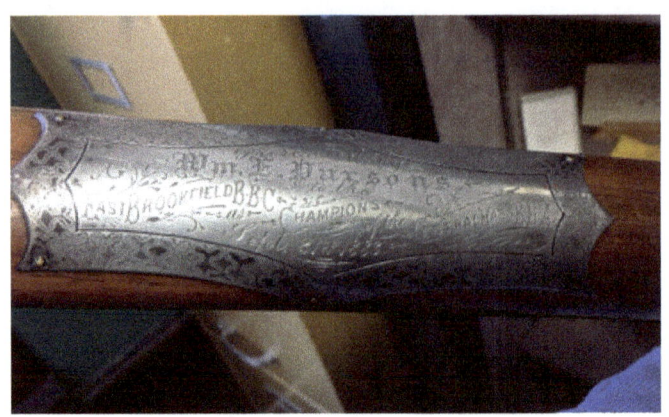

The 1883 Silver Bat awarded to the East Brookfield Team. The bat is currently in the collection of the East Brookfield Historical Museum. Photo by author, 2018.

Oakland Gardens later became known as Ward's Campground and then Tobin's Campground, the site of archaeological excavations over the course of the last several decades.

Quaboag continues to be popular with boaters, kayakers, and fishermen and is accessible via a concrete boat ramp on the north shore of the pond. There are a variety of game fish in Quaboag which make it popular in both the summer and winter months. Largemouth bass, species of pickerel, bullhead, Northern Pike, and perch are native to the pond, all of which have been caught in sizes that meet minimum sizes for recognition by the Sportsfishing Awards Program. (Massachusetts Division of Fisheries and Wildlife, MassWildlife. "Quaboag (North) Pond,"<www.mass.gov/eea/docs/dfg/dfw/habitat/maps-ponds/dfwquabo.pdf> 2016.)

Lake Quacumquasit, or South Pond, is the southernmost of the lakes in East Brookfield. It is a 218-acre body of water with an average depth of thirty-one feet though some areas are as deep as seventy feet. Quacumquasit was the name of a leader of the local American Indian tribe and some sources report that it means rock of black ducks. This body of water is named "South Pond" on maps up until 1898 when it is titled, "Quacumquasit Lake" ("Part of the Town of Brookfield," Atlas of Worcester County, 1898.)

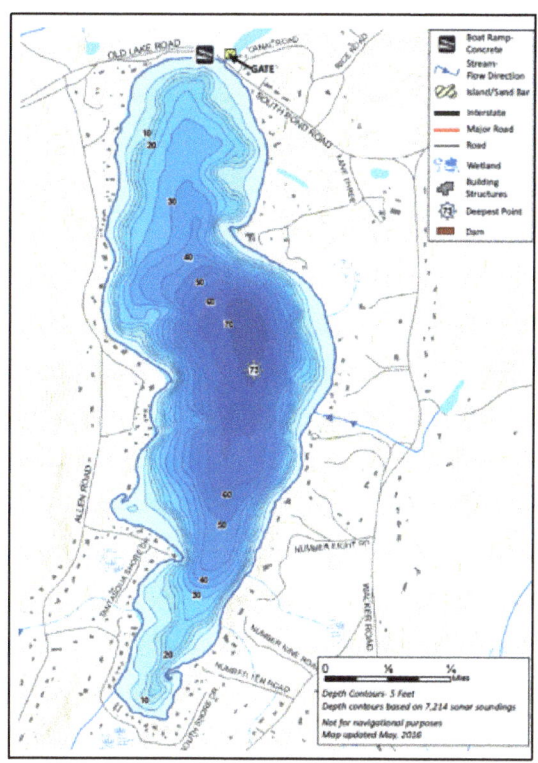

Massachusetts Division of Fisheries and Wildlife, MassWildlife. "Quacumquasit (South) Pond,"www.mass.gov/eea/docs/dfg/dfw/habitat/maps-ponds/dfwquacu.pdf> 2016.

The Point of Pines was a popular recreation area on the shores of this lake at the end of the nineteenth century. It was originally called "Carpenter's Point" as it was part of the Carpenter Farm. This location became the site of outings for Sunday School and other local groups. In 1884, the land was purchased by local business owners Gleason and Allen who named their new resort after a stand of tall pine trees overlooking the lake. Point of Pines included a restaurant, ball field, horse racing in the winter on the ice, and other recreational activities like boating, swimming, bowling, and dancing. The farmhouse was converted to a twelve-room hotel. In the first summer of operation, an estimated 30,000 people visited the resort. *(Brookfield Weekly Times, July 10, 1884.)*

Point of Pines was more difficult to reach than Oakland Gardens on Lake Quaboag as travel by road was the only way to get there at first. Later, a steamboat was able to access Quacumquasit via a canal from Lake Quaboag. The length of the trip did not deter visitors, perhaps because Brookfield was the only "wet" town on the Boston and Albany line between Worcester and Palmer *(Brookfield Times, May 14, 1886)*. Point of Pines received a reputation as a 'party location,' and even lost their liquor license in 1886 as a result of excessive rowdiness, while William Vizard, the owner of Oakland Gardens, marketed his resort as family-friendly and alcohol-free.

In 1916 Point of Pines was purchased by the Newton Y.M.C.A and renamed Camp Frank A. Day. It is named for the man who made the recreation area possible. The camp was built so boys from Boston could enjoy the fresh air of the country and grew in size over several decades from almost ten acres to its current size of fifty-two acres. The Point of Pines's dance hall was converted to a dining hall. The bowling alley remained until it was destroyed by the 1938

Hurricane; it was rebuilt as an arts and crafts center. While originally a boys' retreat, Camp Frank A. Day is open for seven weeks every July and August for boys and girls aged seven to sixteen from the greater Boston area. In 2006, the camp got a $750,000 makeover, with new bathrooms, two new bathhouses, four new cabins, a climbing wall, and new basketball courts.

A once-successful brick yard operated by Twitchell and Brewster was located on the shores of South Pond. Bricks manufactured here were used to constructed Trinity Church in Boston, the Boston Latin School, the dorms at Harvard University, and the Worcester State Hospital. A steamship transported up to 80,000 bricks a day to the railroad located five miles north in the center of East Brookfield. In order for the barge to get to the railroad tracks, a canal was built connecting Lake Quaboag and Lake Quacumquasit and another canal cut through the twisting East Brookfield River to make the journey shorter. When not hauling bricks, the steamship could carry three hundred passengers and transported vacationeers to camps on South Pond from the train depot. In 1925, all that remained of this brick yard was a tall chimney, that collapsed during a windy day. ("Stack at Lake Quacumquasit, Relic of Once Prosperous Plant, Felled," Worcester Telegram, September 27, 1925.)

Lake Quacumquasit is popular with boaters, water skiers, sailers, and fishermen. It is accessible via a concrete boat ramp at the north side of the pond; a small public beach is located here as well. The pond is stocked each year with trout and has been designated a special Brown Trout Water by MassWildlife. Other fish found in the pond include Large- and Smallmouth Bass, Pickerel, and different species of trout and perch.

The lakes and rivers in town certainly had many positive benefits, but were also impacted by large-scale weather events over the years. Two of the largest were the Hurricane of 1938 and the Flood of 1955.

Hurricane of 1938

The Hurricane of 1938 was also known as "The Great New England Hurricane" and was one of the deadliest and most destructive tropical cyclones to impact New England. Forming off the coast of Africa, it made landfall on Long Island as a Category 3 Hurricane on September 21. It made landfall a second time near New Haven, Connecticut and then followed the Connecticut River north through Massachusetts and into Vermont. The Blue Hills Observatory, south of Boston, recorded winds of 186 miles per hour, some of the highest gusts in history. The hurricane killed between 600 and

700 people and damaged or destroyed 57,000 homes from New York to Canada. ("The Great New England Hurricane." History.com, A&E Television Networks, www.history.com/this-day-in-history/the-great-new-england-hurricane.).

The damage to East Brookfield was significant and nearly isolated the town. When the dam at Doane Pond in North Brookfield gave out, it caused an already flooded Lake Lashaway to overflow Route 9. The water reached four feet deep over the roadway until the dam gave way, taking with it two hundred feet of the road, one of the Maclan Hat Company's buildings, a portion of another, and the railroad bridge on the main line of the Boston and Albany line.

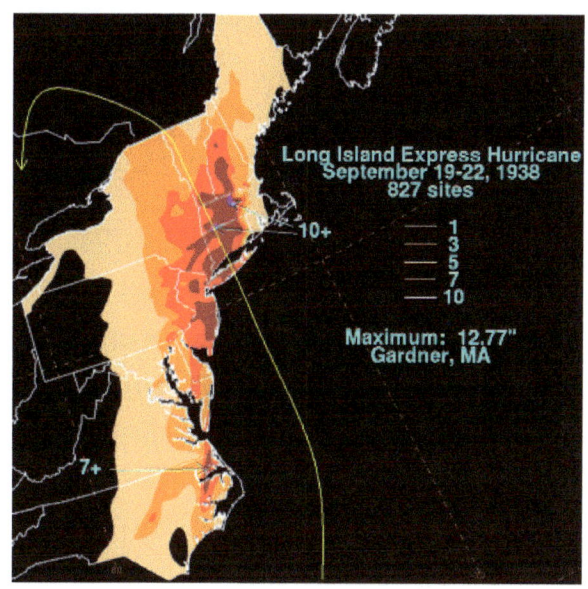

US Department of Commerce, and NOAA. "The Great New England Hurricane of 1938 - Meteorological Maps and Data." National Weather Service, NOAA's National Weather Service, 14 June 2018, www.weather.gov/okx/

The railroad tracks between East Brookfield and North Brookfield were washed out, though by this time, they only carried freight and not passengers. One of the buildings that was part of Varney's Garage (now Parsons Auto) was so damaged by fire shortly after the flood that it had to be torn down. The millions of gallons of water that poured out of the lake raised the level of Lake Quaboag by twelve feet. The smaller bridge on Shore Road at the northern end of Lake Lashaway was also damaged. Emergency repairs were made to it and traffic was re-routed along this road until the more extensive repairs that were needed could be made to the Route 9 road and bridge at the southern shore.

Flood waters overcome the dam at Lake Lashaway and undermine the Maclan Hat Factory. Photo from personal scrapbook at the EB Historical Museum.

The hurricane tore the steeple off the Baptist Church and damaged the roof. Services were held in a private home and in Red Men's Hall until repairs to the condemned building could be made. Services were able to resume in the repaired building for Easter Sunday in 1939. Only three trees in Evergreen Cemetery were left standing. Phone lines were damaged as was the water main. This caused the standpipe to fall over, and the reserve tank on the top of Doane Avenue was emptied. Drinking water had to be provided by a tank on a truck to residents until the main was repaired. (Report of the Water Commissioners, Town of East Brookfield Annual Reports, Year Ending December 31, 1938)

In her written account to the Historical Commission, Pauline Dilling, who lived in the house that is now the Harrington Center across from the Baptist Church, recalled, *"In September 1938 was the terrible flood and hurricane, and I remember sitting with my grandmother as we watched the steeple of the Baptist Church sway back and forth and finally go over. I remember the road washed out near the bridge and the Maclan Hat building, followed by desks, typewriters and everything going down the river... We went by boat for 10 cents to the other side of the lake when the road was closed."*

View from the southern shore of Lake Lashaway, looking east. Route 9 is washed out and Varneys Garage is on fire. Photo from collection of East Brookfield Historical Museum.

Looking east on Route 9 from current fire department. The washed out dam can be seen on the right and the burned Varneys Garage in the background. (from EB Historical Museum Collection)

When the Lake Lashaway Dam gave way, the water rushed down the East Brookfield River, into the Seven Mile River and then into Lake Quaboag, or Podunk Pond. The water level rose by twelve feet, covering the road. (Photos from Dan Hamilton's Brookfield's Research, www.brookfieldsresearch.com.)

Flood of 1955

In 1955 the region was severely impacted by flooding caused when two hurricanes passed by southern New England. Hurricane Connie dumped between four and six inches of rain throughout the southern portions of New England, raising the water level in lakes, streams, and other bodies of water. One week later, Hurricane Diane brought as much as twenty inches of rain to the already drenched region. Connecticut saw the most damage, but in Massachusetts over 200 dams either gave way entirely or were damaged. (US Department of Commerce, NOAA, National Weather Service. "Historic Flood August 1955." National Weather Service, NOAA's National Weather Service, 21 Sept. 2015, www.weather.gov/nerfc/hf_august_1955.)

The Lake Lashaway dam held during this storm, due mostly to the efforts of the Fire Department, the Civil Defense Department, and many volunteers who reinforced it with sandbags. It was the Stevens Dam on the Seven Mile River Bridge at the end of Howe Street that would wash away this storm. The Podunk section of town was isolated for days. In addition, the town was without drinking water for over a week after the pumping station flooded.

Several people in town were veterans and had experience with Bailey Bridges, which were portable bridges used by the military to cross rivers. One was requested and was used to reconnect the Podunk section of town with the main town. It was installed by Highway Superintendent Joe Perry and assistant Mr. Woodis and ready for use within one week of the flood! It remained until a permanent bridge was completed the following year.

View of the Seven Mile River overflowing the bridge at the intersection of Howe Street and Podunk Road, 1955. (Photo by Ernest Benoit, donated to EB Historical Museum)

View of the Seven Mile River overflowing the town shed (current recycling center) on Stevens Road, 1955. . Photo by Ernest Benoit, donated to EB Historical Museum.

View of workers replacing the bridge over the Seven Mile River at the intersection of Howe Street and Podunk Road, 1955. (Photo by Ernest Benoit, donated to EB Historical Museum)

These natural disasters marked the end of the industrial period of East Brookfield. The mills and factories were slowly being replaced by buildings run by electricity rather than water. The Flood of 1938, coupled with the Great Depression, served to close some of the once-thriving factories in town for good. There was no money to rebuild and even if there were, water power was no longer needed to operate factories. Those that were rebuilt were also relocated. Any that remained after this first disaster were permanently closed after the flooding in 1955. East Brookfield transitioned to the bedroom community it is today: a small town where most people commute to other areas for work, returning to this now quiet town in the evenings and weekends.

One outcome of the flooding was the improved state and federal funding of flood control projects to prevent damage from future weather events. Brookfield Athletic Shoe Company donated a piece of land on the bank of the East Brookfield River to the town in 1963 for the construction of a flood wall. The wall was built by the Department of Conservation and finished in 1964.

Part 3

THE FLATS

The area known today by residents as "The Flats" is just that, a large area of very flat land in the midst of the typically rolling hills and rocky outcroppings of a traditional New England landscape. Beginning at the juncture of Main Street/Route 9 and North Brookfield Road and continuing west to the town line in Brookfield, the land lent itself to agriculture and later became an ideal location for an airport and a golf course, and later a small housing development and a lumberyard, along with a variety of other businesses and restaurants.

The original use of the land was mostly agricultural, though the triangular shaped piece of land that is bordered by Route 9, North Brookfield Road, and Blaine Avenue was used as a ball field. Called Houlihan's Field, it was playing on this field that gave Connie Mack his first taste of professional baseball. The Chicago Nationals traveled through town on the way to a game in Boston and played an exhibition game against the East Brookfield team, for whom Connie Mack was catcher. While the Chicago team won, according to those who were there, Connie Mack's superb catching was the talk of the game and made the Chicago team's win at least a bit more difficult.

The first farm located on the Flats was the Stoddard Market Garden, run by Emerson Stoddard and his son. In 1911, Mr. Stoddard hired a 15-year-old Italian immigrant named Louis Petruzzi to work on his farm. Louis would purchase the Stoddard Farm in 1923 and build what was once one of the largest market farms in Massachusetts. Starting with thirty acres on the Flats, the farm grew to 160 acres and included a farm on Cove Street along with eleven greenhouses, an automated packing house and refrigerated storage rooms. The main product was celery at first, but the farm grew a little bit of everything, including spinach, cabbage, beets, and carrots for local markets, a distributor in Boston, and for sale at the iconic farm stand on the side of Route 9 in East Brookfield. Many young people got their first job working in the fields or at the farm stand. Richard Jaskoviak, Telegram reporter, recalled the hard work on the farm, pulling weeds, and then jumping in the nearby Clay Pit Pond to cool off. (Jaskoviak, Richard H. "Down on the farm with Louis Petruzzi." Worcester Sunday Telegram, 19 Nov. 1972, pp. 16–18.) Today, the farm continues to be family-owned and operated and is a popular landmark in town. The stand sells flowers for Memorial Day, starter plants, and a wide variety of vegetables. It is officially summer when Petruzzi's sells corn-on-the-cob for the first time. Their season ends with pumpkins and mums for sale for the fall.

Postcard showing arial view of Petruzzi Farms. (From Collection of Howard Drake donated to East Brookfield Historical Museum).

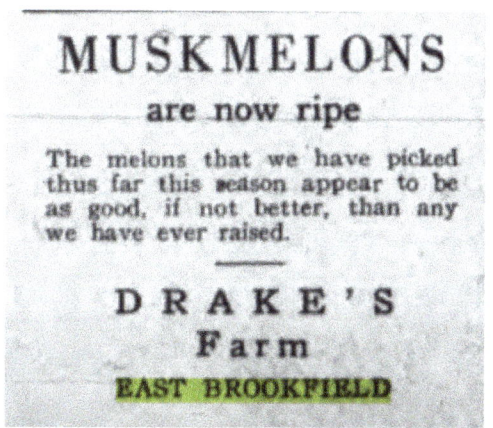

Ad in Spencer Leader, 1930.

Ficociello's Farm was located on the triangle of land between Main Street, North Brookfield Road, and Blaine Avenue. They sold corn at their farm stand.

Another well-known farm to take advantage of the flat land was Drake Gardens. Located on North Brookfield Road, on the current site of Bay Path Golf Course, Drake Gardens was well-known for their production of melons, vegetables and even chickens. This family-owned farm produced as much as twenty tons of melons per year. (Brookfield Union, August 27, 1892) When A. Howard Drake died in 1939, he was the third "Drake" to run the farm.

The bowling alley and golf course were added in 1959 and 1964, respectively, and took the place of the Drake farm. Barbara Drake, an avid athlete, had become interested in bowling but there was no place nearby to practice so her husband, Franklin, built an 8-lane alley for her. Barbara designed the alley and took on the responsibility of running it as a business while Franklin took care of any maintenance needs. Previously called Bay Path Fun Center, when new owners purchased it in 2003 they changed the name to Bogey Lanes and added an 18-hole miniature golf course, pool tables and an arcade.

In 1964, Franklin joined his brother Howard in turning his driving range into a 9-hole golf course. Adjacent to the bowling alley, Bay Path Golf Course is a popular weekend recreational activity for many. Rumors in 2019 were that the golf course was closing though what would take its place was not yet known though at the time of this writing, speculation in town was running rampant!

This was not the only golf course on the Flats. Mid-Way Golf Range took advantage of the flat land when they opened in 1940. It was built by George Rogers and Andrew Campion, Jr., who were managers of other golf courses in the state. They installed lights that allowed for golfing after sunset.

George Mosher operated an airport on the Flats from 1920 until the mid-1950s In 1948, on the thirtieth anniversary celebration of the first airmail service in the U.S., a ceremony was held at the airport. Air mail service from this town took off amid a large crowd of people, some of whom who had purchased postage and sent letters on the flight. One letter was sent to baseball

Advertisement, Spencer Leader, October 19, 1945.

Airmail souvenir, from collection of Larry Gordon. Donated to East Brookfield Historical Museum, 2018.

manager and former East Brookfield resident Connie Mack in Philadelphia. People purchased air mail envelopes and mailed them to themselves as souvenirs.

Many in town, kids included, took rides on the planes from the airport for $10.00 a ride. Eva Perron remembers going for a plane ride one day. She recalls, *"I had a short ride in 1946. I was scared beyond words..The plane, so light, I couldn't wait to land. It was on a Saturday afternoon. Business was good; about ten other people were waiting for take their turn. An experience! The pilot urged me to take a second ride - no way!"* (Eva Perron, written account, April 2019.)

Arthur LeDoux, a prominent businessman in town, was responsible for the homes built on North Brookfield Road. He chose to build small, modest homes that would be affordable to families who worked in town. The homes were close to the town center, churches, railroad, and schools and were located on the bus line. His houses did not stay on the market for very long as they were so affordable and Mr. LeDoux helped with financing by offering a low down payment and a repayment plan. Ten houses and two gas stations were built in the 1920s. In 1939, he continued the project, taking advantage of low lumber prices, a shortage of housing in the area, and an economy that was slowly recovering from the Great Depression. He used lumber and stones from his land in building the homes, further lowering the cost. Most of his houses were sold before they were even finished. His forward thinking and generous spirit enabled many families to purchase their first home.

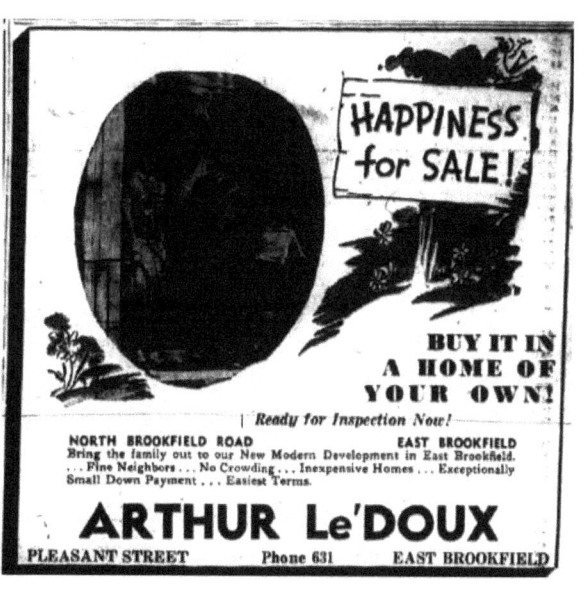
Advertisement in The Spencer Leader, April 19, 1940 for new homes on North Brookfield Road.

In addition to building homes, Arthur LeDoux ran a grocery store in Depot Square. He purchased this store from Warren Tarbell in 1921 and operated it for several decades. He also held many town offices, including being part of the committee to separate from Brookfield. He was a selectman for seven years and organized the Worcester County Selectmen's Association in 1927, in addition to serving on the Finance Committee, the Board of Public Welfare and as director of the Southbridge Cooperative Bank. He was on the board of the North Brookfield Savings Bank and a member of the Lassawa Tribe of Red Men.

The current Mobil Station was formerly Joyce's Colonial Station, a service station run by Roy Joyce, who also served as a selectman in town for several years. His wife ran a tea shop in the house that was attached to the service station. It then became Shorty's Garage, named for owner Francis Eastwood who was just over four feet tall. This garage moved to North Brookfield Road when Mobil bought the station.

Joyce's Colonial Service Station. Photo donated to East Brookfield Historical Museum by Lisa Grace, Roy Joyce's daughter.

An early photo of the service station run by Roy Joyce. Donated to East Brookfield Historical Museum by Lisa Grace, Roy's daughter.

This mostly agricultural area almost had a very different use. In the 1950s, the land was sold to investors from Boston who planned to build a horse racing track. Their rather grand plans included a four-lane highway connecting the race track to the Massachusetts Turnpike and the promise of lower taxes and jobs for residents of town. The plan was controversial in town as some residents felt the town needed the revenue, while others were skeptical of the promised funds, and still others felt the use was immoral and should not be allowed in town. Those opposed to the project organized the "East Brookfield Civic Association" under the leadership of Franklin Drake. A referendum vote in March of 1949 resulted in the voters defeating the project by ten votes. 595 of the town's 668 registered voters turned out for the election which the local reporter called, "the most exciting day in town since the surrender of Japan." (Spencer Leader, March 11, 1949)

The possibility of a race track was again before the town in 1955 when voters approved dog and horse racing by sixteen votes. This vote prompted the Selectmen to give their approval to the project which allowed Walter A. Griffin of Worcester the right to apply to the State Racing Commission for a license. His plan was to build a 4,000 seat stadium, a quarter-mile dog racing track, and a half-mile horse racing track on one hundred acres of land that was owned by George Mosher and John Ficociello. This land included the former East Brookfield Airport. After a public hearing in which clergymen of town led the opposition and members of the American Legion were in favor of the track, the State Gaming Commission rejected the application.

The land was next sold to a Palmer developer in 1979. Ninety acres of the original 120-acre lot was sold to K-Mart, who planned to build a warehouse distribution center. At the time, the planned warehouse would enclose forty-six acres and be the largest single-story building in Massachusetts. It came with the potential of creating 2,000 new jobs and $200,000 in local taxes, one-third the amount collected annually in East Brookfield at the time. A controversial decision by the selectmen to give K-Mart a 50% tax break resulted in a court case against one of the selectmen for conflict of interest. While those who brought the case to court were unsuccessful, the resulting delay was enough to stop the project in another way. Sales in New England did not meet expectations so the distribution center was not needed and the land was put up for sale.

A plan for a race track resurfaced in 1982 when investors, who planned a similar facility in Spencer and were denied, looked to this property for a dog racing track. Their proposed 4,500 seat facility and shopping center would employ 200 full-time and 200 part-time workers at the race track and adjoining shopping area. They planned to purchase a total of sixty acres, half from K-Mart and half from an investor from Palmer. Within six months, the developers were in financial trouble and the bank took some of the 30-acre parcel. A non-binding referendum showed an overwhelming majority of voters opposed the race track and the developers went no further in their plan.

On July 2, 1952, St. John's was established as its own parish, separate from their mother church, St. Mary's of Brookfield. A home on Blaine Avenue was purchased that same year to serve as a rectory for the priest who would lead the church. Even though the church building on Church Street, currently Connie Mack Drive, had been recently renovated with new paint and pews, the parishioners proposed plans for a new building and fundraising began. $67,000 was pledged by house-to-house canvassing, and construction of St. John the Baptist Catholic Church began. The church, located at the corner of Blaine Avenue and North Brookfield Road, was built by the Minuteman Corporation of Lexington at a cost of $233,000, and was dedicated on April 20, 1969. The building seats over four hundred people for Mass and includes a social hall and other meeting rooms in the lower level. The previous St. John's Church was torn down in 1978 as it was structurally unsound. The stained glass windows from that church are in storage at the East Brookfield Historical Museum with one on display.

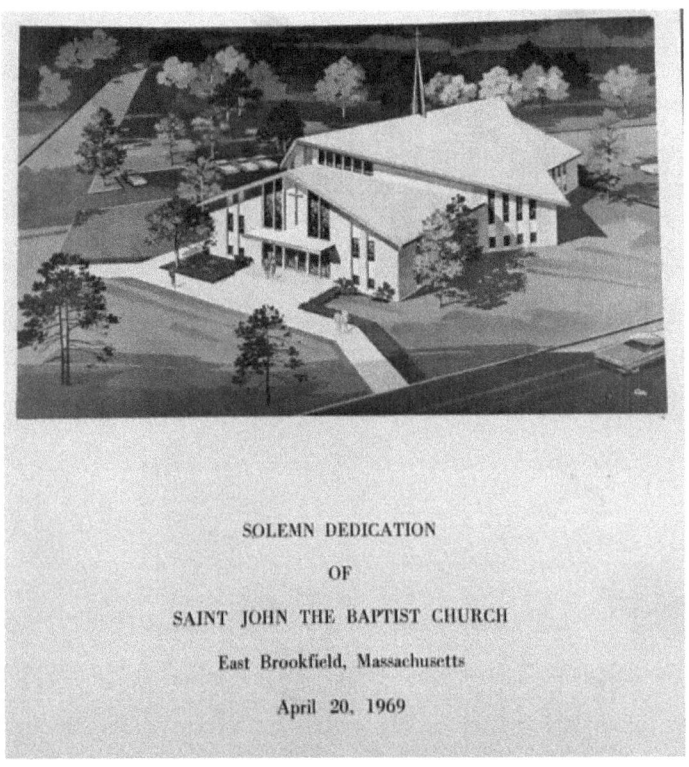

Cover of dedication pamphlet for Saint John's opening. From collection of East Brookfield Historical Museum.

Many who have lived in town for years remember Wilson's Pony Farm on the Flats where children could ride ponies. A teepee near the pony farm sold Native American jewelry and other souvenirs. Oak Grove Luncheon was located on the Flats, just east of Blueberry Lane. It was owned by Fred and Anna Corbett and was commonly referred to as Hot Dog Annie's by locals.

The open area of the Flats remained a potential area of commercial growth for the town. In the late 1980s, Russell DiBara developed thirty acres of land on the Flats, near the Brookfield town line. He opened a driving range, a small engine repair shop and a strip mall. The strip mall has had a variety of businesses in it over the years, but is currently occupied by Panda Garden, a Chinese food restaurant; The "Rise N Shine" breakfast diner which opened in 2005; and a coin shop. DiBara sold land on which a restaurant called Boondocks was built. Scott and Grace Conner purchased the building in 2006 for their own restaurant, EB Flatts.

In 1993, Conrail purchased seventy-six acres on the Flats between the main rail line and Route 9 which has yet to be developed. In 2005, Howe Lumber opened a second location on the Flats and then moved their entire operation there in 2016.

One of the businesses on the Flats, Quaboag Sporting Goods, was destroyed by a fire in April of 2007. The business had been run for forty years, first near Lake Quaboag, before moving to their location on the Flats. A brush fire that started outside in the rear of the building quickly spread to the attached business and home. Adding to the difficulty in fighting a fire which was inside the walls of a building that housed propane tanks and ammunition, was the lack of access to water. The closest hydrant did not have enough water pressure to be effective and tankers had to pump water from Lake Lashaway to be used on the fire, over a mile away. Route 9 was closed for over six hours as over one hundred firefighters battled the blaze. Despite efforts by East Brookfield, Spencer, and almost twenty other area fire departments, the store and home were a complete loss.

Part 4

PODUNK

Depending on where you look for a definition of the word Podunk, you will encounter a variety of definitions; none of them particularly pleasing to those who live in this area of town.

Wikipedia defines Podunk as an insignificant, out-of-the-way, or fictitious town.

The Urban Dictionary describes Podunk as a small, insignificant town and expounds with the following "related words": boondocks, boonies, small town, middle-of nowhere, rural, and hillbilly to name a few. Some are not fit for print.

Merriam-Webster's Online Dictionary lists the definition as a "small, unimportant town," but adds in its "full" definition the word "isolated." Merriam's does, however, acknowledge that the origin of this term is the name of a village in Central Massachusetts or Connecticut.

While everyone is in agreement that the word is derived from a native word, there is a wide variety

Photo taken by the Massachusetts Department of Natural Resources and gifted to Alva and Helen Silliman in appreciation, December 23, 1959.

of interpretations of what "Podunk" meant to the native residents. A few of these interpretations are "river-which-comes-back-to-itself" referring to the winding Seven Mile River, relatedly "long-narrow-neck-of-land," "a boggy place," "the-low-land-beyond." The most commonly used in earlier years is "place of burning." Early in the 1900s, people attributed this "place of burning" to the erroneous belief that the Quaboag Indians burned their captives at the stake. They probably did burn areas as a means of clearing land, so perhaps that is where this definition originated. Clues to the true meaning of the word can be found on two deeds. The term Podunk appears on the original deed given to the English settlers by the Native Americans in 1665. On this deed, a small meadow near the northern shore of Lake Quaboag was labeled "Podunk." It also appears in another deed giving the English land in Connecticut. That land is also a meadow and like the land in our town, it also has a stream running through it that turns and meanders until it is flowing in almost the opposite direction as it begins. Therefore, one can hypothesize that the term "Podunk" means an area of meadow land where a river or stream turns back upon itself in its travels through the land.

What is certain, though, is that Podunk does, in fact, exist. It may seem strange for those who have grown up in this area to read this, for they will certainly question why anyone would think it didn't. However, at varying times in both the 19th and 20th centuries, just such a thing was debated as well as to where the "real" Podunk is located. The place-name of Podunk first appeared in the historical record in the mid-1600s and referred to two meadows on the aforementioned deeds. A tribe of natives named the Podunks lived in these areas, though it is unclear whether they called themselves this or whether it was

> *"Not to care whether a man 'comes from Boston or from Podunk' has always been understood to be the supreme proof of strict impartiality, but it was never meant to mean that it was desirable to come from Podunk." -Harold Fraser, Boston Sunday Globe, November 23, 1924*

a name given them by the English. While not much is known of this tribe, having disappeared from history in the mid-1700s, they were part of the Algonquin nation, were both hunters and farmers, built longhouses, and were eventually decimated by the combination of smallpox and King Phillip's War.

In 1846, a Buffalo newspaper, the Daily National Pilot, ran a series of fictitious letters called "Letters from Podunk," resulting in the perception of Podunk as a backwards, boring place where nothing ever happened. In these letters, which were reprinted on a national scale, residents of Podunk were depicted as unintelligent, dull, and ignorant of current events. Mark Twain even referenced Podunk in an 1869 article titled "Mr. Beecher and the Clergy" in which he stated "they even know of it in Podunk, wherever that may be" in reference to criticism directed at a friend.

Vaudeville entertainer George M. Cohen spent summers in North Brookfield and visited Lakes Quaboag and Quacumquasit as many tourists

Picture from Neil Hickey's article, "What They Think of TV in Podunk," TV Guide, May 4, 1974

A Day in the Life...

"I remember going to my grandparents' house on Howe Street and their telephone was still on a party line. They shared it with the Larkhams, who lived about a half-mile down the street. If you wanted to make a phone call, you had to pick up the receiver and listen quickly. If someone else was already talking, you had to carefully hang up and try again later. This was in the 1980s."

- Heather Gablaski, 2018

did. He incorporated the term "Podunk" into his comedy routines.

Perhaps this nationwide attention on "Podunk" is why so many places across the United States claim to be the "real" Podunk, when it is obviously the small section of East Brookfield that rightfully owns this claim (perhaps shared reluctantly with the Podunk of Connecticut). As of 2017, there were twenty-five geographic features in the United States that include the name "Podunk" and an additional thirteen whose historical place name included the term "Podunk." (U.S. Department of the Interior (2017). Geographic Names Information System. Reston, VA, https://geonames.usgs.gov/.)

In 1933, a Boston Herald article stating that Podunk did not exist, was promptly challenged by E.A. Plimpton, who had a summer home in Podunk. Etymologist Allen Walker Read countered with an explanation that brooks, meadows, ponds and creeks throughout Connecticut, Central Massachusetts and New York carry the name "Podunk" so therefore, it is a real place. It was not until 1941 that the Herald followed up to correct their mistake, challenging the Worcester Telegraph to make the final determination of whether or not Podunk existed. The Telegraph assigned William Moiles to head west and not return until he had either proved or disproved the existence of Podunk. After entering East Brookfield, stopping at a bar to ask directions, and then heading in the general direction of those directions, Moiles came across a boy hitchhiking. The boy indicated that he was going to the Podunk School and then informed Moiles that he was already in the elusive Podunk that he sought and therefore had proven that there was, in fact, a Podunk.

H.L. Mencken, one of the most influential American writers of the first half of the twentieth century, wrote an article titled, "The Podunk Mystery" about what he called, "The Booth-Moiles Expedition of 1941" for The

New Yorker in 1948 as part of his series called "Postscripts to the American Language." His telling of the so-called 'expedition' concluded that this Podunk and one near Hartford, Connecticut were the only authentic Podunks. In the 1950s Webster's Dictionary added the phrase, "a village near Worcester, Massachusetts" to their definition of Podunk.

In 1959, excitement came to Podunk again when a spruce tree, cut from Alva and Helen Silliman's farm on Howe Street was chosen to be the Rockefeller Center Christmas Tree. This story is told in more detail in another chapter.

In 1974, Podunk attained national fame again. In response to criticism from a TV Guide writer that television offerings were crude and "drivel," an unnamed television executive made the off-hand and derogatory comment that "We've got the facts and figures which tell us exactly what they want to see out there in Podunk." This aroused the ire of Neil Hickey, writer for the TV Guide, who remembered the 1948 article by H.L. Mencken that identified Podunk as a real place in Central Massachusetts. Apparently leaving New York that very day, Hickey arrived in East Brookfield via Route 9 through Ware, crossed the bridge on Cottage Street and was informed by a pedestrian that he had arrived in Podunk.

Hickey spent six days interviewing approximately fifty "Podunkians" about their opinion of television. John Treadwell stopped working his oxen to tell Hickey that he usually falls asleep when watching television after spending a long day on his farm. He said, perhaps prophetically that, "The nighttime shows are all the same - police and crime. If they keep detailing how to commit crimes, we'll soon have a nation of criminals" and "you get fat going to the refrigerator during all those commercials." Alva Silliman reported similar distaste for current programming, lamenting the loss of Arthur Godfrey and Ed Sullivan and commenting that "They must be really hard up for programs if they keep showing the same ones over and over." His wife, Helen, was concerned about the impact of violence and slinky costumes on young people. [In my second favorite quote from my grandmother, my first being the admonishment when doing dishes that there was nothing you could get on your hands that you couldn't wash off,

Worcester Telegram & Gazette, May 7, 1974, photo by George P. Cocat

she questioned the need for television at all, what with the exhilarating fall colors that could be seen by simply looking out the window.] John Terry, Jr. commented that he "had better things to do," citing a recent turkey raffle. Joe Perry lamented on news reporters who did not let the viewing public make up their own minds, but added too much editorializing to the news.

In six days of interviews, Hickey met residents he described as "uniformly gracious, hospitable and - more important - articulate, opinionated and well-informed;" none of whom were overly excited about television offerings. Following the TV Guide article, which brought nation-wide attention to Podunk, four billboards were erected with the message, "Welcome to Worcester: Gateway to Podunk."

So, those who have lived in this area have always known that Podunk exists, but *where* is it? There are no boundary lines, not even any "Entering Podunk" signs now, though there used to be! There is no school for current Podunkians, though there were two until the 1930s, no post office; so how does one know when they are within the borders of this illustrious place? Podunk is about six square miles in area, roughly the area from the Podunk Pike to Lake Quaboags and Quacumquasit and just over the town lines to Sturbridge and Charlton. Depending on who you talk to and when, the boundaries appear to get larger. Alva Silliman said the boundary was just past Young Road on Howe Street and cut through the woods to Podunk Road and extended out to South Pond and to a small portion of Sturbridge and Charlton on the southern border of the town. Today, as soon as you cross the bridge over the Seven Mile River, some would say you are in Podunk.

Podunk had an Upper and Lower section with the Upper Section being the section near the cemetery and Podunk Chapel and the Lower Section somewhat along West Sturbridge Road. Lower Podunk, or "Lower Dunk," had two main settlements of houses, one called Rice Corner on West Sturbridge Road and one near the intersection of Draper Road, Shore Road, and

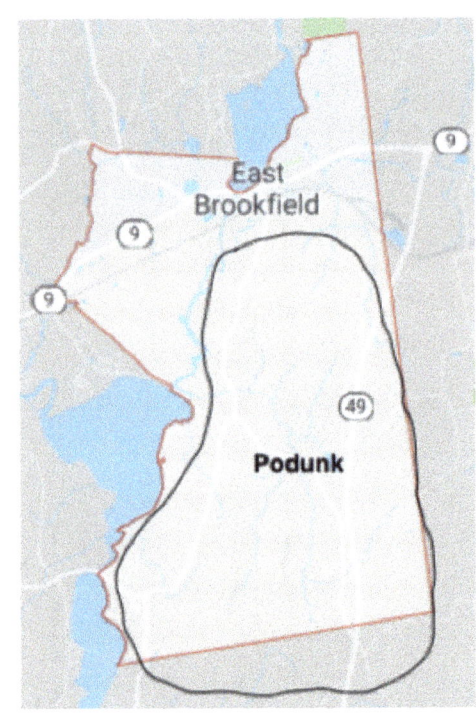

According to a hand-drawn map in 1963 and various oral accounts, this is the rough outline of the "Podunk Community." Created by author based on map and accounts from collection of EB Historical Museum. Created by author.

Podunk Road.

The earliest European settlers to Podunk may have been the Hamilton brothers, who moved to the area in 1660 and settled on the northwest shore of Lake Quaboag. In a presentation to the Quaboag Historical Society in 1926, Walter Terry stated that brothers with the last name Hobbs settled in the Podunk area around 1675 near Draper Road. Ellis Draper mined for ore and carted it to the furnace in East Brookfield, which was near the dam at the southern shore of Lake Lashaway. Shortly before 1700, a road, if it could be called that, was created connecting the Podunk area and the town of Brookfield along the northern shore of today's Lake Quaboag. Podunk was also on the main route between Springfield and Providence, which provided both connection to others and a means of trade for those settling in the area. As early as 1720, farmland was cleared for the settlers who were moving to the area that would come to be known as Podunk.

> *"Don't ask me why, but you go uphill to get to Lowerdunk and downhill to get to Upperdunk." -Mrs. Milton A Putnam as quoted in New York World Telegram, May 3, 1956, article by Murray Robinson*

The Adams Family was also a prominent one in Podunk. Abraham Adams was born in Medfield, Massachusetts in 1701, moved to Brookfield in the 1730s and married Mary Cummings of Oxford. They had five sons and three daughters. It was their home "over south," where Adams Road is today, that held one of the first schools in the area. Abraham built a small one-and-a-half story home within sight of the family farm for his son Eleazar in 1767. This home was passed on to Eleazar's descendants until it was sold in 1993 and moved from the property on Adams Road to become an addition to a home on Podunk Road.

The settlement was so established by 1793 that residents asked to be incorporated as their own town, citing their size in addition to the distance to the meeting house in Brookfield. Their request was denied, but had it been approved, the question over whether there really was a Podunk would be a moot point!

Men from Podunk have formed militias several times, the first in 1675 to combat attacks by natives during King Philip's War. A militia from Podunk fought the British in the Revolutionary War, then in Shay's Rebellion and the War of 1812. Men from Podunk fought in twenty-five battles during the Civil War and formed for the last time during World War II.

Union Hall, artist rendering. Source: Photo East Brookfield Historical Museum.

In close proximity to the bustling Henshaw Tavern, described earlier, was a brick kiln, a grist mill and a saw mill with accompanying houses for workers. Remains of one mill and two houses could still be seen in 1910. ("Historic Podunk: Written for Meeting of Historic Society, June 23, 1926, held at "Gray Ledge" alias "Indian Rock House" in Podunk"; W.O. Terry.)

The Second Universalist Society in Brookfield was formed in 1819 and a church was built in 1820. This church became the religious, social, cultural and political center for "Podunkians," hosting religious services of different denominations, political rallies, concerts, and dances. Plays were put on by the "Podunk Literary Society."

Podunk Chapel, 1920. From Collection of EB Historical Museum.

After Union Hall was destroyed by fire, the residents of Podunk raised funds to build another hall and Union Chapel opened in 1882. The 30 by 40 foot building was heated by a wood stove and lit with kerosene lanterns. There was no water on site so neighbors would bring water as needed for various functions. Services, including a Sunday School, were held on Sunday afternoons. Attendance was fairly small, as were the offerings collected, but social events were quite popular and raised most of the operating costs for the Chapel, which mostly included a token amount given to whichever local preacher was engaged for the weekly service and for the accompanying organist.

The Podunk Community Club and the Podunk

Women's Club organized community service projects in the area including renovations to the Podunk Chapel, which was the social hall of the area. Mrs. Elizabeth (Bettie) Macia recalls that the traveling ministers would sometimes bring their own organist or soloists along for the service and that the Sunday School classes were quite small, her class consisting of herself and one other student. (Macia, Elizabeth Putnam. "Letter to Betty." Received by Bertina Brennan, 30 Sept. 1986, East Brookfield, MA. letter to Historical Commission about Podunk Chapel.) The Podunk Community Club held annual Strawberry Festivals in June; Old Home Day celebrations on Labor Day with food, dancing, and games such as three-legged races and softball; Chicken Pie and Harvest Suppers in the Fall; and a Christmas Tree Social, which was the highlight of the year for the local children.

The Hurricane of 1938 damaged the chapel, requiring a decision as to whether to abandon the building or restore it. Due to the amount of donations of money and materials, as well as a leftover $80 from a Union Hall account, the decision was made to restore the building. On April 16, 1939, thirty men and eight women volunteered their time and skills to help with repairs to the roof. Other residents donated such materials as nails, cement, and lumber. Donations were also received to update the building. Dr. John Fowler donated wiring, a local electrician, Ambrose Tower, donated his time, and Arthur LeDoux and the East Brookfield Baptist Church donated light fixtures. Card parties and suppers were held to raise money to purchase paint, repair the basement floors, built new cupboards, and install dining tables. Mr. and Mrs. Arthur LaCroix donated material to repair the ceilings and replaced the wood stove with a hot air furnace. Eventually, the foundation was repaired and concrete front stairs were built; these were the only repairs that required funds from the savings of the Chapel, all others had been funded by donations. Later, in

The Chapel after restoration. Photo: Ed Gablaski, May 2017.

1949, a well was dug on the property, the exterior was repainted, and landscaping was done. All the work on the chapel was done by volunteers. (Historical account, East Brookfield Historical Commission, c. 1949.)

In 1974, the Chapel was only occasionally used for community events and was in need of repairs again. A 99-year lease was signed with the Brookfield

Lodge of Masons, who completed the necessary repairs and held meetings there for many years.

By 2014, Podunk Chapel was closed and in need of serious repairs. Animals had gotten into the building and the roof was leaking and falling in in places. The five churches who were trustees of the building, the East Brookfield Baptist Church, the Congregational Church of Spencer, the Congregational-Evangelical Society of Brookfield, the Methodist-Episcopal Society of Brookfield, and the the Methodist-Episcopal Society of Charlton, decided that their lack of use of the building combined with the cost of repairs that were needed, made it a better option to sell the building. While the East Brookfield Historical Commission and several town members were interested in acquiring the building, the charter required that the building be used for religious services and could not be fulfilled if the town owned the building. In 2014, Podunk Chapel was sold to Mr. David Sweet of Spencer, a member of the Masons group that had used the building for meetings. He completed extensive renovations on the building and it has regained its place as a community gathering space.

Restored sanctuary, Podunk Chapel. Photo by author, 2017.

On November 13, 2016, Mr. Sweet held an Open House after refurbishing the building by getting donations of pews, statues, and lighting fixtures from churches as close as Spencer and as far away as North Carolina. (Spencer New Leader, November 25, 2016, Kevin Flanders.)

On May 21, 2017, Mr. Sweet rededicated the Podunk Chapel in honor of Virginia "Ginny" Allen, longtime Town Clerk of East Brookfield and an ardent supporter

Rededication of Chapel in honor of Ginny Allen. Pictured (left to right) Selectman Shaun Richards, Selectman Ted Boulay, Ginny Allen, David Sweet, State Senator Ann Gobi, State Representative Donnie Berthiaume. Photo: Ed Gablaski, May 2017

of his attempts to purchase the building. Ginny, along with her family, friends, and co-workers attended a surprise rededication ceremony.

Since that time, the Chapel has returned to its original use as a community gathering center: hosting weddings, anniversary and holiday parties, workshops, and yard sales. Plans for resurrecting the famed Strawberry Festivals along with other community events so fondly remembered by Podunk residents and many others are anticipated as well.

An interesting historical anecdote relates to the brothers John and Jairus Wood, whose family were among the earliest European settlers of Podunk, having been granted land in 1720. The brothers lived a rather isolated life on a farm in the woods between Howe Street and Podunk Road on the side of Teneriffe Hill. It was a journey of nearly a mile from the main road, Howe Street, to their homestead. They lived on this isolated farm with their parents and several brothers and sisters, only four

Emerson, Paesiello. Jairus Wood's house "Podunk" southwest. 1901. Web. 11 Oct 2017. <http://ark.digitalcommonwealth.org/ark:/50959/4t64hh70b>.

of whom survived to adulthood. The foundation of one of their houses can still be seen on land adjacent to the town-owned open space property called "Pelletier Woods." The original house was possibly one of the oldest homes in the area and was dragged to this remote location by twenty yoke of oxen. ("Podunk is Real," W.A. McLaughlin, Jr. The Springfield Massachusetts Sunday Republican, July 16, 1967)

Due to this isolation, John and Jairus Woods were constantly together. They worked on the farm, hunted and fished, and were inseparable. In fact, they were called the Woods Twins, even though Jairus was four years older, as they looked nearly identical and one was rarely seen without the other. According to the story, Jairus fell in love with Charlotte Squires, a resident of nearby Spencer and began spending time courting her. His younger brother, jealous and curious of the young woman who had taken his brother's attention away from him, traveled to town to see Charlotte. For him, it was love at first sight. Both brothers began courting Charlotte, who was flattered by the attention of both young men.

There are two versions of the story of what the brothers decided to do next. One tells of an unusual competition: a walking race. The brothers planned to set out in opposite directions from the intersection of Wood Road and Howe Street, and whoever completed the loop and returned first to the location would marry Miss Squires. The other version, and the one that is told in earlier accounts and therefore most likely more accurate, is of a fistfight to determine a "winner" for Ms. Squires's hand in marriage. Neither man would ever speak of what had actually happened so the truth has been lost. However, a 1922 Boston Sunday Post article written about Podunk includes a quote from a Mr. Benson, who said, *"The only duel those two ever had was by word of mouth and they did certainly jaw each other. I knew 'em but they never fought."* (Dare, Elmer. "Post Man Finds Podunk, Jokesmiths' Butt, A Real Town Rich in Romance." Boston Sunday Globe, 2 July 1922.)

Regardless of how it was determined, Jairus won and married Charlotte; ruining the once close relationship between the two brothers. Eventually, John forbade Jairus from speaking to him again and Jairus and Charlotte moved to town for a few years. John remained with his mother, who deeded him the property, but one day left without a word to anyone. Jairus and Charlotte moved back to the farm to care for his mother and the property. After traveling for seven years, John returned to the family home, and demanded that Jairus leave. His mother and Charlotte convinced him to give Jairus some land, and Jairus built another house less than one hundred yards away on a half acre of land for himself and Charlotte. The two never spoke again, even though they cut hay to sell, chopped wood, and lived within close proximity of each other for the next forty years. If a decision needed to be made regarding an aspect of the farm, it would be communicated through notes or through Charlotte. Jairus seemed

Jairus Wood House. Rock formation called Devil's Kitchen is to the right of where this picture was taken. The path the can be seen between the house and the man leads to Draper Road. Alva Silliman recounted stories of using this route to walk to and from school. (Photo from collection of EB Historical Museum.)

to be a bit of a recluse, spending most of his time on the family property. For thirty years, Charlotte spent weekdays in town, working at a shoe factory in Spencer. It was her brother-in-law John who drove her to and from the trolley on Friday afternoons and Monday mornings. When she was home, she would cook meals to last the whole week for both of the men.

In all this time, their anger did not diminish. Jairus kept chickens on his small plot of land and if they strayed onto John's land, he would send his dog to drive them off. Even when they were old men, they did not speak to each other, but would loudly exclaim within ear shot of the other about how lazy or mean the other was. There were frequent visitors to the homestead, both to see the strange living situation of the brothers and to visit the nearby rock formation known as "Devil's Kitchen." The brothers were happy to share stories with visitors, but would not speak of the origins of their feud.

John, who never married, died in 1908, nursed on his sickbed by Charlotte, but he and Jairus both refused to reconcile before his death. A funeral service was held on the family's property; Jairus refused to sit with the other mourners, but sat close enough to hear the service. Jairus and Charlotte moved back into the original home, where Jairus died six years later at the age of 83. Charlotte's brother moved into the isolated house with her and found her dead in her bed at the age of 74. The original house burned to the ground in 1930 and the house Jairus built was also destroyed by fire, but not until the early 1990s. All three are buried in Evergreen Cemetery, Jairus and Charlotte near the north wall and John on the opposite side.

The Wood Homestead is also the location of "Devil's Kitchen," a formation of rocks that appears to have footprints and a hole from a staff embedded in one of the rocks. Local legend, though of unknown origins, tells that the devil was pushed off the higher rocks and his feet and staff burned into the rock on which he landed. The prints are much less clear today, but many local residents have memories of trying to fit their own feet into the marks on the rocks. These

Photo showing one of the "footprints" and the "staff" imprint. (Photo from collection of EB Historical Museum.)

marks are most likely the result of Native Americans using the large, flat surface as a means of grinding grain as there is more than one stone with these markings. One is still on site and the other was purchased from Jairus Wood by Dr. A.A. Bemis and donated to the Spencer Historical Museum. It was on display at the Richard Sugden Library, but is currently missing.

Another legend told of a hoard of gold and silver buried under the rocks at Devil's Kitchen by an American Indian and at the time the Woods Brothers lived here, people would try to find this hoard of riches. Behind the flat rock on which the marks can be found are two boulders which form a small cave about six feet deep and five feet wide. A small root cellar is also found on the property across from the foundation of Jairus Wood's house. A visit to this site today gives a good impression of the isolation of these brothers as there were no other homes besides theirs in the area.

Grey Ledge is a large rock formation south of Podunk Road that includes an overhang at its base and a rock "stairway" at his southern end. It runs along a fault line that is oriented north to south and is a similar geological formation as the more commonly known High Rocks area, located just to the south. (United States. Department of Conservation and Recreation. CMRPC. Upper Quaboag Watershed and North Quabbin Region Landscape Inventory: Massachusetts Heritage Landscape Inventory Program. Boston, MA: Massachusetts Department of Conservation and Recreation, 2008, p. 15 Print.)

This area was the location of a Boy Scout camp run by Reverend Walter O. Terry. Remnants of the camp are still visible, including a well and a chimney from a cabin. Reverend Terry theorized that the trails in this area, which lead to High Rocks and Wells State Park, were originally native foot paths that were enlarged by European settlers. In a written account, *"History of Grey Ledge,"* Reverend Terry recounts a 1923 conversation with Willis Gleason, a long-time resident of Podunk. In his conversation with Terry, Gleason shares stories his grandfather Calvin Hobbs, an early settler of Podunk, had told him. According to this account, the last members of the Quaboag Indians, Long John and Red Jacket, lived under the ledge with their families in the 1820s and 1830s. The

Aerial view of Grey Ledge Area. Mass. Heritage Landscape Inventory Program, EB Reconnaissance Report, P. 16)

natives earned their living hunting and trapping in the winter and tending small gardens in the summer. They also worked at Henshaw's Tavern and visited area fairs where they earned money showing off their skill with a bow. According to this third-hand account, Long John was buried in "the old burying ground," whether he is referring to the Podunk Cemetery, the Adams Cemetery, or a different burial ground is unclear. When Red Jacket died, he was buried in a small cave, the entrance of which was then covered with rocks. Gleason, hearing this story from his grandfather, went on a search for the tomb and found a small cave that contained an old sword and stone tools. The sword is on display at the Quaboag Historical Society's Museum in West Brookfield. After Red Jacket's death, the remaining members of his family left the area.

In a tour with the Quaboag Historical Society in 1926, Reverend Terry shared more history of the Grey Ledge area. According to Terry, a man named Thomas Mansby, who died in 1916 at the age of 95, told of a settlement of several houses in the Grey Ledge area and near the iron mines on Teneriffe Hill. Terry told of the remnants of cellar holes and possible farms of settlers who most likely moved west to Ohio when the area opened to English settlers. Terry contends that when these houses were abandoned, squatters moved in and continued mining. He said it was still possible to find piles of iron ore, abandoned before it could be processed. ("Historic Podunk: Written for Meeting of Historic Society," June 23, 1926, held at "Gray Ledge" alias "Indian Rock House" in Podunk," W.O. Terry) The area is currently privately owned by the Allen Family.

At the end of Draper Road is a graveyard where members of the Adams Family were buried. The stones are very simple, being only field stones with little obvious shaping or carving, even names and dates have faded. The only known identification comes from oral histories from older residents or in passing accounts in a variety of newspapers. A 1922 Boston Sunday Post article on Podunk references a cemetery, "now abandoned, back of Teneriffe Hill" and reports hundreds of Adamses there with the latest legible date on a stone of 1795. A Spencer Leader news article in 1931 states that one of the headstones was marked 1793. (Spencer Leader, January 16, 1931, "There is a Podunk

This picture, taken in 1944, shows the engraving from one of the stones, outlined with chalk. Carving into fieldstone was not an easy task, and while these stones were readily available, it is uncommon to see them used as gravestones. Photo from EB Historical Museum

in Massachusetts.") Photos taken in the 1940s and in the collection of the East Brookfield Historical Museum clearly show a date of 1806 on a stone. In his interview with the Historical Commission in 1984 Alva Silliman recounts seeing twenty-two stones, including one with an inscription that stated, "A.A. 1801." A written account in the Historical Commission by Edith Hall Plimpton, an Adams descendent, states, "Abraham Adams gave his son, Jesse, the old homestead (house over 'South') to his son, Abraham, Jr., the house known as the 'Moses Adams' place; and to his son William, the place where Elijah Adams lived; Elijah, Sr., Many of these Adams are buried on a knoll between this old place and the 'Benjamin Wood lot' which we still own." Further in the account, it is written, "Eleazar and his wife were buried on the knoll. Their daughters...were buried in Podunk Cemetery..." We also know that at one point the vast majority of residents of the surrounding area had the surname of Adams, with every school-aged child at one point having that same last name. Pictures show the extent of the encroaching forest on the graveyard, especially since logging done in the early 2000s cut down large trees, allowing saplings to grow and mostly obscure and in some cases bury the stones under a large amount of decomposing leaves and pine needles. Sadly, during the logging, some of the stones were knocked over. In May 2018, the graveyard was declared abandoned by the Board of Selectmen and efforts were begun to preserve it.

In Fall 2018, members of the Historical Commission and the 100th Anniversary Committee worked to clear the brush and decades of leaves and

Pictures like this one taken between 1920 and 1925 show how open the land was. Photo from album of Alfred Stoddard, former president of Quaboag Historical Society.

These pictures taken in January 2017, show the overgrown forest which has encroached on the stones and the moss and lichen which cover the stones. Photo taken by author, 2017.

pine needles that were obscuring most of the stones. Using photos taken in 1920 and 1944, they worked to uncover over forty stones, including what is most likely headstones and foot stones. The work to rescue this cemetery will hopefully include a simple fence and sign to keep it from falling into obscurity again and to show respect to these first settlers of Podunk.

It was certainly not unusual for people to be buried in family plots or individual graves. An unnamed member of the Adams family who died from a disease, potentially smallpox, was buried between the current McCrillis's farm and Route 49. The location was marked with a stone, which has since been moved. James Hamilton, an early settler of Podunk, wanted to be buried in a location where the sunrise and sunset would be visible. He is buried on the McKeon's property on Podunk Road; a stone marks the grave.

James Hamilton's gravestone. Photo by author, 2019

In the late 1940s, two large chicken farms were in operation in the Podunk section of town. One was built by Wallace Fish, a World War II veteran, who raised up to 10,000 chickens on his farm on Draper Road. George Payne raised several thousands chickens on his farm near the mid-point of Howe Street, and Hilario Far built a four-story building that could house up to 20,000 chickens. His modern facility, located on Adams Road between Howe Street and Podunk Road, included a grain elevator and automatic heating system. The eggs produced at these farms were sold all along the eastern coast of the United States. (Spencer Leader, October 8, 1948)

At least three dairy farms were located in Podunk. Wally Grimes's farm was on Adams Street, George McCrillis's and Effentee (or FNT for owner Fremont N. Turgeon) Farm were both on Howe Street. In addition to selling milk, Effentee Farm was also a horse farm. Mary Turgeon was an accomplished and award-winning horsewoman who bred, raised, and trained Morgan horses until 1958. She also hosted several gatherings in the 1930s on the Effentee Farm called Gymkhanas in which typical party games like musical chairs, balloon races, and croquet were all played on horseback. Jumping exhibitions were also part of the day's entertainment. These events were open to the public and were free for anyone who arrived on horseback. A nominal fee of 15 cents was charged if you arrived without a horse. Ms. Turgeon moved to Vermont and this horse farm was then run by the Steedmans, who offered horseback riding lessons. The barn on this property is empty today and the land that was once used for riding rings has since been inundated by flooding caused by beaver dams.

Podunk still comes to the attention of those living outside the community whenever a reporter is looking for a news story with a rural twist on it. Podunk was featured in a 2014 edition of the television show, Chronicle. (http://www.wcvb.com/article/podunk-massachusetts-its-for-real/8035442) In 2016, in the midst of the highly contentious Republican and Democratic National Conventions, a reporter from FOX News came to hear the opinions of people in Podunk. Unfortunately, they interviewed no one who actually lived in the Podunk section of town and went to the Trolley Stop on Main Street, which is not in Podunk. Articles over the years have been in Massachusetts and national publications. Each begins with the surprising statement that there is such a place as Podunk and that the people who live there are kind, intelligent, normal people, as if that were a surprise to the readers.

CHAPTER 5
Notable Events and People

Our quiet town of East Brookfield has had its share of notable citizens. Those in this section are not meant to be a comprehensive listing, but a sampling of those residents who have left their mark on the town and the world in small and large ways.

Some early settlers who used some "Yankee ingenuity" to make their lives easier and even turn a little profit included Edward Drake, who was one of the first to develop carbonated beverages. He operated the Aerated Water Works Company near Mud Pond. William Whitney made improvements to the hammerless gun, Orin Henshaw build a windmill to pump water on his farm, and Albert Smith created an incubator for hatching chickens. Read on for more notable people and events!

Part 1

NOTABLE CITIZENS

James and Henry Plimpton were related to some of the earliest residents of the area that would become East Brookfield. They were descended from Abraham Adams, a veteran of the French and Indian War, and one of the first settlers of the Podunk area of town. Their original home was located on the section of Adams Road that runs perpendicular to Howe Street and connects Route 49 to Podunk Road. The house, referred to as the 1767 Farm by the family, was the oldest still standing in Podunk when it was dismantled in 1993. It was built by Abraham Adams, an ancestor of the Plimptons, in 1767 for one of his sons. Sixteen descendants of Abraham Adams were born in the house over the course of generations. Members of the Plimpton Family continued to use the house as a summer home through 1979 when a fire, perhaps started by vandals, caused damage to the empty house. The fire destroyed a shed and damaged part of the back of the house. The owner at the time, Elizabeth Plimpton, feared vandalism and damage would continue to plague the empty house. She offered to donate it to Old Sturbridge Village, but there was no interest. The house was disassembled in 1993, the pieces labeled, and reconstructed as an addition to a house at 742 Podunk Road.

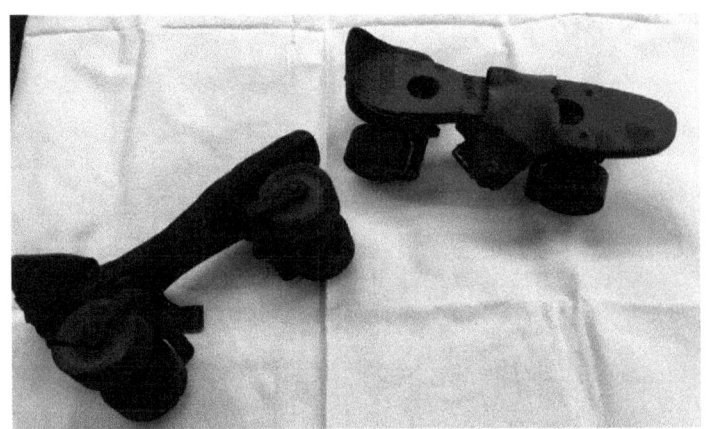

Photo of Plimpton's improved design on roller skates. Skates on display at EB Historical Commission, photo by author 2017.

James Leonard Plimpton patented roller bearings for roller skates that allowed them to turn corners more easily. This invention caused a boom in the roller skating industry. His son, Henry, attended MIT and improved upon his father's design. He and his sister Fannie demonstrated the capabilities of the new skates to the Queen of England in 1875. Henry also worked with noted inventor Thomas Edison to construct an electric generator, which powered his home in 1888, the first to use electric lights in Worcester County. He was also the first in the area to have an indoor shower and bath tub after creating a gravity-fed apparatus that held water on the second floor of his home. In an interview in 1979, John Plimpton recalled, "Dad was the first to have a bathtub. I can remember people coming to the house carrying towels, asking if they might use our Bathtub." ("Plimpton's Grief Shared by Many," Spencer New Leader, July 20, 1979) The father and son duo worked together to design and patent a piece of furniture that could be used as a bed, desk, or dressing table.

Jeduthan Stevens is a man who is responsible for the most notable feature in town: Lake Lashaway. Stevens was a lieutenant in the American Revolution from Connecticut who moved to Brookfield in 1790. He built his home on the corner of Main Street and North Street and ran Stevens Tavern, the first tavern in the village of East Brookfield. He had a grist mill along the Five Mile River near what is today the northern shore of Lake Lashaway. He wanted to flood the low-laying meadow south of his mill by damming the Five Mile River in order to create the opportunity for more mills to be built and boost the economy of the village. He eventually purchased land around the Five Mile River from the Haire Family, and built the dam to power mills. In April 1825, the dam was completed and the area was flooded. This dam was originally just a pile of logs blocking the flow of water. Logs would be added or removed to control the flow of the water. The lake came to be known as Jeduthan Stevens' Pond. Once the water froze over in the winter, men walked out on the ice and cut the trees off at the surface, leaving stumps sticking up from the waters until they eventually rotted or were cut in later years when the water was low. The dam and the water power that was produced allowed Stevens and others to build another gristmill, a saw mill, a machine shop, and several houses nearby. Thus, the center of the village was gradually established at the southern shore of the new lake, where it is located today. Lake Lashaway is essentially a memorial to a man whose name few remember today.

The Hodgkins Building, one of the most easily recognizable buildings in town, is named for **David Webb Hodgkins,** a doctor and citizen of the town who was involved in local and state politics as well as a variety of community organizations. David Hodgkins was born in Maine in 1834. He was a direct descendent of Plymouth settlers; his father fought in the War of 1812 and his grand father fought in the American Revolution. He moved to New York City to pursue a medical education and received his medical degree in 1862 from the College of Physicians and Surgeons. He then taught at Rutgers Female Seminary in New York. Hodgkins served as a surgeon in the Union Army from 1863 to 1865, mainly on a hospital transport ship but also at Fredericksburg. After the war, he remarried, his first wife having died two years after they wed, and moved to East Brookfield in 1868 where he served as community doctor for thirty years. In addition to this work, he served on several local boards, including Selectman, School Committee Member for over twenty years, member of the Board of Health and Water Department, trustee of the cemetery fund, and trustee of the Merrick Public Library. At the state level, he was a medical examiner for the state of Massachusetts from 1877 to 1898 and served in the State House of Representatives from 1882 to 1883. (http://library-archives.cumc.columbia.edu/finding-aid/david-webb-hodgkins-papers-1820-1898-bulk-1858-1870, Columbia University Health Sciences Library; Special Collections)

DAVID W. HODGKINS.

Men of Progress: One Thousand Biographical Sketches and Portraits of Leaders in Business and Professional Life in the Commonwealth of Massachusetts by Edwin Monroe Bacon New England magazine, 1896

Dr. Hodgkins was also a deacon in the Baptist Church, superintendent of the Sunday School, and an outspoken advocate of the temperance movement. He led talks in the village about the negative effects of alcohol on health. This accomplished citizen was also one of the founding members of the Brookfield Medical Club and a leader in the failed 1888 movement to separate from Brookfield. Interestingly, he served as a personal physician to an elderly couple during their travels to Japan in the late 1880s. (Bacon, Edward Monroe. "Men of Progress: One Thousand Biographical Sketches and Portraits of Leaders in Business and Professional Life in the Commonwealth of Massachusetts." New England Magazine 1896: n. pag. Print.)

A collection of Dr. Hodgkins' personal letters, diaries, photos and other memorabilia are currently in the archives of Columbia University. These papers include mainly personal letters to his father while he was in New York and in the Army. There is also a detailed description of the failed Union attempt to capture Fort Fisher in North Carolina and reports of his travels in Japan.

The Hodgkins Building was built in 1883 as a replacement for the brick school house that served the children of the center of town. It operated as a school until 2002. The land it was built on was purchased from Richard Sugden of Spencer and then Hodgkins himself designed the building. The total cost for the building was $7,286.53. It originally housed students in first through eighth grades, though sometimes ninth graders attended their first year of high school here. Teachers had either one or two grades in one room depending on enrollment numbers. When Memorial School opened in 1957, students in grades six through eight remained at Lashaway Junior High with students traveling to the adjoining Memorial School for lunch, physical education class, and assemblies. The school sustained some damage from a fire in the attic in 1978, but was repaired.

In 1983, teachers and students held a 100th year celebration of the building, with essay contests, a gathering in front of the building by all the students who each released a balloon with a postcard attached, and tours for the public. A highly anticipated Jacob Knight painting honoring the building and the town was unveiled, the original auctioned and prints sold.

The Hodgkins Building, 2016. (Photo by author.)

At the time of its closing in 2002, it was the oldest wooden school house still in operation as a school. The building is currently the home for a variety of community organizations including the Historical Commission, the Massasoit Art Guild, the Quaboag Valley Railroaders, and Boy Scout Troop 238. While a historic building, the Hodgkins Building is not on the Register of Historic Buildings. The second and third floors are not open to use due to a lack of safe fire exits.

Sarah Henshaw was born in the Podunk section of town in 1803 and became the first licensed woman preacher in the Reformed Methodist Church in 1830. She preached in ten states over the course of her life, giving an average of one hundred sermons a year. ("Podunk: Special Correspondence." Spencer Sun [Spencer] 2 July 1880: 8. Print.) While it was not uncommon for women to be licensed to preach in the Reformed Methodist Church, Ms. Henshaw had a prolific career, continuing to preach well into her seventies. In 1984, a stone was placed near her birthplace on Podunk Road with the inscription: "Birthplace of Sarah Henshaw 1803-1885. First licensed woman preacher in the Reformed Methodist Church." It was placed by the Reformed Methodist Church of Charlton.

Stone in its original location on the northerly side of Podunk Road. Photo by author, 2016.

In 1990, the movie "Glory" told the story of the 54th Massachusetts Volunteer Regiment. This regiment was led by Robert Shaw and was comprised of African-American soldiers. While arming African-Americans caused a controversy, many Northerners signed up to serve in this regiment. **William Henry Young**, a resident of Spencer, signed up for service in the 54th Massachusetts in July of 1863. Depending on the source, he was either drafted or volunteered for service and was assigned to Company F. While Young joined the 54th Massachusetts after their famous and tragic attack on Fort Wagner, he joined knowing the policy of the Confederacy was to execute any black Union soldiers who were captured rather than keeping them as prisoners of war.

Memorial to Robert Gould Shaw and the 54th Massachusetts, located across from the State House, Boston, MA. Photo: National Parks Service, open source.

William Henry Young's gravestone in Evergreen Cemetery. Photo by author, 2016.

Young was born into slavery in Wilmington, North Carolina and escaped at age 29 by stowing away on a ship heading for Boston. Prior to enlisting, he worked as a farmhand on the Tyler Farm on Greenville Street. (Smock, Frederick A. "Civil War Recruit from Spencer Felt Freedom for Himself Wasn't Enough." Telegram and Gazette [Worcester] 17 Apr. 1990: n. pag. Print.) Young spent two years in the army before being honorably discharged at the end of the war in 1865. He returned to Spencer and worked as a farmhand on Joshua Bemis's farm.

Young is included in this history because he is buried in Evergreen Cemetery in East Brookfield. While it is not clear why he is buried in East Brookfield, one account tells that when he was older he may have lived in Brookfield. His life and service, little that we know of them, are an important chapter in the history of our country.

His gravestone is located in the older section of Evergreen Cemetery in the the far corner. His stone is relatively isolated, but marked with an American flag and a now-faded inscription which reads, "William Henry Young Co F 54 Regt Mass Vol 1820-1896." While there, wander respectfully and note the number of other veterans from East Brookfield who served in wars from the Civil War to the Vietnam War.

Perhaps the most famous resident of our small town is **Cornelius McGillicuddy**, better known as Connie Mack although his other nicknames include: *"The Grand Old Man of Baseball," "Mr. Baseball," "Mr. Mack," "The Noblest Sportsman of Them All,"* and *"The Tall Tactician."* He was the son of Irish immigrants who came first to Boston and then to Central Massachusetts during the potato famine that forced many Irish to immigrate. Born in East Brookfield on December 22, 1862, Connie Mack would revolutionize

Birthplace of Connie Mack, corner of Maple Street and Main Street, Photo by author,

the game of baseball, changing some of its most basic rules into those familiar to most Americans today. Cornelius was born into challenging times. His father was away fighting in the Civil War when he was born in a rented house at the corner of Maple and Main Streets. They moved about a mile west to a home near the junction of Routes 9 and 67 when Cornelius was four years old.

Connie Mack in the Dugout. (Mack, Connie. Photograph. Britannica Online for Kids. Web. 15 Feb. 2016. <http://kids.britannica.com/comptons/art-155941>.)

The McGillicuddy Family had their fair share of tragedies and challenges. There were eventually five boys and two girls in the family. His two sisters, one-year-old Mary and thirteen-year-old Nellie died of either scarlet fever or diphtheria during an outbreak in the 1870s.   His father, Michael McGillicuddy, returned from the war unable to work much. As a result, the children needed to pitch in and help with adding to the family finances. Cornelius started working at age 9 to help support his family. He spent the summers working at the Brookfield Manufacturing Company where he ran errands, operated the freight elevator and delivered

> *"The country town is the soil in which great athletes grow."*
>
> *- Connie Mack*

supplies from one end of the mill to the other. He earned $6 a month to help his mother with family expenses. This money, along with his father's military pension and money his mother earned baking, allowed the family to purchase the house they were renting. He also picked vegetables during harvest time, earning ten cents a week, keeping this money for himself. He left school at the age of 16, never entering high school, not uncommon in those days, to work in the Green and Twitchell Shoe Factory in Brookfield and then in the George H. Burt Shoe Company. The mills and factories of Brookfield allowed for a relatively quick recovery in the area from the Panic of 1873 and provided jobs for residents.

Even though much of his time was spent at work, Cornelius spent his free time, even his one-hour lunch breaks during his twelve hour work day, playing baseball with others in the neighborhood at Houlihan Field near his home. This field was located on the triangular-shaped piece of land bordered by Main Street, North Brookfield Road, and Blaine Avenue. Here, he earned the nickname, "Slats" as a result of his tall, lanky frame. These early games were played by the first rules of baseball. The players would stand in one circle, hit the ball, and try to run to a second circle without being tagged out with the ball. The bat was flat and made of wood and the ball was made of rags covered with leather. Later, the game was changed when home plate and three bases were added, though the baselines were different. In his autobiography, Connie Mack fondly remembers his youth in a "typical American village" as a "rich inheritance where he learned what it meant to be an American." (Mack, p.8)

Connie Mack baseball card from his time with the Washington Statesmen. (Goodwin & Co., Sponsor. [Connie Mack, Washington Statesmen, baseball card portrait]. to 1890, 1887. Image. Retrieved from the Library of Congress, <https://www.loc.gov/item/2007686426/>).

In 1879, when he was sixteen, Connie Mack tried out for and made the town baseball team as catcher. Town baseball was serious business in those days, with players traded and cut from teams just as they are in the Major Leagues today. He played for the East Brookfield Baseball Club, which played exhibition games against the Worcester Ruby Legs and then the Chicago White Stockings as they traveled through East Brookfield on their way to Boston. Even though the town team lost both games by a large margin, Connie Mack's performance and stature caught the attention of Cap Anson, leader of the Chicago team and perhaps caused Connie Mack to think of a career as a professional baseball player. In 1883, the East Brookfield team became champions of the Central Massachusetts Baseball Association after defeating North

Connie Mack, while manager of the Philadelphia Athletics. Thompson, Paul, photographer. Connie Mack, mgr., Phila. Am. Jan 7, ca. 1911. Image. Retrieved from the Library of Congress, <https://www.loc.gov/item/2008678872/>

Brookfield 2-1. This rivalry continues to this day with both towns fielding teams every now and again and competing to see which residents have the stronger ball players.

After the 1883 championship win, Connie Mack quit his factory job to join the Neriden Club in the Connecticut League and the following year moved to the Hartford Club. It was during his time in Hartford that Connie Mack, playing as catcher, made two key changes in how the game was played. First, he convinced the pitcher to change his style of pitching from underhand to overhand and then he moved the pitcher's mound back fifteen and a half feet from home plate to the 60 feet, 6 inches baseball players and fans are familiar with today. Another change attributed to Mack was changing the batter's count from seven balls and four strikes to four balls and three strikes. Finally, Mack changed the catcher's position to directly behind the batter, rather than being fifteen feet behind the plate and catching the pitch on the bounce. This famous East Brookfield resident certainly left his mark on the game!

In baseball's off season, Connie Mack continued to live and work in East Brookfield, managing the bowling alley in Vizard's Hall. He married Margaret Hogan in 1887 and they had three children before she died in 1892. He would remarry in 1910 and have another five children. In 1891, Connie Mack was signed to the Pittsburgh Pirates, for whom he played catcher for two years until becoming the team's manager from 1893 to 1896. In 1900, he raised funds to build a new ball park and created a new team. Originally called the "White Elephants," the team's name soon changed to the Philadelphia Athletics. Under Mack's management, the team won nine American League pennants and five World Series Championships. He managed the American League All-Star Team in the first ever All-Star Game in 1933 and in 1934 was the manager of an American exhibition team that played in Japan, the Philippines, and China. He was elected to the Baseball Hall of Fame in 1937. He was known for building championship teams. He shared in "The Shell Chateau" radio program in 1937 that he did not like selling off players, but his budget could not afford to pay them what they were worth. (https://youtu.be/83YIVTvfKec)

Connie Mack was an innovator in the development of America's pastime and a man of strong moral character. He was one of the first to add lights to the stadium and play night games, one of the first managers to scout high school and college teams for new talent, and he introduced the bullpen and relief pitcher to the game. When he surprised his mother at the age of twenty-one with his decision to leave home and become a professional baseball player in order to better support her and his siblings, she made him promise not to pick up any bad habits and never to drink. He kept his promise and became known as a fair and kind person who could be trusted to make sound decisions. In a letter to the editor in the New York Times on February 28, 1930, Connie Mack is described as "a man of the highest integrity and modesty, and is beloved, as a person, by everyone who is attached to the game." In the introduction to Connie Mack's autobiography, American writer and film-maker Francis Trevelyn Miller described him as "the truest exemplification of the American Spirit," in acknowledgment of his rise to success from humble beginnings due to his passion and hard work.

> *"Humanity is the keystone that holds nations and men together. When that collapses, the whole structure crumbles. This is as true of baseball teams as any other pursuit in life."* - *Connie Mack*

In his obituary, The New York Times lauded Mack's new style of managing, writing: "The old-time leaders ruled by force, often thrashing players who disobeyed orders on the field or broke club rules off the field. One of the kindest and most soft-spoken of men, he always insisted that he could get better results by kindness. He never humiliated a player by public criticism. No one ever heard him scold a man in the most trying times of his many pennant fights." ("Connie Mack, Mr. Baseball, Dies in Philadelphia at the Age of 93," New York Times, Feb. 9, 1956, 1, 36.)

Over the years, both before and after his death, the towns of East and North Brookfield held several commemorations for "the Grand Old Man of Baseball." These days usually included an old-style baseball game between the two towns in remembrance of the 1883 game. Connie Mack returned to the

Brookfields in 1934 and the town of North Brookfield held a "Connie Mack Day" on July 10 in conjunction with his visit. Members of the pennant-winning Philadelphia Athletics and fellow Brookfields native and Broadway star, George M. Cohen accompanied him to town. In his autobiography, Mack speaks with great happiness of this visit, thankful for the opportunity to "relive the happiest days of our lives" (Mack, p. 12) with Cohen and other former men with whom he first played the game of baseball.

In 1948, Connie Mack was honored by the creation of a town baseball league in his name. The first game of the Connie Mack Sportsmen's Club of the Brookfields was preceded by a parade from Blaine Avenue, past his former home, and on to the newly renovated baseball diamond on School Street where the North Brookfield team played against the East Brookfield team. In 1970, Church Street was renamed Connie Mack Drive and the town's baseball field was renamed "Connie Mack Memorial Ball Field" as part of the town's Fiftieth Anniversary Celebration.

Most recently, the town of East Brookfield celebrated their most famous resident's 150th birthday on September 14th and 15th, 2012. On Friday the 14th, "An Evening with Connie Mack," organized by the Philadelphia Athletics Historical Society was held at East Brookfield Elementary School and included a display of Connie Mack memorabilia and several speakers. Norman Macht, Connie Mack biographer and author of three biographies of Connie Mack, spoke on the topic of Connie Mack's early life to 1900. Dick Rosen, chair of the Philadelphia Athletics Historical Society, shared information about Mack's career and Richard Armstrong, former Public Relations Director of the Athletics, shared personal memories of Connie Mack. The evening ended with Brandon Avery of the North Brookfield Historical Society speaking on the exhibition game in 1934 featuring Connie Mack and the A's.

Dick Rosen speaks to the audience at EB Elementary on the career of Connie Mack. (Photo by author, 2012.)

On Saturday September 15, 2012 a full day of events was held at the Town Complex on Connie Mack Drive. East Brookfield Baptist Church kicked off the day with a Pancake Breakfast and a parade made its way from the elementary school to Bay Path Estates. Hot air balloon rides, an antique car and tractor show at St. John the Baptist Church, games, book signings, bands, and food vendors were enjoyed throughout the day. At 1:00 the field was rededicated with an unveiling of a new Connie Mack Field Sign painted by Jacobs Design of East Brookfield. Essay contest winners read their work, and all enjoyed a piece of birthday cake in honor of Mr. Mack's birthday. Guests of honor included members of Connie Mack's family: grandson Senator Connie Mack III of Florida, great-grandson U.S. Representative Connie Mack IV of Florida, and great-great-grandson Connie Mack V.

The afternoon was capped by a baseball game played according to old time rules between residents of North Brookfield and East Brookfield, with East Brookfield winning 32 to 4, perhaps due to the help of former Red Sox pitcher Bill "Spaceman" Lee. The rules in 1883 were that the team who reached one hundred runs was the winner, but this game was called in the third inning. The day ended with the Quabbin Community Band playing during a chicken barbecue put on by the fire department.

Members of Connie Mack's family, Connie Mack III, Connie Mack IV, and Connie Mack V enjoyed the hospitality of town during the anniversary celebration. They threw out the ceremonial first pitch of the game. (Photo by author, 2012.)

Selectman Larry Gordon, far right, presents commemorative bat to the winning East Brookfield team, which included former Red Sox player Bill "Spaceman" Lee. . (Photo by author, 2012.)

Sign unveiled at rededication of Connie Mack Field, by Ken Jacobs. Photo by author, 2012.

Notable events in the career of Connie Mack

1883	Wins Central Mass Association Championship
1884	Entered professional baseball with Meriden CT team
1885	Joined Hartford, CT team and then Metropolitans (NY team)
1886	Joined Washington Senators, National League Team
1891	Joined Pittsburgh Pirates
1894	Became manager of Pittsburgh Pirates
1900	Established Philadelphia "Athletics"
1902	Won first pennant
1905	Won second pennant
1910	Won first World's Series
1911	Won second World's Series
1913	Won third World's Series
1929	Won fourth World's Series
1930	Won Fifth World's Series
1939	Accepted into Baseball Hall of Fame as "Builder of Baseball"
1941	May 17th established as "Connie Mack Day" in Pennsylvania
1949	Honored in New York City with "Connie Mack Day" Parade

Warren E. Tarbell lived on West Main Street in East Brookfield and was a well-known community member who was instrumental in East Brookfield's independence movement. Born in Worcester, he served in the Civil War in Company C, 2nd regiment of the Massachusetts volunteer militia where he earned the rank of first lieutenant. He moved to East Brookfield in 1886 and operated a general store in town for fifteen years at the location of the former L & N Warren Store in Depot Square. He was also part owner of the New England Brick Company. Senator Tarbell was a deputy sheriff in town and also president of the Massachusetts Sheriff's Association. He was also an active participant in town affairs, lobbying for and getting a town water system when East Brookfield was still part of Brookfield. He served as a selectman in Brookfield and East Brookfield for twelve years, with six of those years as chairman. He was on the water commission for eighteen years, all but one as chairman.

Campaign poster from collection of EB Historical Museum.

He was elected three times to serve in the House of Representatives, once in 1906 and again in 1915 and 1917. He was elected to the Massachusetts State Senate in 1919. He served a five-year term and was then re-elected in 1929. He was on many committees including the Mercantile Affairs Committee and Committee on Agriculture. Under his leadership, the Western Worcester District Court was formed serving the towns of Spencer, Brookfield, East Brookfield North Brookfield, West Brookfield, and Warren, with a court house in East Brookfield.

Senator Tarbell was a key leader in the separation of East Brookfield from Brookfield and became one of the first selectmen of the newly formed town, along with George Daniels and A. Howard Drake. As a justice of the peace, he called the very first town meeting to order.

At the time of his death in 1931, he was a sitting State Senator who was unopposed in his campaign for another term as a senator for the Worcester-Hampden District. The funeral was held from his East Brookfield home and was one of the largest held in town. A special train was scheduled to bring mourners from Boston.

The **Drake Family** operated Drake Gardens on North Brookfield Road. Members of the Drake family moved to Brookfield about the time of the American Revolution. **A. Howard Drake** was instrumental in the separation of East Brookfield from Brookfield and served on the first Board of Selectmen. His father and grandfather operated Drake Gardens starting the late 1700s. He and his son, **Francis H. Drake**, were prolific collectors of American Indian artifacts and together amassed a collection of over 3,000

Drake Farms, photo from Drake Family collection, donated to East Brookfield Historical Museum.

arrowheads, pestles and mortars, spearheads and other weapons, and other such relics. **Howard "Bud" Drake** was born on the family farm in 1904, went to Cushing Academy and graduated from Rensselaer Polytechnic Institute, followed by a career at Norton Company. He served as a selectman, town treasurer, was on the Finance Committee, the Board of Health, and the Cemetery Commission. He collected postcards, some of which are in the East Brookfield Historical Museum, political campaign buttons, and antique clocks. He worked for more than thirty years to protect the Franklin mile markers along the Old Boston Post Road. Only weeks after his death in 1986, the legislature approved $25,000 to preserve the markers.

His brother, **Franklin Drake**, and his wife **Barbara**, built Bay Path Alleys in 1959. Barbara had picked up the sport of bowling and wanted somewhere closer to home to practice her new hobby. The bowling alley originally had eight lanes and automatic pin-setters, a novelty for the area as previous alleys used boys to reset the pins. Franklin was responsible for fine-tuning and fixing the machinery and Barbara ran the leagues and managed the finances. After a few years, the management of the bowling alley, with the addition of Bayberry Lanes in Spencer, became their full time job. They ran the alley

Drake Farms, photo from Drake Family collection, donated to East Brookfield Historical Museum.

in East Brookfield until 1971 and the alley in Spencer until 1973.

It was around this same time that Howard and Franklin decided to transition the remaining farm land into a 9-hole golf course. Bay Path Golf Course opened in 1964.

The Drakes were integral parts of the East Brookfield Community. Howard served as selectman for many years and Franklin was an assessor for seven years. Franklin was also active in the church, serving as deacon in the East Brookfield Baptist Church.

Barbara (Howe) Franklin was an impressive athlete who held the title in the women's running high jump while a student at David Prouty High School. Her record was five feet, one and a half inches. In 1935, at the age of 19, she competed in the National Track Meet in New York City, and won first place in the high jump with a jump of four feet, eleven inches. (Spencer Leader, "Barbara Howe Wins National Jump Honors," Sept 20, 1935) Barbara, along with Dorothy Lyford of Spencer, practiced daily with the athletic coach from David Prouty High School to prepare for the 1936 Olympic finals at Brown University in Providence, Rhode Island. Annette Rogers, of Chicago and a 1932 Olympian, won the high jump with a height of five feet, 2 and a half inches. Barbara married Franklin Drake, in 1944.

> *"I don't own this land. My name is on the deed, but I really don't own it. The good Lord lets me use it and expects that I will leave it in better shape than I received it." - Louis Petruzzi*

The Petruzzi Family's name is synonymous with farming in East Brookfield. **Louis Petruzzi, Sr.** immigrated to the United States as a teenager in 1911 from Castelvetere, Italy. He joined his sister, who lived in the easterly section of the town of Brookfield. His father had come to the area and worked on the railroad as so many Italian immigrants did at the time, but had returned home. Louis Petruzzi's life story is a true example of what the American Dream meant to so many during the 1900s. He worked hard, first getting a job as a farm hand on the Stoddard Farm, earning $4 a week for a 10-hour, 6-day work week. He would eventually earn $30 a week when he became a boss on the farm. He got married, bought a house, married Margaret Ficociello, and started a family. When the Stoddard Farm was for sale in 1923, he sold his house, took out a loan from the bank, and bought the very farm which had provided him with his first job in America.

He and his family worked the thirty acres and expanded it to 160 acres, making it one of the largest market farms in Massachusetts. He and his wife had nine children who helped with the work on the farm. One son, **Louis Petruzzi, Jr.**, served as a selectman in town for nearly three decades and has a meeting room in the town hall named in his honor. He gave back to his community, not only through public service, but he donated $50,000 to the David Prouty High School Scholarship Fund to support the college dreams of East Brookfield residents.

The Petruzzi Farm Stand is still a popular place for East Brookfield residents and others from surrounding towns to purchase fresh vegetables and flowers.

John M. Treadwell was a well-known oxen owner in New England. In 1943, he purchased a 185-acre farm formerly known as the Underwood Farm in the Podunk section of town in the home that is currently located at 771 Podunk Road. Part of his farm included a rock formation known as High Rocks. His former farmlands have been sold and High Rocks Estates is built on the land today. He bought and sold hay and ran a dairy until 1950 when he became one of the best oxen breeders in the country.

John Treadwell and his oxen leaving the East Brookfield train depot to shoot, "The Way West." Photo from collection of EB Historical Museum.

He was probably most well-known for his Durham oxen, one of the original breeds used in colonial New England, which he supplied to Old Sturbridge Village. He also competed in oxen pulls and appeared in local parades. In 1966 he spent six months on the west coast to train oxen and ox drivers for the movie, "The Way West," starring Kirk Douglas and Robert

Mitchum. He also worked on the movie "Hawaii," portions of which were filmed in Old Sturbridge Village. In 1976, he led oxen on a recreation of Henry Knox's trip from Fort Ticonderoga to Boston. When his oxen weren't featured in these types of activities, they ran the sawmill on the family farm.

Raoul J. LeBeau, who would become known in town as "Doc LeBeau," was a 1947 graduate of David Prouty High School and attended Clark University as a pre-med student, majoring in both biology and chemistry. His college education was interrupted by the Korean War, in which he served as a combat medic. He was a biochemist and director of research at Memorial Hospital for eighteen years and created and patented an artificial kidney in partnership with Dr. Richard Meyer. Doc built a dialysis machine with materials purchased at Spags, a general goods store in Shrewsbury. He was honored in Stockholm, Sweden in 1966 at the Seventh International Conference on Medical and Biological Engineering for his work attempting to solve problems related to vascular surgery and spoke about his work in many countries, including Ireland, Germany, and Turkey. He was a Fellow of the Royal Society of Health in London, a member of the Massachusetts Association of Clinical Laboratory Directors, and a former national chairman of the American Heart Association. He published twenty-one medical journals over the course of his career.

Mr. LeBeau was very active in town politics and community life. He served as town moderator for thirty years, stepping down only three days before his death. He was on the Town Hall Committee, the Board of Health, the Planning Board, and the Water Needs Committee, in addition to being a volunteer firefighter for fifteen years, Civil Defense Director, and the town's first EMT. He and four other residents purchased the Keith Block at auction with the purpose of selling it to the town for use as a town hall when bylaws prevented the town from doing so itself. He was also on the committee that brought 4th of July celebrations to town, along with Richard McNeaney, Nick Worthington, and Richard Jaskoviak. He was chairman of the town's 50th Anniversary Committee and worked with Senator Ted Kennedy to arrange a flyover during the parade by the Air Force. This parade took two hours to pass by the reviewing stand and included thirty-eight floats.

Doc was also a musician and played the clarinet and saxophone in several bands including the Flying Fortress Swing Band. He was the director and saxophone player of the Hofsbrauhaus Bavarian Band, which traveled to Germany to play. He took several high school students, including his son, to Germany to perform. He was an organist at St John the Baptist Church. This musical talent runs in his family as nearly everyone in town has heard an enjoyed the bands in which his son and grandsons play. (George, Erin, and Craig Holt. "'Doc Leaves Longtime E Brookfield Legacy Behind.'" Spencer New Leader, 11 May 1999.) Any band with Dennis and sons Tommy and Paul are crowd favorites, especially Big Gunz, which frequently includes other local musicians. Rosie Porter and the Neon Moons, a band which includes Thomas LeBeau, is also a popular band at local venues.

Roger Jaskoviak, more famously known as Jacob Knight, grew up in East Brookfield and graduated from David Prouty High School. After graduation, he moved to California and worked in several films as an extra. He returned home for a visit and never went back to Hollywood, instead, attending Leicester Junior College on a basketball scholarship. At the age of twenty-six, he moved to Greenwich Village and sold his art on the street and in local fairs and taught art classes. It was during this time that he adopted the name of Jacob Knight and became a nationally known artist. His work was featured in Women's Day, Ladies Home Journal, McCalls, Family Circle, Smithsonian, Playboy, and TV Guide in addition to being displayed in the United Nations building and Sax Fifth Avenue in New York City. He moved to West Brookfield and spent his time creating works of art from what others might call trash. He exhibited his work in New York.

He is best known in East Brookfield as the artist who created the commemorative painting for the 100th Anniversary of the Hodgkins Building. The painting depicts key locations in town in addition to the Hodgkins Building, where he attended school. These include Lake Lashaway, High Rocks, and a Petruzzi farm truck. Dr. Hodgkins and Connie Mack are featured in the corners of the painting. Similarly-styled paintings were completed for several area towns.

Not only was Jacob Knight a talented painter, he was a generous person as well, giving to those who were in need. According to friend Stephen DiRado, "He'd put food on the table and clothes on their back. He'd help them pay their rent." (Sheehan, Nancy. "A Knight to Remember.'" Telegram and Gazette, 3 Oct. 2004.)

Though not a person, the **Solomon Richardson House,** a model home for the late 1800s at Old Sturbridge Village, was once located in the Podunk section of East Brookfield. It was located on the Underwood Farm, near Podunk Cemetery, but today stands on the common at Old Sturbridge Village and represents what a pastor's home might have looked like in the 1830's.

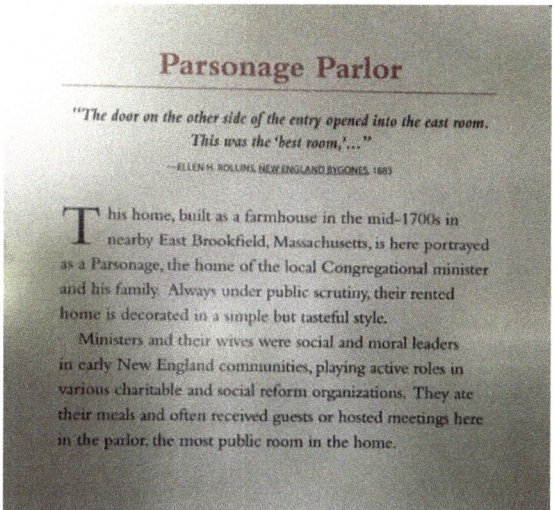

Sign inside Solomon Richardson House, Old Sturbridge Village. Photo taken by author, 2017.

Solomon Richardson House at Old Sturbridge Village once stood in Podunk. Photo taken by author, 2016.

Part 2

PODUNK SENDS A TREE TO NEW YORK CITY

The Rockefeller Center Christmas Tree Lighting has been a tradition and tourist attraction since 1933. In 1931, construction workers who were lucky enough to have a job amid the Great Depression erected a 20-foot tall tree in what would become Rockefeller Center. Two years later, in 1933, the first official tree lighting was held and an American tradition begun. Today, the tree is lit in the days following Thanksgiving and remains lit until the first week of January. But did you know that our town has a connection with what has been called the "most famous Christmas Tree in the world?"

Helen Silliman looking at the tree the day it was chosen to go to Rockefeller Center.

The tree as it appeared in December 1959, fully decorated for the holiday season.

In 1959, the idea that the village of Podunk, known in popular culture as a backwoods, backwards place, would be contributing to the holiday season in the largest city in the United States, made quite the news story. Titles of articles included: "N.Y.C to Get Its Yule Tree From Podunk" (Southbridge Shopping News, October 29, 1959), "Christmas Tree for Manhattan" and "Podunk's Mighty Christmas Tree."

The evergreen used in the Rockefeller Center is typically between 70' and 100' tall and has upwards of 30,000 lights on it. The tree from Podunk fell at the lower end of this range at exactly 70'. In 1959, Massachusetts was selected to supply the Rockefeller Christmas Tree which was, according to Governor Foster Furcolo, "a great honor for our state." He directed the Commissioner of Natural Resources to "conduct a search in all parts of the Commonwealth for a tree that will be suitable for such a majestic setting." Harold O. Cook, the oldest active forester in the United States, is credited with locating the tree. It was then submitted for consideration by Harry C. Smith. Smith was the owner of Spencer Decorating Company, which supplied Christmas trees and decorations to major cities across the nation. Smith had used Alva and Helen Silliman's farm for trees in the past and stated, "I took an option on that tree three years ago, and knew it was headed for Rockefeller Center." ("Christmas Tree for Manhattan, 1959 newspaper article.) The tree's height and near perfect proportions can be attributed to the fact that it grew on the edge of a pasture with no large trees around it to block the sun.

According to the Public Relations Department of Rockefeller Center, the 70-foot Norway spruce tree had a branch spread of 40 feet and a trunk 2-1/2 feet in diameter, weighed three tons and was approximately 80 years old when cut down. ("1959 Christmas Fact Sheet." Rockefeller Center 320 (1959): 1. Print.)

According to Nancy Armstrong in her 2010 book:

> "In 1959, the seventy-foot, eighty-year-old Norway spruce from Podunk, Massachusetts, stood proudly in Rockefeller Plaza. Harold O. Cook, the oldest living forester in the United States at the time, made a gift of the tree to Rockefeller Center after a statewide hunt by the Massachusetts Department of Natural Resources that lasted for several months. They finally found the tree on the property of Alva Silliman in Podunk, and the spruce was felled amidst heavy rains on a Saturday in late November. It made the long trip to Manhattan in the rain and snow and twenty men spent an entire week erecting scaffolding and decorating the three-ton evergreen.
>
> This was the most extensive search for a tree yet, and the coveted evergreen made for another breathtaking display in the plaza that December. Lit on December 10 of that year, the tree's stunning beauty made the arduous search worth every moment." (Armstrong, Nancy, The Rockefeller Christmas Tree, Cider Mill Press, 2010, p. 49.)

All the attention led to some miscommunication as the Governor of Massachusetts erroneously stated that the famous tree was grown in Brookfield, not East Brookfield. Of course, as the tree was approximately eighty years old, it had begun its life in the town of Brookfield but Raymond F. Burke and Charles A. Fahey of the Boulette-Skyten American Legion crafted a letter to the governor stating that, "We, of East Brookfield's Boulette-Skyten American Legion Post 386, are proud that the seventy-five [sic] foot tall Norway spruce should come from this area. We are, however, deeply insulted that publicity on the tree would give credit to the wrong town as the origin…We feel that this, the youngest and most active town in the state, should get recognition due us, and request that your office rectify this mistake as soon as possible." (Telegram and Gazette, October 28, 1959). Of course, the governor's office promptly blamed the State Department of Natural Resources and in a reply to Burke and Fahey stated that the governor had a "warm spot in his heart" for the town of East Brookfield. (unknown newspaper article)

Three men from a New Jersey tree cutting service made the trip to Podunk to cut the tree. They were the same men who cut the tree the state of Maine sent to Rockefeller Center the year before. Working from the top down, they spent three days tying up the tree's branches so its 45' diameter could be narrowed to the 15' required for the 165-mile road trip to New York City. A tree-cutting ceremony scheduled for Saturday, November 28 was attended by about 200 people in the pouring rain, including state representative Philip A. Quinn of Spencer, state senator Paul Benoit of Southbridge, Raymond Burke of the Boulette-Skyten American Legion, representatives of the Department of Natural Resources, Rockefeller Center, the Department of Commerce and the Worcester Chamber

Bulldozer pulling crane out of the mud for loading. Photo: personal Silliman Family Collection.

of Commerce and a variety of neighbors. The hundreds of visitors prompted one resident to note that there was more traffic in the area on this one day than in the previous three months. (*"Rockefeller Center Tree Will be Cut Tomorrow"* Unknown newspaper, November 27, 1959) The scheduled 10:00 cutting was delayed until 2:30 when the rains that had fallen for several days turned the field to mud and the crane became stuck. A bulldozer had to be called in from Worcester to drag the crane out of the mud.

View of the tree tied and ready to be lowered by crane onto the flat bed truck.

By 3:30 the tree was loaded on the trailer and ready for its trip along route 9 to the West Springfield entrance to the Massachusetts Turnpike and from there to the New York Thruway.

The tree arrived in Rockefeller Center on Monday morning, November 30, and spent the next two weeks being decorated before the tree lighting on December 10. Thirty-nine residents of East Brookfield chartered a bus and traveled to New York City for the occasion. There they were taken on a guided tour of Radio City Music Hall and had a reserved overlook for the tree lighting. Those at home could not see them when the lighting was televised, but could hear their cheers when their attendance at the ceremony was mentioned by announcer Ben Grauer. They left New York City that evening and returned to East Brookfield at 2:00 AM, tired but bearing Christmas gifts for friends and families.

...Proud Podunkians ensured everyone knew where the tree was from by attaching this banner to the truck accompanying the tree. The banner now hangs in the EB Historical Museum.

In a newspaper article titled, "Podunk's Mighty Christmas Tree" from an unknown paper, the author alludes to the tree's origins in Podunk by writing, "And so, farewell splendid tree. You have only a few short weeks or days left in which to savor the New England atmosphere that gave you your special quality. Always be proud of your origins, even though some New Yorkers may claim that your birthplace does not exist."

Newspaper articles and programs on the Rockefeller Center Christmas Tree continued to mention Podunk, as in 1984, when an article picked up by the Associated Press and included in newspapers from New York to California stated that "Over the years, from sites ranging from Podunk to Canada - trees have been shipped in from New Jersey, New York, Maine, Connecticut and Pennsylvania. In 1959, the tree came from Podunk, Mass." Podunk is still a term whose uniqueness almost demands special attention.

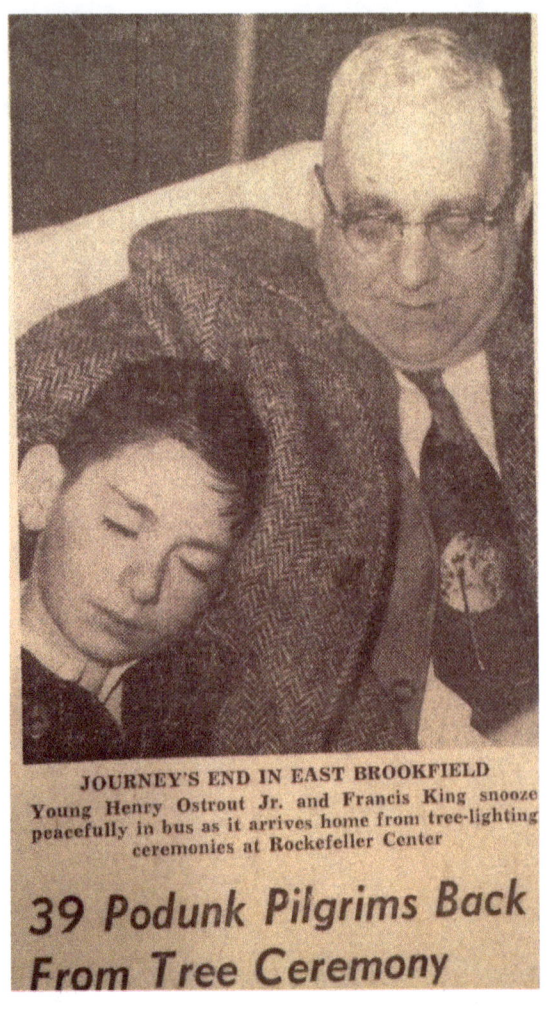

JOURNEY'S END IN EAST BROOKFIELD
Young Henry Ostrout Jr. and Francis King snooze peacefully in bus as it arrives home from tree-lighting ceremonies at Rockefeller Center

39 Podunk Pilgrims Back From Tree Ceremony

> "The citizens of East Brookfield can be proud that a native of our woodlands, dressed in all its traditional glory in Rockefeller Plaza, will silently reflect the glory and beauty that is Christmas" ("East Brookfield Norway Spruce Chosen For Rockefeller Center Christmas Tree," Unknown newspaper article, 1959)

All photos courtesy of Silliman Family personal collection.

CHAPTER 6

Development in the Late 20th and Early 21st Century

There is no doubt that East Brookfield today is not the industrial center that it was in the 19th and early 20th centuries. The Great Depression resulted in the closing of many mills in the town and the loss of jobs. The Hurricane of 1938 and the Flood of 1955 damaged some of the remaining businesses and the town continued its transition from an industrial center to a residential community. East Brookfield today is known as a generally quiet little town with houses nestled among the trees.

Increasingly, development has not been that of businesses, but of housing. East Brookfield today, with its population of nearly 2,200 is mainly a "bedroom community" as most residents work in surrounding town and commute to work. The relatively close proximity to major thoroughfares like Route 20, Route 9, and the Mass Pike, and shopping centers in Sturbridge and Spencer make it an attractive location for commuters.

Since the transition from industrial center, several businesses have been established in the town and continue to flourish here. In addition, municipal projects have added to the quality of life and the services available to residents. Following is a description of some of those businesses and projects. This is not meant to be a comprehensive listing; but does include some of the larger businesses and projects in town since 1970.

Howe Lumber (1965)

Howe Lumber is a family owned and operated business that first opened its doors in 1965. Founded by Henry Howe and his son Stephen of North Brookfield, the business began small with a pick-up truck and one other employee. In 1974, the business expanded and moved to 555 East Main Street in East Brookfield, near the Spencer town line, the current location of Timberyard Brewing Company, which got its name from the lumber company from which it purchased the land and buildings for its company. Henry Howe, his wife Barbara, and son-in-law John Lofgren ran the North Brookfield store while Stephen Howe and his sister, Joyce Lofgren, operated the East Brookfield location.

In 1988, the North Brookfield location closed and the business operated solely from its East Brookfield location for several years. Then, in 2005, they expanded again, building a delivery yard and showroom at 225 West Main Street, in the Flats area of East Brookfield. In 2013, Steve retired as President of Howe Lumber and handed the reins over to Scott Norrie, his son in-law, who had joined the business

Howe Lumber's first East Brookfield location at 555 East Main Street. Photo from Howe Lumber's FaceBook page, 2018

in 1998. Although Steve had officially retired, he continued to enjoy working a few days a week until his death in 2014.

From the very beginning, Howe Lumber was run as a family business. Steve's children, Kate and David, joined the business early on, eventually stepping into the shoes worn by John and Joyce Lofgren upon their respective retirements. Dave made the decision to leave the business in 2012, but Kate continues to run the business along with her husband Scott Norrie.

https://howelumber.com/gallery

For years, the company's plan was to consolidate the East Brookfield locations and run the business solely from the location they had nicknamed "West." In 2015, Scott and Kate started the process of adding a new retail store behind the existing showroom and officially opened the new store on May 1, 2016.

Since it opened in 1965, Howe Lumber has been a go-to place for contractors and do-it-yourselfers, selling lumber for any size project as well as doors, windows, general building supplies, and offers assistance in designing any building project. In addition, the business has been a strong supporter of the town, donating materials for building projects such as the Connie Mack Snack Shack, supporting local Cub Scout and Boy Scout Troops and was the main sponsor for the town's 100th Anniversary Celebration.

Special thanks to Kate Norrie for writing the majority of the above section about Howe Lumber.

Route 49 (1972)

The State Highway known as Route 49 or the Podunk Pike was built in 1972 to connect Route 20 in Sturbridge to Route 9 in Spencer. Previously, access from the Brookfield and Spencer to Sturbridge was via back roads. This two-lane state highway parallels two Podunk Roads, one in East Brookfield and one in Sturbridge, for much of its 7.4 mile length. The portion of Route 49 that runs through Spencer and East Brookfield also carries the name of the "Philip Quinn Memorial Highway" in honor of the state senator from Spencer.

The portion of Route 49 that connected Podunk Road in East Brookfield to Route 20 in Sturbridge was completed in 1972. The northern portion connecting Sturbridge to Route 9 in Spencer was completed in 1974. Before the highway officially opened, young drivers would sneak onto it and enjoy the relatively straight road to try out the speed of their cars.

In the years since, Route 49 has been the site of many serious and fatal accidents which resulted in a safety study in late 2017. New signage was posted alerting drivers to upcoming intersections, where most of the accidents occur. A center turning lane was created at the intersection with Putnam Road. Unfortunately, Route 49 remains a dangerous road; one which needs drivers' close attention while traveling.

Lamoureux Ford (1977)

In 1977, Lionel Lamoureux was a thirty-one year old husband and father of two young children who worked for Ford Motor Company but had a dream to own his own dealership. At the time, Varneys Garage, located on the corner of Mechanic Street and Route 9 where Parsons Auto Body is today, was a licensed Ford dealer. Donald Varney had decided to sell his dealership and Lionel Lamoureux borrowed $80,000 to buy the dealership, not knowing how this risk would pay off for him. Within three years, the dealership expanded from selling twenty to twenty-five vehicles a month to outgrowing their location. In 1980, Lionel purchased two acres of land less than a mile east of his original location between the town cemetery and Route 9. This was the former location of Wagner's Farm. The green house on the corner of Main Street and Evergreen Street being the farm house and the buildings in the rear the former chicken coops. Lionel Lamoureux completed construction on his new dealership in 1982. A later purchase of an additional 4.5 acres allowed for continued expansion, which the quickly growing business would need!

In 2004, with sales continuing to increase, a one million dollar renovation was completed that included a new facade, four new service bays, and an

Lamoureux Ford dealership, 2018

expanded sales lot. The expansion allowed Lamoureux Ford to accommodate three hundred vehicles.

Lamoureux Ford has grown from eleven employees to averaging between forty and fifty. Annual sales started at three hundred sales of new and used vehicles per year to a current average of 1,100 to 1,200 per year. If asked, the Lamoureux family would most likely report that the secret of their success is treating employees and customers with respect, dignity and integrity. Many employees have worked at Lamoureux Ford for over twenty-five years and their slogan of "where friends send their friends" is a result of the superior customer service and low pressure, knowledgable, and friendly sales staff.

Lamoureux Ford has been the proud recipient of the Ford President's Award for twenty years in a row. This award is given to fewer than ten percent of dealers in the country and represents acknowledgment of dealers who provide the highest level of sales and service satisfaction. Lamoureux Ford is also a large supporter of community events. They loan cars for the use of veterans during the Memorial Day Parade each year, support the Summer Concert Series as well as other local organizations and charities and were a sponsor of the town's 100th Anniversary Celebration.

Special thanks to Marc Lamoureux who shared some of the information above in the form of a speech made by his father on the occasion of Lamoureux Ford's 40th anniversary in 2017.

COURT HOUSE (1995)

Since its incorporation in 1920, East Brookfield has been the site of the regional courthouse, with the exception of several years in the 1980s and early 1990s. For a few years the court house was located in a factory building in North Brookfield, and then it moved to a renovated car dealership on Route 9 in Spencer, across from the Spencer Country Inn near the Leicester town line. The first court house of Western Worcester County was originally on the second floor of a wooden building that was the former train station. It was located on the opposite side of the Keith Block as the train tracks. Later, it moved to a small brick building on Mechanic Street where space was leased from a private citizen. The location of the district court being in East Brookfield was mostly due to the efforts of Senator Warren Tarbell, who was in office when the town gained independence from Brookfield.

Site of original Western Worcester County Courthouse on Mechanic Street. Photo by Jordan Gablaski, 2018.

The current courthouse is a $7.3 million two-story brick and concrete building located on Route 9 near the Spencer town line. Construction began in 1993 and was completed in 1995. It was designed by Moore-Nolte Associates, Incorporated and built by R.W. Granger and Sons. The entrance is rounded with glass panels, flanked by an east and west wing.

"East Brookfield District Court." Mass.gov, Commonwealth of Massachusetts, 2018, www.mass.gov/locations/east-brookfield-district-court.

The Western Worcester Country Courthouse serves the communities of Spencer, Paxton, Rutland, Oakham, Hardwick, Leicester, Barre, New Braintree, Warren, and all the Brookfields. The new building allowed for jury trials to take place in this courthouse, thus alleviating the crowded courts in Worcester and Dudley.

In 2011, the courthouse was rededicated in honor of Judge Francis H. George, a WWII veteran, Associate Justice of the East Brookfield Court from 1974 to 1984, and First Justice of the East Brookfield Court from 1984 to 1989. (Deacon, John E. "Worcester County - East Brookfield." American Courthouses, 2017, www.courthouses.co/us-states/m/massachusetts/worcester-county/worcester-county-east-brookfield/.)

In 2014, a victims' waiting room was added to the court house so those who would be testifying in court would have a safe, comfortable place to wait. The room was the idea of Victims' Witness Advocate for the District Attorney's Office, Amy Law, who along with colleagues, donated items for the room including toys, stuffed animals and a television. (NECN. "Courthouse in East Brookfield, Mass. Adds Special Room for Victims." NECN, NECN, 27 June 2014, www.necn.com/news/new-england/
 NECN Courthouse in East Brookfield Mass Adds Special Room for Victims NECN-264108151.html.)

SECOND CHANCE ANIMAL SERVICES (1999)

In 1999, Animal Control Office Sheryl Blancato realized the need for a means to re-home animals that were stray or unclaimed by their owners and in the custody of the town. She first established Second Chance Animal Shelter as a non-profit organization that was a network of foster homes who cared for dogs and cats until permanent homes could be found for them.  This network developed into a shelter in 2002 when land and materials were donated and volunteer work resulted in a physical building on Young Road in East Brookfield.

Second Chance originally operated as an adoption center, but incorporated educational outreach into its mission to reduce the number of unwanted pets in the area. It soon became obvious that in order to affect a dramatic decrease in the number of homeless animals, a third component needed to be added to the mission of the organization. Second Chance established a low-cost spay-neuter program which offered low- and no-cost procedures to owned animals and feral cat colonies.

Through the dedication and perseverance of volunteers and paid staff, Second Chance expanded immensely in the years since its inception. Second Chance currently operates the Adoption Center in East Brookfield, Wellness Clinics with low-cost veterinary services in North Brookfield, Springfield, and Worcester, and partners with PetSmart to offer adoption days at its area stores. The organization is planning to expand into Southbridge and work to help veterinary technicians get practical experience while in school.

Second Chance Animal Services Adoption Center, photo by author, 2016.

Second Chance has three mobile vehicles that help promote adoptions, their spay/neuter program, and mobile veterinary services. After Sheryl went to Louisiana to help with the recovery after Hurricane Katrina, the shelter formed a partnership with the Humane Society of the United States to help in cases of animal hoarding, abuse, or in times of natural disasters. The shelter deployed staff and brought donations after the hurricanes in 2011 that hit Florida, Texas and Puerto Rico. Second Chance sent supplies to the shelters located in these areas and brought pets to Second Chance that were already in shelters to make room for those that had been displaced by the storms.

Second Chance estimates that through all of its programs, it directly supports approximately 37,000 pets each year. Today, it is the third largest animal services program in the state after the MSPCA and Boston Animal Rescue League. Due to the variety of services offered, Second Chance Animal Shelter changed its name to Second Chance Animal Services in 2018.

EAST BROOKFIELD ELEMENTARY SCHOOL (2004)

By 1996, it was time for upgrades to Memorial School. In addition, the over one hundred-year-old Lashaway Junior High was quickly reaching the end of its lifespan as a school. A proposal for an addition was defeated by voters in May of 1996, but in 1999, voters overwhelmingly supported building a new elementary school in a 170 to 52 vote. After this show of support, town officials proposed the purchase of twenty-three acres of land on Route 9 and negotiated a selling price of $160,000 which was approved at a special town meeting in September 1999.

East Brookfield Elementary School, photo from school website, 2017.

The two-story building includes a combination gymnasium/auditorium, a separate cafeteria, and educates students in Kindergarten through Grade 6. The Pre-K for the Spencer-East Brookfield Regional School District is also housed in this building. The grounds include a playground area, tennis courts, ample space for soccer fields, and a softball field. In 2009, the field was dedicated as "Fahey Field" in honor of Charles "Bud" Fahey who served on the Regional School Committee for more than forty years. He was involved in the building of the school as a member of the School Building Committee. He was also a volunteer firefighter and on the Recreation Committee and served in the Honor Guard on Memorial Day.

NEW ENGLAND AUTOMOTIVE GATEWAY (2004)

Planning for an $11 million auto processing and distribution center on 200 acres of land in Spencer and East Brookfield with access off Route 49 began in 1994. The center would be a hub for auto distribution in the northeast with vehicles arriving on trains from the west and being distributed by tractor trailer truck throughout New England states. This site was in an ideal location, being located between Route 9 and Route 20, with easy access to Route 84 and the

Mass Pike, where the vast majority of trailers would head after picking up vehicles. The center was built with the capacity of handling 130,000 vehicles per year with about seventy-five tractor trailer trucks loading up each day.

George W. Bell, the owner of the East Brookfield-Spencer Railroad, originally planned the center and purchased the land for it. Once it was built, he and his partners sold it to CSX, who then leased it back to them to handle the operation of the center. CSX brings vehicles in on railroad cars, up to 100 car carriers per train, and East Brookfield-Spencer Railroad's engines pick up the cars and bring them onto the 300 foot spur track that leads to the distribution center where they are unloaded.

New England Automotive Gateway, Aerial View. "TransDevelopment Group." New England Automotive Gateway , TransDevelopment Group, www.transdevelopment.com/?project=new-england-automotive-gateway.

The distribution center was more successful than anticipated, resulting in extended hours that caused upset in the first years of operation. Selectmen from East Brookfield and Spencer held several town meetings regarding complaints from residents of noise, lights, and fumes all hours of the day and night and on every day of the week. The original plan for locomotives to sound their whistle when approaching the distribution center to warn workers who might be close to the track served to disrupt many nights of sleep for residents on Howe Street, Cove Street, Young Road, Harrington Street and areas in South Spencer. On certain nights, the train whistles could be heard throughout town. At one community meeting with residents of East Brookfield and Spencer and representatives of the railroad, then Senator Stephen Brewer warned that if conditions were not remediated, "We're going to give you problems that you don't want." (David Dore, "Locals screaming mad at train whistles," *Spencer New Leader*, 6 July 2007.)

Soon after that meeting, changes were made to address the concerns of neighbors. These changes included scheduling when cars were delivered, upgrades to the engines used on the site to prevent idling, the use of radios and a flagman to signal an approaching train, fines for engineers who did not follow company procedures regarding blowing their train's whistle, and planting additional trees to serve as sound barriers. After residents acclimated to the additional lights, these improved conditions lessened the complaints of residents.

A year after opening, the facility was expanded to include parking for six hundred more vehicles. The TransDevelopment Group is the development manager for the center. Their website states that 400,000 vehicles go through this center each year and that there is fifty acres of paved vehicle yards and tracks capable of holding 240 railcars. Their site also states that planned expansions will result in a total of ninety developed acres at the site. ("TransDevelopment Group." New England Automotive Gateway , TransDevelopment Group, www.transdevelopment.com/?project=new-england-automotive-gateway.)

EB FLATTS (2006)

Scott and Grace Conner, owners of "EB Flatts" are both veterans of the Coast Guard who always enjoyed entertaining friends and family. When Scott retired, their family moved to Massachusetts and ran a food truck at the New England Truck Stop in Sturbridge. In 1999, their food truck became a restaurant near the same location, also called "Gracie's." During this time, they also operated another "Gracie's" in Charlton City.

"Home." E.B. Flatts Restaurant, 2018, ebflatts.com/.

In 2006, Scott and Grace purchased EB Flatts on West Main Street in East Brookfield. The restaurant not only serves fantastic breakfasts, lunches, and dinners, but also supports a variety of community events. The post and beam building, previously a restaurant called "Boondocks," is filled with an eclectic assortment of knick knacks, and transmits a cozy atmosphere, a perfect match for the traditional classics served at the restaurant.

Scott and Grace are supporters of town events, donating use of their restaurant for town events and fundraisers, sponsoring the town's 100 Anniversary Celebration, catering events at cost and supporting the summer concerts, tree lighting and other town events.

PELLETIER WOODS (2007)

"Pelletier Woods" includes 118 acres of wooded land which the Town of East Brookfield purchased with the help of a state grant in 2007 to preserve open space for the citizens of East Brookfield and their families and friends to continue to enjoy. After being up for sale for several years by the Pelletier family, the town decided to pursue state grant funds to help pay for the purchase of the land. It was felt that protecting the land for open space rather than the seventy houses that could be built on the property was more in line with the recently completed Master Plan and the desires of the town's residents.

The space gets the "Pelletier" portion of its name from Romeo and Richard Pelletier, who purchased pieces of this land over the course of many years until it reached its current size. The "Woods" portion of the name refers to the Woods Brothers, who lived just outside what is currently "Pelletier Woods." The private road which is shown on some older maps, "Wood Road" gets its name from these brothers as well.

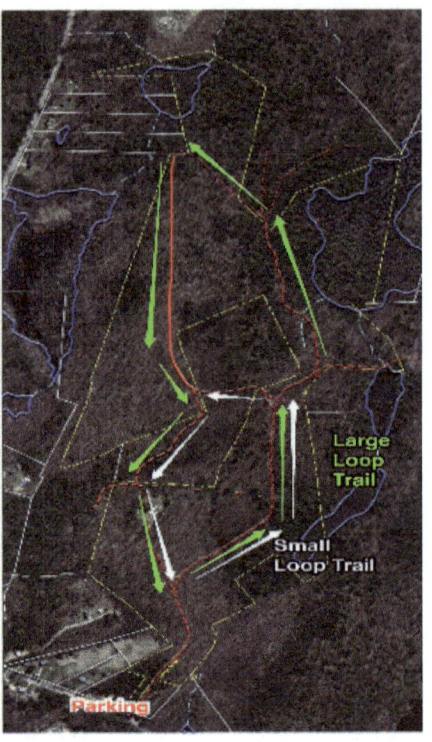

Trail map of Pelletier Woods. The Large Loop Trail is 2.1 miles in length and the Small Loop Trail is 1.25 miles in length.

The trails and cart roads that traverse Pelletier Woods were used by people of the village of Podunk to get from Howe Street to Podunk and Draper Roads. Many people walked these cart roads to get to and from school and church.

Much of this land was open pasture used by local farmers as grazing land for their livestock. Cattle would be brought here to graze during the warmer months. If you walk the trails, look for the stone walls that mark these different pastures. Alva Silliman shared that his family owned one acre of land here, most likely for grazing livestock, whose borders were marked by "a large oak tree"

In 2016, Tom Gilmeister completed an Eagle Scout project to build a welcome kiosk and map the trails. Photo by author, 2016.

and other such impermanent natural boundaries. As he was paying taxes on land he could no longer identify, he sold it for $1 to the Pelletiers. Most likely, others did the same or simply forgot about the land.

Today, the open space is accessible off Howe Street via a fifty foot easement. Hikers and mountain bikers enjoy the trails as it is open for passive recreation only, meaning motorized vehicles are prohibited. Hunters also have access to the land and it is a popular place for deer and turkey hunters.

MEMORIAL TOWN COMPLEX (2008) and DEPARTMENT OF PUBLIC WORKS BUILDING (2010)

With the construction of East Brookfield Elementary School, the town was left owning the former Memorial School. The building was in good shape despite being almost fifty years old, and in considerably better condition than the 1880's-era Keith Building which housed the town offices, police department and library. The Keith Block had been heavily damaged by poor drainage over the years resulting in mold and air quality issues. With an empty town-owned building and a building deemed unsafe, the decision was made to move all town offices to the former elementary school. In 2005, voters approved $1.4 million to renovate and furnish the building.

Department of Public Works Building on East Main Street, between Lashaway Drive and Harrington Street. Photo by author, 2018.

The renovation of the former elementary school took place in stages with the town offices housed in the former cafeteria/gymnasium/auditorium while the rest of the building was renovated. The classrooms on the north end of the building became the police department, those in the middle of the building housed offices for each of the town departments, and the former cafeteria/gymnasium/auditorium served as the new town library. The former stage was transformed into a reading area.

The official opening of the Memorial Town Complex was held in May of 2008, even though municipal offices had crowded into the former gymnasium at the end of 2005 when mold forced them out of the Keith Block.

Just two years later, the town completed upgrades of municipal facilities when they purchased a forty-year-old, 8,000 square foot building formerly owned by Verizon that abutted town-owned land on which East Brookfield Elementary School had been built. The previous town barn, located on the site of an old mill on Stevens Road, was described by selectmen as "beyond repair" ("For Highway, It Will Be Home Sweet Home," David Dore, May 21, 2010, The New Leader). Costing $950,000, the building seemed made for the purpose of housing the Highway and Water Departments as it included a large truck bay, office space, and a fenced storage area and was in near perfect condition for the Highway Department to move into with little preparation work. After power washing and a fresh coat of paint, costing about $600, the building was ready for the Highway Department to move their operations there.

Town Gazebo (2008) & Summer Concert Series (2009)

In 2006, the Friends of the Community, led by Sandy Kady, Tricia Durand, and Debbie Morgan, began a campaign to raise funds to build a gazebo behind the Hodgkins Building on the town field. After several years of hard work, the project was completed in 2008. Typical of area businesses and residents, the building was a result of generous donations of time, money, and materials. Howe Lumber donated building materials, John Rossi of the Finance Committee donated the architectural designs, and others volunteered to make the brick walkway that is inscribed with donors' names and to complete the electrical service.

Concert at the Town Gazebo, 2014. Photo by author.

In 2009, Joan Bedard and Dennis LeBeau planned a series of free concerts for the people of East Brookfield and the surrounding towns. In the next year, and in the years since then, her granddaughter and grandson-in-law, Amanda and Dan Lambert and a group of their friends ran the project. Over time, the Bandstand Committee raised more funds through donations, grants from the

Cultural Council, and the sale of food and drinks at concerts to bring more expensive bands to the concerts.

The first few years of the concerts included the sale of lemonade and popcorn, donated by the Lions Club of Brookfield. Then, hot dogs, hamburgers, and pulled pork sandwiches were added to the menu. In 2015, the Bandstand Committee decided they needed to build and outfit a concession stand adjacent to the field. The committee had been cooking from the back of a trailer that was brought to and from the field each Thursday night. East Brookfield residents Larry Gordon, Mark Carpentier, and Ted Boulay, along with State Representative Donnie Berthiaume spent several days constructing the 'shack' and the committee painted the building. Generous local businesses made donations that covered all the materials needed for the project. Republic Waste made a cash donation, Howe Lumber again donated building materials, Rick Hill donated the concrete for the slab on which the shack was built, an anonymous resident donated a refrigerator and did electrical work, and members of the Bandstand Committee painted the building. Named the "Connie Mack Snack Shack," the building is used during concerts and also at the Independence Day Celebration and by other town groups who have events on the field.

A band plays while the Boy Scouts present the flag to open the concert. Photo by author, 2012.

Nathan Gershman and Dean Iacobucci preparing food for the audience at the Summer concerts. Photo by author, 2019.

Today, the concerts continue each Thursday in July and August following the Independence Day Celebration. The concerts attract between one hundred and two hundred visitors each week to enjoy such bands and artists as Noah Lis, the Island Castaways, the Otters, and the local town favorite, Big Gunz, a band comprised of the LeBeau family and special guests who always bring in a large crowd. The concerts represent what it means to live in a small town: extended family and neighbors meeting at the field, having dinner together, enjoying great music, while children play in the background.

308 LAKESIDE (2013)

In 2013, a group of local family members purchased the Lashaway Inn from the Merola family who had owned the restaurant for the previous forty-two years. The site had held an inn/tavern-type business for decades. The first tavern was built in 1864 and was named the Lakewood House. The  named changed in 1885 to the Crystal house but changed back to the Lakewood House after renovations necessitated by a fire in 1909. In 1928 it was renamed the Lakewood Inn. In 1948 new owners changed the name to the Lashaway Inn, a name it retained until ownership changed hands in 2013 and the restaurant was renamed the 308 Lakeside.

Following months of discussions and planning meetings, the dream of 308 Lakeside began to take shape. Over fourteen months, architects, designers and expert builders transformed the aging building into the relaxing and welcoming waterfront environment it is today. The restaurant boasts an open layout, complete with dining room, large bar, outdoor deck and lower level patio, and is perfect for small and large functions, live music and gatherings of friends and family from near and far. Aluminum docks welcome countless boaters throughout the warmer months, with the frozen lake providing easy access for snowmobilers and cross country skiers alike.

Rear of 308 Lakeside. Photo from 308 Lakeside Facebook page, August 2018.

The owners of 308 take great pride in supporting the local communities, so appreciative of the tremendous support they receive from their many loyal customers, now friends. The annual golf tournament raises thousands of dollars for local events, particularly the Independence Day Fireworks and the 100th Anniversary Celebration. They support organizations by hosting coupon fundraisers where a percentage of proceeds are donated to the organization. They have also worked to help slow the speed of cars through the center of town through the use of speed monitoring signs.

Visitors to the 308 Team enjoy drinks, delicious meals or homemade desserts, with the backdrop of Lake Lashaway providing scenic views from nearly every seat. The owners have worked hard to create an atmosphere that results in relaxed and satisfied customers and friends.

Special thanks to MaryEllen Brunelle for her assistance in writing about the 308 Lakeside.

LAKE LASHAWAY OVERLOOK (2014)

In 2014, the Lake Lashaway Overlook opened to the public. It includes a covered patio and two boat docks, allowing lake residents and other boaters to dock their boats and enjoy the restaurants in downtown East Brookfield. It was the final phase of a $2 million dollar, years-long project that included rebuilding the dam, the spillway, and the Route 9 bridge, along with new lighting along the bridge and a new draw-down gate. The gate allows the level of the lake to be lowered every fall for weed control. The overlook was dedicated to Robert Monyon, the founder of the Lake Lashaway Community Association.

Representative Ann Gobi, Selectman Leo Fayard, and Senator Steve Brewer at the ribbon cutting ceremony. Photo by author, September 24, 2014.

The State Department of Transportation paid for a majority of the project, as did a MassWorks grant for $594,000. The cost to the town of East Brookfield was only $70,000.

The Overlook in a popular fishing spot as well and is heavily used in the spring, summer, and fall months.

SOLAR FARM: HARRINGTON STREET (2017)

In 2017, a solar project that was years in the planning and construction opened in what was a large gravel pit at 229 Harrington Street. The facility, when opened, was run by NuGen but had gone through several different owners. The first was Ansar Energy of Scituate, followed by CleanGen Partners of Hollis, New Hampshire, then Olson Energy Corporation of Minneapolis. This company was purchased by HydroChina of Beijing.

The initial six-megawatt project eventually expanded to 13-megawatt project that spread into the neighboring town of Spencer. At the time of its proposal, it was the largest solar farm in the state. The project is tied directly into pre-existing National Grid high-tension lines though a substation built on the property. The company estimated that one megawatt of solar power can provide the necessary electricity for one hundred fifty to two hundred homes and after twenty years, the facility will still be operating at eighty to eight-five percent efficiency. The company was required to submit a decommissioning plan and a bond to pay for taking down and recycling the panels should it become necessary to do so. They also had to provide training for the fire department and work with neighbors to screen the property from view.

The site had previously been under consideration for a large, low-income housing project, "East Brookfield Village" which would have almost doubled the number of homes in town. This plan was changed to a combination of senior housing and assisted living facility, but fell through. The option of a solar farm was more palatable to residents and town officials as it would not put strain on town services, such as fire, police, and schools, that a large increase in population would have.

Aerial view of solar facility, courtesy of Eric Aubrey, project manager, 2017.

TimberYard Brewing (2018)

In 2017, Matt Zarif purchased the former Howe Lumber property near the Spencer town line on Route 9 and began planning renovations to open an on-site brewing company. After much planning and work with town agencies and holding a public hearing, the brewery held their grand opening the weekend of October 19, 2018. The facility opened with a brew house and taproom with a bar made from the original sales counter from Howe Lumber. Beams used in the renovation came from a farm owned by the Howe Family. Their mission is to brew beer using local ingredients and create a family-friendly, community-oriented business. Live music is held throughout the weekend. This business has also been a strong supporter of town events and is a sponsor of the 100th Anniversary Celebration.

Bar at Timberyard Brewing repurposed the original sales counter from Howe Lumber. Photo by author, October 2018

Brewing room at Timberyard. Photo by author, August 2018.

CHAPTER 7

Remembrances

"Wherever you go, your memories from the place you grew up always remain special."

- Guru Randhawa

One of my favorite parts of writing this book was reading anecdotes and talking to people who grew up in town who had their own stories to share. I discovered that people do not necessarily think to record information about the times in which they live. I came across many pictures without labels, businesses no one remembered, and short articles in newspapers with little or no follow-up. Technology today has made sharing information easier and it was as much fun reading a written account from decades ago as it was reading memories from a few years ago. Enjoy!

Part 1

Facebook

> You know you grew up in East Brookfield, MA if......
> 🌐 Public group

Many people had fun finishing this sentence! See if any of these memories are familiar to you. Join the group on FaceBook and continue the conversation!

August 8, 2011

Lakeside church services at EBBC...brrrrr....

 1

August 5, 2011

...you went to Washington DC for your 8th grade trip!

August 6, 2011

Hearing the fire whistle blow and riding to the fire station to read the chaulkboard on where the fire was.

August 7, 2011

Going to the dump on Saturday morning for entertainment after cartoons. Or when Harry's Pizza was actually run by a man named Harry?

August 4, 2011

The fruit stand across the street from EB Pizza that is now just a garage.

2

August 4, 2011

Getting Donuts downtown before there was a Pizza Shop there

 November 14, 2015

It's getting cold out....we used to go skating on "Mud Pond!" Anyone remember where that is?
My sisters and I would sometimes bring a hot dog or a potato to bake if someone was making a fire, (probably on a weekend) and our Aunt Joan would always make us cocoa and let us come in to thaw out!

👍 Like 💬 Comment ↗ Share

 August 7, 2011

have tried to dial 8675309

 August 7, 2011

Not having cable TV until around high school!!

August 7, 2011

You financed your dentist's home with all the penny candy ya bought at Ernie's....🙂

👍 Like 💬 Comment ↗ Share

August 6, 2011

Remember going to Sturbridge when there was no Rt 49?

👍 Like 💬 Comment ↗ Share

August 8, 2011

Watching the 4th of July waterski show.

👍 Like 💬 Comment ↗ Share

August 9, 2011

Turning Lashaway School/Hodgkins School into a Haunted House. Having kids believe that Dr. Hodgkins was walking the halls. Although it wasn't hard believing it yourself when you were all alone in that school!

August 10, 2011

You spent three nights a week watching your dad and Franny Petruzzi mow the entire Connie Mac baseball field with a push mower and then water it with a garden hose. He sure loved the kids. True story.

September 18, 2011

How about the chicken farm that used to be on Adams Road? I think it was Farrs but not sure of that or the spelling. It would have been located where Kitty G. lives now.

3 Comments

👍 Like   💬 Comment   ↗ Share

it was the Farr farm. Vinny was older than me, but I knew him from the bus, and he had a younger brother whose name I can't recall. There was also an older brother who died. I don't know if I ever heard how, but it was at the time when Korea... See More

7y · Like

Back then there were several farms in East Brookfield. For chickens there was George Payne at the Sturbridge line on Podunk Road, Farr's, George McCrillis Payne Sr. and Turgeon's on Howe Street, and I think Tuttle on West Sturbridge Road. Dairy cows were at Cole's on the No. Brookfield Road, Tredwell's on Podunk, Benoit on Adams Road, (Grimes farm) George McCrillis Sr. on Howe Street, plus John Thomas and my father and probably several others who had enough cows to supply our own family and sell some to neighbors. Oh yes, Bugbee, Jacobs, and Fred McCrillis would be in that list as well.

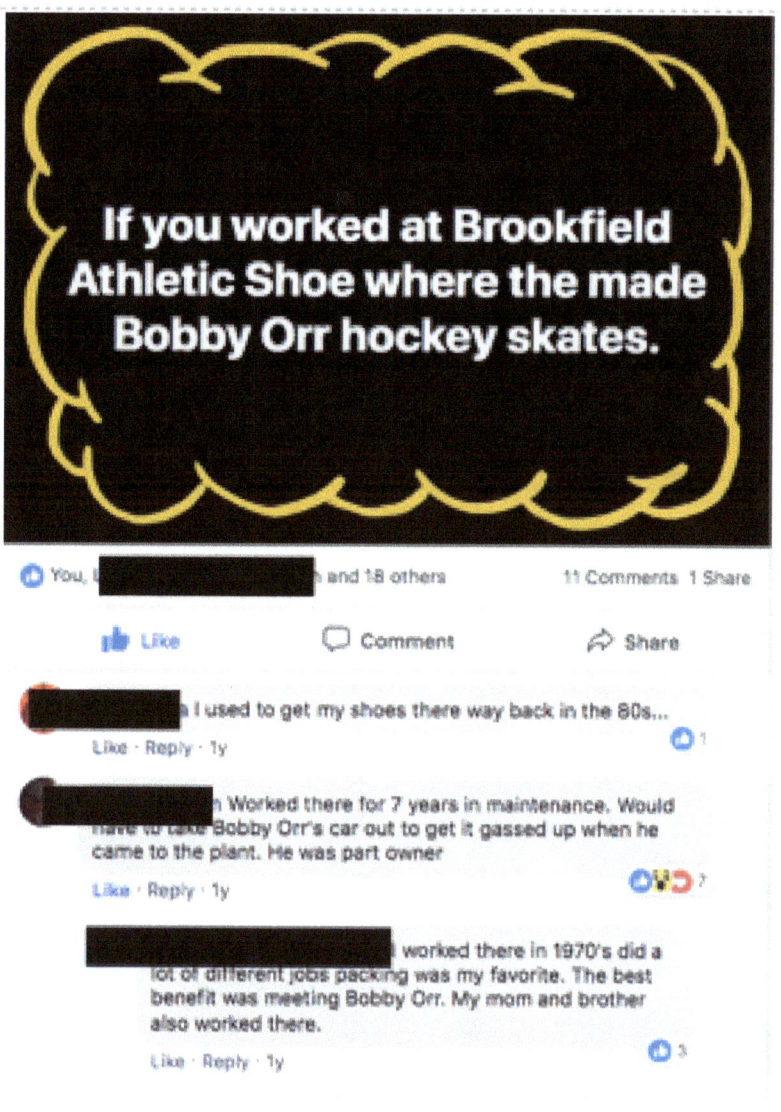

I used to get my shoes there way back in the 80s...
Like · Reply · 1y

Worked there for 7 years in maintenance. Would have to take Bobby Orr's car out to get it gassed up when he came to the plant. He was part owner
Like · Reply · 1y

worked there in 1970's did a lot of different jobs packing was my favorite. The best benefit was meeting Bobby Orr. My mom and brother also worked there.
Like · Reply · 1y

August 4, 2011

You went to Happy Days for kindergarten..

Like   Comment   Share

August 6, 2011

Remember when there were two farm stands on the flats? The old Petruzzi stand and Ficciccolo's

Like   Comment   Share

January 9, 2012

I remember when local kids use to pick vegatables at Petruzzi Farms and others on the Flats.

👍 Like   💬 Comment   ➤ Share

Heather
December 18, 2018

Christmas songs always remind me of the Memorial School gymnasium the day before vacation. Our dear Mr. Robertson would wheel his piano in, and the whole school would join in chorus singing Frosty, Rudolph, and many other Christmas classics. This was always followed up by a Disney movie on the old reel. Joyous memories of a precious teacher and a small town school.

August 9, 2011

buying fish & chips at Leblanc's on the flats, where the current Petruzzi's stand is

August 5, 2011

when Camp Atwater played the bugles at dusk

👍 Like   💬 Comment   ➤ Share

August 4, 2011

you ever got a slush puppy from Ernie's Variety

👍 Like   💬 Comment   ➤ Share

December 19, 2017

Whites, Days store (penny candy, newspapers, coffee, sandwiches) downtown Main St, Lashaway side...same place. Which name was first? Do I even have the names right? What did YOU buy there?...OK, so, we've recollected that KINGS, Ernies and Days were the variety store downtown and located and reconstructed much of EB's downtown and changes there...Town Library to Guppy World to Pizza, Varneys to Lamoreaux to Parsons, etc.

> My memory is failing me. I remember Ledouxs grocerys store. Trahans icecream and Paul Derricks grocery store. Ledouxs store was close to the post office..I remember a dog named Kansas that was so friendly and I loved him but dont know who owned him...Laahaway inn where I had my wedding reception and watched the water skiers on lake lashaway..many good childhood memories..names not so much

> Yes, I also remember Ledoux's by the Post Office...another haunt. Whites (and later called Days I believe) was just a few doors down from Lashaway Inn, between the Inn and the waterfall bridge; right smack dab in the center of that block on Main St. I agree, lots of great memories. It's tough years later trying to piece the town back together the way it was and recall what everything was (for me, the 70s/early 80s). Nearly everything I remember is something different now...but the same buildings are all still there.

> I can remember the Post Office being in the small building on Main Street. It was the Lashaway Inn, a house, the P.O. Derrick's grocery, Kings Variety store, and Trahan's, with the Red and White package store across the street, then the library and Varney's Mobil station and Ford dealership. Later the Post Office moved into a section of the multi family building on Mechanic Street, next to the current post office.

August 21, 2011

Benoit's Blackshop on Bridge st

👍 Like 💬 Comment ➤ Share

April 7, 2012

I remember driving past the Hayes farm and seeing all the pumpkins in the field one day and the next day the fields were empty. They were all made into pies by Tagle Talk pies in Worcester.

👍 2   1 Comment

👍 Like   💬 Comment   ➤ Share

I am pretty sure my dad worked at picking those pumpkins (and squash) for table talk. I have heard the stories.

6y · Like

October 7, 2011

living next to the "shoe shop" remembering it was still manufacturing, the back parking lot was chock full of cars...early in the morning watching everyone arrive for work, and then again in the afternoon when they went home...it's sad so many lost their jobs when it closed. My special needs sister worked there and absolutely loved it:) Also, remember the big green bus that drove through town picking up employees for Wright's in Warren.

👍 and 3 others   1 Comment

👍 Like   💬 Comment   ➤ Share

My grandmother rode on that green bus to work at Gavitts in Brookfield. In the 70s there were 450 people who worked at Brookfield Shoe. For the time they actually paid fairly well.

7y · Like   👍 1

Part 2

East Brookfield Historical Commission Facebook Page

Another page on social media, run by the Historical Commission, posted photos and asked for people to enter their memories or share related stories. Follow their page on FaceBook for more posts!

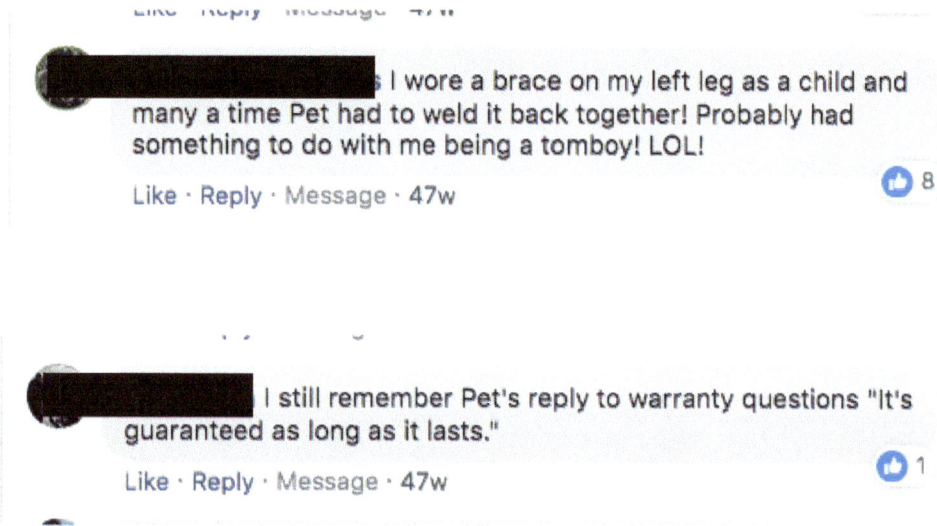

Oak Grove Lunch was located at 196 West Main Street. It was owned and operated by Frank and Anna Wells. Anna (Boucher) Wells was known as "Hot Dog Annie" before there was another establishment in a nearby town with that name! The store was sold in 1953 and eventually torn down in the early 1960s.

> Yes that was a great spectator sport..i remember watching the jumps...remember watching "winky" Varney jump...think it was like 90 ft if my memory is correct. Thinking early-mid 60's

> I remember watching the ski shows on Lashaway. Lex Carroll of the Carroll Moters in West Brookfield use to ski in the show and his wife use to get onto his shoulders. Was a great time, my father even skied with him a few times in the show. Long time ago. Thanks for posting.

From FaceBook Page, "You know you grew up in EB, if..."

East Brookfield Historical Commission added 3 new photos.
March 28, 2018

Drake's Gardens were famous for their melons, honey, and other vegetables. It was located where Bay Path Golf Course is today. Any memories of this farm to share?

When I was a little girl we'd love to go into the fields and eat the melons. When we did this we didn't think the Drakes could see us hiding in the fields. Of course they probably did! The melons were so, so sweet and good!

Like · Reply · Message · 46w 👍 2

East Brookfield Historical Commission added 2 new photos.
September 8, 2018

Any ideas on this shoe I found in a box at the museum? A metal attachment on the heel and looks like there was a similar one on the toe. Cleats?

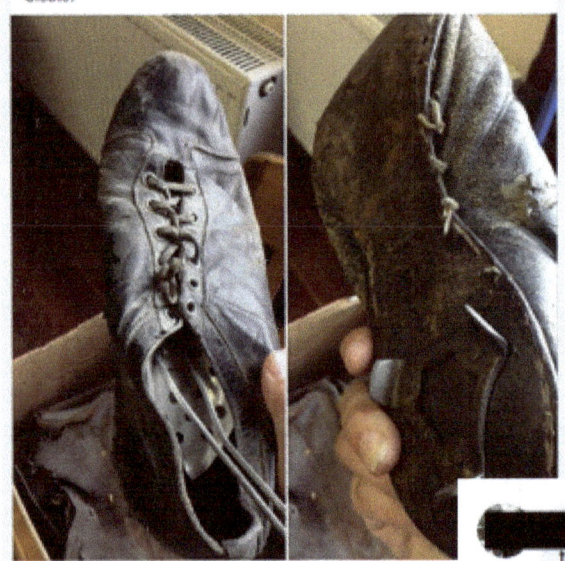

Very cool, old and I think kind of rare. Looks like they are missing the front cleats. Ty Cobb was famous for sliding into home "With my steel showing" to intimidate the catcher into backing off.

Like · Reply · Message · 23w 👍 1

Looks like one that was made at the shoe shop back in the day. They did more than ice skates. However, there may be a story as well

Like · Reply · Message · 23w 👍 1

East Brookfield Historical Commission
September 24, 2018

Last Hurricane of 1938 photo. The Hurricane severely damaged the Podunk Chapel and residents joined together to donated money and supplies to repair it. All the work was done by volunteers.

My sister had her wedding there! Loved the square dances there on Saturday nights and all the suppers they had! Good Old Days!

Like · Reply · Message · 11w   2

Part 3

Journals, Notes, and Interviews

Some of the most interesting information gathered for this book came from reading the journals of residents, notes and letters written for the purpose of sharing memories of town, and interviews and informal conversations with current and former residents. Visiting the Senior Center always resulted in new knowledge. People don't always recognize that they have knowledge that cannot be found anywhere else and adds to our understanding of the past.

Memories of Podunk
Account of Linda Ciejka, April 2019

My grandfather, Horace Terry, owned and operated a Gulf gas station on the old Podunk Road, and I have so many happy memories, like after school, he would let us cousins go in for a free ice-cream. What a treat to look forward to! ... I used to love to hear his laughter. He was wonderful! (circa 1955).

Horace Terry's Gulf Service Station, located in Podunk. From collection of East Brookfield Historical Museum.

An Account of Podunk School as told to Eva Perron by Elizabeth (Betty) Putnam Macia.

"School began promptly at nine with the ringing of a hand bell. Classes began with a prayer and the Pledge of Allegiance. There were never snow days or one sessions. There was no central heat, no electricity or running water, and no telephone or radio But they did have the wood stove, two small buildings in the back (one for the girls and one for the boys) and a spring at the foot of the hill.

"The bigger boys had to task of 'going to the spring' to bring back the daily water supply. There was a dipper and each child had his and her own drinking cup. Girls and younger boys had chores such as sharpening pencils, clapping erasers, and helping first and second graders with buttons and boots.

"For games, they had two seesaws, one swing and many trees, pines and maples for climbing and birches made for swinging. In the winter they took their sleds to school and some youngsters were lucky enough to have skis. The usual games of hide and seek, marbles, jump rope, red rover and fox and geese.

"A favorite place to hide was a shallow, dry well nearby; however, it wasn't as shallow as thought and story has it that while two boys were hiding in it, the bottom dropped. Their clothes had to be dried near the stove, while they sat in class in their underwear. In the woods they learned how to identify birds, wild flowers, and trees. There were lots of falls from trees and stone walls, and skinned knees were often the order of the day.

"The one room school would be frowned upon by today's standards, but they got an early education that served them well; they made many lifelong friends and had lots of fun."

The gracious and knowledgable lady who shared this story with me was Elizabeth Putnam Macia who passed away in 2002 at the age of 86. Elizabeth's mother, Mrs. Mary Putnam was the teacher, and today, town residents who were taught by Mrs. Putnam at Hodgkin's school speak fondly of her and have lots of happy memories.

Perron, Eva. "Podunk School." Received by Heather Gablaski, 29 July 2017, East Brookfield, MA.

Memories of Podunk Chapel by Betty Macia

My Sunday school teacher was Mrs. Eva R. Terry (Phil's grandmother). This class consisted of myself and Donald Terry. I think my mother and Mrs. Mary Q. Ainsworth taught other Sunday school classes, and possibly Mrs. Nichols had a class (all small classes).

Organists were Mrs. Ruggles and Mrs. Astrid Wray. Sometimes the visiting minister would bring his own organist, and perhaps a soloist or quartet.

Attendance was small, as were monetary gifts. The minister received a pitifully small amount.

There were a few Sturbridge residents who were faithful attendants, among them my grandparents, Milton and Alice Putnam, and the Nichols Family.

Gradually people began attending other area churches, principally the East Brookfield Baptist Church, but some in Brookfield, Spencer and Sturbridge.

From time to time, social events were held at the Chapel, including an occasional public supper, a Memorial Day Program, and a Community Christmas tree which was the highlight of my life.

Heat was provided by wood stoves, and kerosene lamps supplied the lighting. Water was supplied by neighbors.

The long-gone horse sheds in the rear were a wonderful place for children to play while the adults visited after church services.

Macia, Betty. "Podunk Chapel." Received by Bettie Brennan, EB Historical Commission, 30 September 1986, East Brookfield, MA.

Podunk Chapel, Secretary's Report
Year Beginning April 1, 1900.

Sunday, July 7, was observed as Children's Day, a pleasing program of recitations and song being rendered by the children, under the direction of Mrs. L.F. Herrick. An appreciative audience of about seventy was present, among whom was Mr. J.H. Ames of Spencer, who addressed a few remarks to the children. ...

On the evening of Nov. 21st, a pleasing program was rendered under the efficient management of Mrs. Lynde Stark and Mrs. Albert Hobbs. The farce "Not a Man in the House" was presented to an appreciative audience, followed by a supper of chicken pie, to which full justice was done. The affair was pronounced a decided success, financially and otherwise.

Christmas was observed as usual with a tree on the evening of Dec. 25th. The children, under the direction of their devoted teacher, Mrs. Lewis Herrick, gave the cantata, "Story of the Star," including songs and recitations. This was followed by a visit from Mrs. Santa Claus, who brought Mrs. Herrick a gold watch chain as a token of respect and esteem from her Chapel friends.

Feb 6th a Farmer's Institute was held under the auspices of the Worcester South Agricultural Society. An address on General Farming was given. The audience was rather small. Under the direction of Mrs. Lewis Herrick a dinner was served by the ladies.

On the evening of Feb. 20th an entertainment was given, consisting of recitations, harmonica solos, tableaux, and the "Lady from Philadelphia," under the direction of Mrs. Lynde Stark and Mrs. Albert Hobbs. The audience, owning to the bad condition of the roads, was smaller than usual. A bountiful supper of baked beans and cold meat was served, in charge of Mrs. W.D. Corey.

Memories of East Brookfield
Interview with Jeanne LeBeau

Jeanne was born in May of 1931 in the only house on Cottage Street. Five generations have lived in the house starting with her grandparents.

Her grandfather, Alphonse Gaudette, played ball with Connie Mack. He went as far as the Meriden, CT baseball league when he injured his leg. He owned an operated Gaudette's Luncheonette in the same building Dunny's Tavern is today.

Jeanne remembers four grocery stores in town: LeDoux's Market on Pleasant Street, Dillon's Market and the Red and White Market, both on Main Street, and Bousquet's Market in the house to the east of Dunny's Tavern. A bicycle shop was located where the fire department is today.

Her father, Frank Gaudette, was a World War II veteran and worked for the post office for fifty-five years. He took a horse and buggy from East Brookfield to Route 20 to deliver mail, changing horses halfway through his route. Once the roads were improved enough, used his own car to deliver the mail. He also used the car to drive Warren Tarbell around when he was home from serving in the legislature as not many people had driver's licenses as the time.

She remembers buying eggs of all different colors from Alva Silliman and going to Wilson's Pony Farm on the Flats with her friends, Ruth (McNeaney) and Betty Ann (Wells) to take care of the ponies in return for free rides. She would also go fishing and go to the theater in North Brookfield.

LeBeau, Jeanne. "Memories of East Brookfield." Interviewed by Heather Gablaski, 3 Aug. 2017.

Excerpts from Written Account by Pauline Dilling, April 21, 1994, to East Brookfield Historical Commission

I loved that house [currently the Harrington Center] because we were close to everything - we didn't have to go to school till the bell rang because we abutted the school yard. We were only a couple minutes from the Catholic Church. We were across the street from the lake, the Baptist Church and the firehouse, and over the fence to the baseball field. Our family was large and every Sunday we had barbeques and clam bakes.

...

Most of this time was during the depression and my dad was a brick-layer and stone mason, but no one was having this work done, as no one had any money. So during the depression he worked for P.D. Bousquet, carrying ice and shoveling coal. I remember my dad wearing a heavy rubber sheet on his back, carrying a block of ice and of course he's always chip off some little pieces for his little girls.

I will always remember skating on the lake. I will always remember the old ice house and the men cutting the ice. I will always remember crunching thru the snow for 5AM mass on holy days at the old church. I will always remember my grandmother frying eggs and salt pork and making toast on the stove for my grandfather and Great Uncle Joe before they went to cut wood at the wood lot for the day. I will always remember the rows and rows of wood in the back yard stacked so neatly they weren't a half inch out of line. I remember Mrs. Lavigne making her raisin-filled cookies that melted in my mouth.

...

They called them the good old days - and I agree. We didn't have much, but we appreciated what we had, and I personally thank God that I was a part of it.

1970 School Essay Contest Submission: "East Brookfield, Young, Progressive and Promising"
by Sandra Grimes

"East Brookfield is a very young town compared to other towns. Our town is only 50 years old. We separated from Brookfield in 1920, 50 years ago...Podunk has its own cemetery and chapel...East Brookfield is progressive. It has one or two factories. The shoe factory is the largest one out of all the factories. It is growing in population too...every year new families are moving in...New people move in with young children, too. East Brookfield is very promising because of the opportunities it offers. It offers space to develop houses and families. Industries will move in during the future. With more industry we will have more people, more families, with these new things we will need to enlarge the schools to fit the children. EB has two productive dairy farms left. These are Mr. McCrillis's and Mr. Grimes's but when the new Podunk Pike comes there will be only one or maybe not even that. The Podunk Pike may help in some ways but it is damaging too. It is taking Mr. Grimes's two lower field and is going close to Mr. McCrillis's house and barn so he can't get to his land on the other side. But in the other way it will take the big trucks off the small roads... East Brookfield has other farms such as Petruzzi's vegetable farm and Steedman's horse farm. Petruzzi's vegetable farm is very productive, they produce many vegetables and also have some pigs. ... The Steedman's horse farm has about 25 horses, she teaches people to ride, too... This town is the youngest town in this area but it has two grocery stores, LeDoux's and the Red and White, two variety store which are Kings' variety store and Trahans. East Brookfield has a lake, Lake Lashaway, and it has a bowling alley, Bay Path....It has three gas stations, Varney's, Ken's, and Dave Gagne's. Their real names are Mobile, Citgo, and Shell.... We have a library in East Brookfield run by Miss Laven [sic] and we also have two barber shops, one run by Roger and the other run by a man named by Joe. We have two or three beauty saloons...In our small town we also have the district court. There is a small fire station and police department. Plus we have two churches, the Catholic and Baptist. We have a small saw mill run by Mr. Treadwell. Our town may be young and small but we have a lot of small things all working for it..."

1970 School Essay Contest Submission: "East Brookfield, Young, Progressive and Promising"
by Brian Worthington

"…Lashaway Park, as it was called, was located at the end of what is now Lashaway Drive. There was a trolley-car track leading down where the road is now and turning around at the end of where the road is now. There was a stand right next to the track where you could get refreshments. All through this area there were benches made by fastening a board between two trees. Also in this park there was a theater over looking the water where performers and actors would come and perform. The theater was destroyed and the park area was turned into homes and cottages… The hole in the dump was a clay pit where the brick company got its clay to make bricks. Down where the RR station is now there was a coal office and a couple other factories on the other side of the tracks. When one of those factories caught fire, the fifty foot chimney fell across the tracks. It took almost a week to clear the bricks and replace the damaged rails. Where the court house now stands was an Opera house. This opera house showed movies and held many dances. Downstairs there was a bowling alley with four lanes. Instead of machines, boys would set up pins. This was torn down a few years before the whole building was destroyed by fire. The blacksmith shop that is now standing is the sixth blacksmith shop to stand on that spot. In earlier years they had to use fire to heat the materials they were working with. There were a few careless accidents that caused to the burning of the blacksmith shops. Every time one would burn, it would be replaced. The Benoits have always owned the blacksmith shops, even through these hard times. "

Part 4

Newspaper Clippings

I enjoyed reading newspaper accounts from the late 1800s to the mid-1900s. These have been scanned and are accessible on http://www.brookfieldsresearch.com/. They provided a truly fascinating look into daily life during this period. While I used them as resources for previous portions of this book, some were not used, but are interesting just the same. http://www.brookfieldsresearch.com/

May 6, 1887 - The Brookfield Times

Queer Freaks of Lightning.

During the thunder shower of last Friday the lightning struck a stone wall near the house of Alphonzo Howe, at East Brookfield, plowing two furrows in it for a distance of some two rods, and scattering the stones to right and left. It then jumped quite a distance to a well, and striking an iron pipe, (laid to conduct water underground to the house of Julius Howe) followed it 218 feet to the cellar of Mr. Julius Howe's residence, then jumped to one side and tore out a portion of the cellar wall. Many panes of glass were shattered at both houses and at the latter place, one hen was killed, and a cow knocked down. Mrs. Howe, who went to the barn to examine the extent of damage there, fainted from alarm and excitement.

August 19, 1887 - The Brookfield Times

Freshet at East Brookfield.

About four o'clock this morning a freshet carried off the office of Geo. Forbes' mill, the corner of the finishing department of the woolen mill and the blacksmith shop, also undermining the brick building used for a dying room so that it fell in. The road to Podunk was washed out for a space of 30 to 35 feet in width and to a depth of some 15 feet. The loss to the town will be heavy.

The temperance movement was one that continued in town for many years. Factory workers were often young men without families who liked to drink after long days at work. Others in town frowned upon the use of liquor, feeling that it led to poor morals and behavior. This feeling was underscored in 1881 when Officer Edward Hogan shot and killed a man after a drunken disturbance at W.J. Vizard's saloon. According to newspaper accounts in the Worcester Spy, the Spencer Sun, and the Springfield Republican, the officer heard a commotion at the bar around 10:00 PM and entering, saw Corliss Longway, a factory worker, kick the proprietor, W. J. Vizard because he wouldn't serve him any more beer. Officer Hogan arrested the man and a crowd of up to twenty other patrons followed him down the street, throwing stones and other items at him, trying to get him to release Longway. Octave St. John, who had already been kicked out of the bar but returned, raised a club or large stick and Officer Hogan, thinking he was going to be hit, fired his revolver, striking St. John, a 23-year-old factory worker who was familiar to police and had been arrested five times in the past year for a variety of offenses. St. John died three days later. (Spencer Sun, April 29, 1881) Many in the town used this incident to speak out against drinking establishments and call for an end to the sale of liquor in town. Interestingly, many surrounding towns were dry, causing East Brookfield to attract many who visited the drinking establishments in town.

Feb 17, 1888 - The Brookfield Times

Dr. D. W. Hodgkins delivered his valuable lecture on the effects of alcohol on the human system to a good sized audience at Podunk Chapel, Tuesday evening.

W. J. Vizard was arraigned before Judge Hill of Spencer last week, and fined $50 and costs for keeping a liquor nuisance. Let the good work go on.

July 13, 1888 - The Brookfield Times

Charles Langdon was arraigned before Judge Hill Tuesday morning, and fined $100 and costs for illegal rum selling. This is the second time he has been convicted within about a year. The officers are on the track of other offenders, and more arrests are likely to be made before long, and we say "let no guilty man escape."

The opinion of the reporter is pretty obvious!

Even though there were only a handful of liquor licenses awarded each year, the profit to be had was so much that raids were frequent and the fines levied on those selling liquor without a license did little to stop them from continuing to do so.

Two prominent EB men were clearly on opposite sides of the temperance movement as evidenced by these two articles in the *The Brookfield Times*. Dr. Hodgkins spoke several times on the dangers of alcohol.

An article in the same paper in March reported on a meeting of citizens who were against liquor licenses in town. The commentator for the paper wrote that, "The aim of our citizens… is to perpetuate a no license administration, suppress the saloon and kitchen bar room, and redeem the town of Brookfield from the reproach of being a rum community - in a word, swing it into line with West Brookfield, North Brookfield and Spencer, and so far, nearly all citizens not frequenters of the saloon are with us." (*The Brookfield Times, March 30, 1888.*). According to the paper, those in favor of allowing liquor licenses were not permitted to speak at the meeting so held their own meeting the next night.

The town continued to issue liquor licenses and in 1901 increased the number of licenses to two for Brookfield and two for the village of East Brookfield. Previously, it was two for the entire town. (*Brookfield Times, April 19, 1901*).

Dec 12, 1902 - The Brookfield Times

Tuesday the thermometer registered the lowest point that it has reached for 20 years or more. At W. G. Keith's store the mercury fell to 20 degrees below zero and in numerous places the thermometers indicted from 15 to 18 degrees. The temperature until late in the evening varied from eight to 10 degrees below.

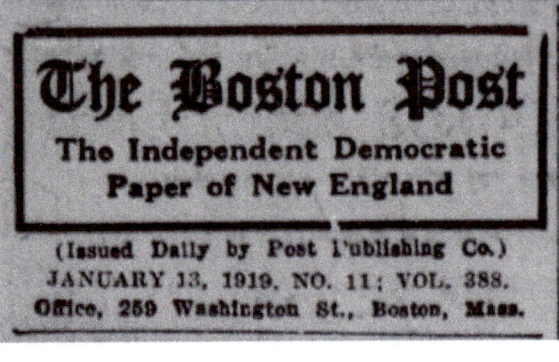

The Boston Post
The Independent Democratic Paper of New England

(Issued Daily by Post Publishing Co.)
JANUARY 13, 1919. NO. 11; VOL. 388.
Office, 259 Washington St., Boston, Mass.

✦ ✦ ✦ ✦
An iceboat driven by gasolene has been launched on Lake Lashway at East Brookfield. The machine is operated by a Ford engine. A propeller rigged forward is geared to make 1000 revolutions a minute and drive the craft 80 miles an hour.
✦ ✦ ✦ ✦

Lake Lashaway Park.

The Casino Merry Makers has been giving a variety show at Lashaway Park, every afternoon and evening this week. They have been drawing large crowds.

A new stage has been built at Lashaway Park. There are two ante-rooms connected and the stage is of quite good size.

The steamboat is again afloat on the lake.

A crowd of several hundred people heard the excellent concert given by the Foresters' brass band of North Brookfield at Lashaway Park, last Sunday afternoon. The traffic on the W., B. & S. electric railroad was so heavy that 20 minute time was run to Spencer and North Brookfield until late in the evening.

Prof. C. W. Oldrelve, the world's champion water walker, gave an exhibition of water walking on the lake, Thursday evening. He will give an exhibition each evening for the remainder of the week and on the afternoon and evening of July 17.

Thursday evening, July 14, there was dancing at the Park, music was furnished by Hoone's orchestra. There will also be dancing Friday and Saturday evenings.

Brookfield Times, July 15, 1898.

Dance ticket, from collection of East Brookfield Historical Museum.

The former Vizard's Opera House, a three-story building that was a factory, then a theater where dances, shows, and basketball games were held, then a factory again, was destroyed by fire on January 28, 1926. (Spencer Leader, January 29, 1926)

EAST BROOKFIELD HARD HIT

Fire Destroys Court House, Dufault Factory, Barn and Blacksmith Shop

Fire which did damage estimated at $100,000 destroyed the Dufault Bros. five-story shoe finding shop, the district court house, a blacksmith shop owned by former State Senator Warren E. Tarbell, and a barn owned by Henry Courtemanche, all in the center of East Brookfield, about 11.30 Friday night.

At 12.30 o'clock Saturday morning the fire was under control, although the ruins and debris were still blazing.

Spencer firemen with the auto fire truck were called to assist and remained on duty until four o'clock in the morning.

The blaze lighted up the sky and could be plainly seen from in front of the Spencer town hall.

Many local people made the trip to East Brookfield by automobile to see the fire. On Saturday and Sunday many others visited the ruins.

The Worcester-Springfield highway was blocked for hours by fire apparatus and lines of hose. Electric wires which threatened the lives of firemen were cut, throwing the entire town into darkness.

The Courtemanche family was driven into the open thinly clad as the flames swept from the factory and courthouse, threatening their home. Firemen fighting the fire as it consumed the courthouse narrowly escaped serious injury when the front wall of the brick building crashed to the earth. Several firemen were struck by falling bricks but none received worse than slight bruises.

Calls for assistance were sent to Brookfield, North Brookfield and Spencer while fire departments in other towns in this vicinity remained in readiness at their stations to answer a call for help.

The fire is believed to have started in the boiler room of the Dufault factory. Rapidly gaining headway, it ate upward through the building and had practically consumed the interior and contents before it was discovered.

With the thermometer hovering around 15 degrees above zero, the firemen were severely handicapped in their efforts to subdue the blaze.

Arriving at the scene, lines of hose were immediately placed from the Lake Lashaway a quarter of a mile away and tons of water poured upon the burning building. The old steamer which had not been used for several years was pressed into service while the local department awaited help from the surrounding towns.

The flames quickly levelled the Dufault factory and with a strong wind blowing swept through the courthouse which because of its brick construction the firemen had hoped would withstand the flames.

The upper story of the courthouse has been occupied by a family until recently and much excitement prevailed when residents who were not aware that the family had vacated two weeks ago, insisted that they were in the building. While firemen made frantic efforts to approach the buildings to determine whether or not it was occupied, nearby residents told of the removal of the family which eliminated the possibility of a catastrophe.

The outbuildings, including the Courtemanche barn and the blacksmith shop owned by ExSenator Tarbell burned like matchwood so intense was the heat from the larger buildings.

With the arrival of the Spencer and North Brookfield pump engins they were sent to Lake Lashaway and four lines of hose fully a quarter of a mile in length were laid. Firemen chopped holes in the ice which was almost a foot in thickness and inserted the suction hose.

When the calls for assistance were sent to North Brookfield and the other towns trucks were pressed into service to gather the firemen and when full loads were obtained they were hurriedly taken to the fire.

State troopers from the Brookfield barracks, under the direction of Corp. Melvin Riley, were quickly on the scene and handled the traffic situation. The hose covering the main highway which is the direct route between Springfield and Worcester, caused a long delay for scores of autos. Countless other automobiles arrived carrying hundreds who had seen the flames which emblazoned the sky for miles around.

The battle of the firemen to save the Courtemanche home from destruction was watched with intense interest by the throng that gathered. After the barn had gone down to ashes the firemen devoted their efforts to saving the house. At one time eight lines of hose were being used to keep the building thoroughly wet down.

The Dufault factory was for years known to the people of this section of the country as Vizard's opera house. It was in this building that all of the social events of importance were conducted. The old-time dances, the high school proms and fraternal events were held there. About ten years ago it was converted into a factory and has remained as such since then. Twenty hands were employed by the Dufault company in the five-story frame structure.

When the fire officials deemed it unwise to allow the firemen to continue fighting the flames while the electric light wires carried current, the lighting company officials cut off the power. The town was thrown into darkness and in the hotel, stores and homes candles and kerosene lamps were pressed into service.

The courthouse building was owned by Oscar Russell, president of the Russell & Peterson Realty Co., with offices at 311 Main street, Worcester. According to information obtained insurance will cover about half the losses on all buildings and contents.

EAST BROOKFIELD

WILL OF GEORGE F. UPHAM

Masonic Lodges of Spencer and Brookfields Are Beneficiaries

Worcester residents and Masonic lodges in Spencer, Brookfield and Roslindale benefit by the will of George F. Upham of Bronxville, N. Y., and East Brookfield, filed for probate in Westchester County Surrogate's Court.

Edith W. Adams of 29 Irving street, Worcester, is left ten thousand dollars and personal property. Beatrice H. Almy of 6 Chatham place, Worcester, receives the same amount and all of the Massachusetts real estate.

The balance goes to the Worcester County Trust Co. as a trust estate out of which twenty-five thousand dollars is to be used to erect "a main entrance to and a wall around the Evergreen cemetery in East Brookfield and an entrance and wall to be similar in material in the cemetery at New Braintree, Mass."

The remainder of the residuary estates goes in equal shares to Spencer lodge, A. F. & A. M., Meriden Sun lodge, A. F. & A. M. of Roslindale. The will directs the lodges to use the money for the relief of the poor.

Mr. Upham died Nov. 20 at the age of sixty-eight. Funeral services were at Spencer. The Central Hanover Bank and Trust Co. is executor.

George Upham was a well-known businessman from East Brookfield. He moved to New York where he worked for a coffee and tea importer and eventually bought the business. He traveled around the world several times before retiring and returning to his home on Pleasant Street. He had one of the best collections of Oriental shawls and rugs in New England and was also a collector of clocks. In his will, he left funds to build an entrance and wall around Evergreen Cemetery in East Brookfield. (Spencer Leader obituary, November 22, 1935.)

Photo of new entrance and wall at Evergreen Cemetery, donated by George Upham in his will. Photo from collection of East Brookfield Historical Museum.

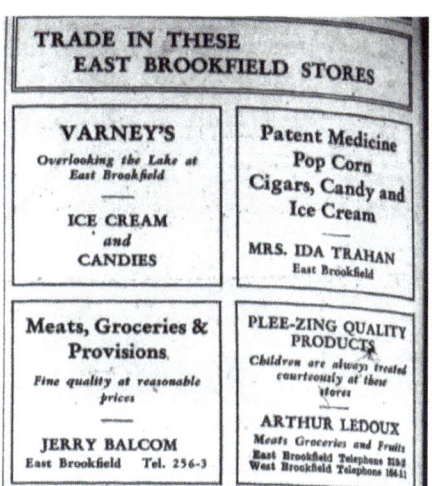

Varney's was located in the building to the east of where the Trolley Stop is today. It was remodeled in 1952 to include an updated soda bar with eight stools and a new 'cooling unit' to sell cold bottles of soda. Ida Trahan's store was in the building that houses the Trolley Stop today, and Arthur LeDoux's store is where the Depot Square Deli is today. Spencer Leader, June 9, 1933

The Handy Store was located on the second floor of the brick building just west of the post office. While first started as a store to sell honey, the owner, Mr. John Buchanan, decided to expand the business to include items needed for the home, like dishes, lamps, and linens to gift items. Ladies in town were happy to be able to buy stockings right in town. Within a year, Mr. Buchanan moved the business to Main Street. (Spencer Leader, October 28, 1949)

This hat store opened in 1895 in East Brookfield. At one time there were two in town, one was located on the corner of Cottage Street and Main Street. (Brookfield Times, June 7, 1895)

Charles Elder opened his homemade donut shop at the end of 1948 in the wooden building just to the west of where the post office is located today. (Spencer Leader, Dec. 31, 1948)

DILLON'S Lakeside Grocery
Main St.   Tel. 2751   East Brookfield

Dillon's Grocery would deliver orders for free to vacationers and residents alike. It was located where Kim's Country Store is today, two houses wet of the 308. (Spencer Leader, July 4, 1941.)

Ryan's Lunch was located near the corner of Pleasant Street and Main Street. It would later be a bar named Peg's Place before being empty for many years until the Thai House renovated the building and established their restaurant there. (Spencer Leader, November, 1944.)

E.R. Varnum's store selling farm equipment was located on the corner of Lashaway Drive and Route 9 where Uncle Sam's Pizza is today. (Spencer Leader, Sept. 3, 1948)

There were many businesses in town as travel to places outside of town was not as easy as it is today. One of these businesses was the Lakeside Diner. It was run by Eva Perron's mother, Eva Comeau, and Eva's husband Norman Perron from 1948 to 1956. The diner was owned by local businesswomen Ida Trahan, who also owned a general store. It was a popular stop for truckers and having only eight stools, there was always a waiting line at lunch time. (Eva Perron, written account, April 2019. Ad from Spencer Leader, Feb 17, 1950.)

CHAPTER 8

In Summary

I hope you have enjoyed reading this book as much as I enjoyed writing it! There is so much history in our small town and I am happy to have shared some of it through this book. If you would like to continue learning, Dr. Roy's <u>A History of East Brookfield, 1686-1970</u> is a great reference as is the website BrookfieldsResearch.org.

Our town is made special by the efforts of many citizens who give of their time to ensure that our town is safe and there are activities and traditions to enjoy. I encourage you to get involved by joining a committee or just by attending the events put on by the variety of town committees. Stop by the Hodgkins Building to visit the Historical Museum and the Quaboag Railroaders on the second Saturday of each month. Commemorate our veterans on Memorial Day with a ceremony at Podunk Cemetery and then a parade in the center of town, a tradition that has continued for over a century. Enjoy the parade, food and vendors on Connie Mack Field and then the fireworks on the first Saturday following the 4th of July for our amazing Independence Day Celebration. Attend a concert or two (or more!) on Thursday evenings in July and August. Hike the trails at Pelletier Woods; swim or boat in Lake Lashaway, Lake Quaboag or Lake Quacumquasit. Visit the Fire Department during their annual open house in October. Honor our Veterans at a ceremony at Depot Square on the Sunday before Veterans' Day. Come sing along and enjoy cookies and hot chocolate at the annual Tree Lighting in December.

I hope that in the next one hundred years, our town continues to be a welcoming place for people to raise their children and to enjoy nature and all that small town life has to offer. East Brookfield is truly a special place to live with a unique history that has made it the community it is today.

References

Annual Town Reports, Town of Brookfield, various 1876-1919.

Annual Town Reports, Town of East Brookfield, various 1920-2018.

Bedard, Joan Leger. All Ya' Need is Love: A Depression-Era Memoir. Self-published. 2015.

Benoit, Lou Ann. [Letter] Received by Blanche, 21 Dec. 1995.

Brookfield Times, various dates.

Brookfield Union, various dates.

"Col. James Philip Terry Obituary - Visitation & Funeral Information." Fairfax, VA Funeral Services - Fairfax Memorial Funeral Home, Dec. 2014, www.fairfaxmemorialfuneralhome.com/obituaries/Col-James-Philip-Terry?obId=2418003#/obituaryInfo.

Bulletin of the Massachusetts Archaeological Society, Volume 27, Massachusetts Archaeological Society, 1965.

Connole, Dennis A. The Indians of the Nipmuck Country in Southern New England, 1630-1750: an Historical Geography. McFarland & Co., 2001.

Crotty, Frank. "Around These Parts." The Evening Gazette, 25 Apr. 1961."Courthouse in East Brookfield, Mass. Adds Special Room for Victims." NECN, NECN, 27 June 2014,

Deacon, John E. "Worcester County - East Brookfield." American Courthouses, 2017, www.courthouses.co/us-states/m/massachusetts/worcester-county/worcester-county-east-brookfield/.

Department of Conservation and Recreation. CMRPC. East Brookfield Reconnaissance Report: Massachusetts Heritage Landscape Inventory Program. Boston, MA: Massachusetts Department of Conservation and Recreation, 2008, Print.

Duffy, Donald. Quaboag and Nipmuck Indians: The Quaboag Indians, a Loup People and the Nipmucks of the Upper Quinebaug River Valley, Self-published, 2014.

East Brookfield Baptist Church 200th Anniversary Pamphlet, 1986

"East Brookfield District Court." Mass.gov, Commonwealth of Massachusetts, 2018, www.mass.gov/locations/east-brookfield-district-court.

East Brookfield School Committee Minutes, September 1, 1921.

Fazen, Curtis C.E. "The Great Ponds of Massachusetts: A Case Study of Quaboag and Quacumquasit." Northeastern University, 2009.

"File:Brookfield1.jpg." Wikimedia Commons, the free media repository. 5 Jan 2015, 09:13 UTC.12 Jul 2017, 13:19

George, Erin, and Craig Holt. "'Doc Leaves Longtime E Brookfield Legacy Behind.'" Spencer New Leader, 11 May 1999.

Hamilton, Dan. "Street Railways." YouTube, YouTube, 4 Dec. 2016, www.youtube.com/watch?v=_ZpMYV_g89g&feature=youtu.be.

Hamilton, Dan. "Wilder Map 24- Brookfield Massacre 1693." Robertwildermaps.com, 2014, www.robertwildermaps.com/Maps/Wilder Map 24.html.

Hodgkins, Martha A. "Address to Quaboag Historical Society." East Brookfield, 3 June 1903.

Holbrook, Stewart H., The Old Post Road: The Story of the Boston Post Road, McGraw-Hill, New York, 1962.

Hollis, Nicholas E. Stephen Jennings: The Brookfield Years (1693-1710). http://www.agribusinesscouncil.org/jennings%20heritage/Brookfield%20Years.htm

"Home." E.B. Flatts Restaurant, 2018, ebflatts.com/.

Jaskoviak, Richard H. "Down on the farm with Louis Petruzzi." Worcester Sunday Telegram, 19 Nov. 1972, pp. 16–18.

Lamoureux, Lionel. "History of Lamoureux Ford, 1977-2017." 2017. Written for the 40th anniversary of the dealership.

Leach, Douglas Edward. Flintlock and Tomahawk:New England in King Philips War. Norton, 1966.

LePoer, Barbara A. A Concise Dictionary of Indian Tribes of North America. Reference Publications, 1991.

Lincoln, William and Charles Hersey; History of Worcester, Massachusetts : from its earliest settlement to September 1836 ; with various notices relating to the history of Worcester County; Worcester, MA, 1862.

Lindsay, George W., et al. "The Official History of the Improved Order of Red Men." Edited by Carl R. Lemke, Davis Bros Publishing, Waco, TX, 1964.

Macht, Norman L. Connie Mack and the Early Years of Baseball. Univ Of Nebraska Press, 2012.

Macia, Elizabeth Putnam. "Letter to Betty." Received by Bertina Brennan, 30 Sept. 1986, East Brookfield, MA. letter to Historical Commission about Podunk Chapel.

Mack, Connie. My 66 Years in the Big Leagues. Dover Publications, 2009.

Martin, Linda. "Search Genealogy.com." Search - Genealogy.com, 24 Mar. 2000, genforum.genealogy.com/cgi-bin/print.cgi?granger::558.html.

Massachusetts Division of Fisheries and Wildlife, MassWildlife. "Quaboag (North) Pond,"<www.mass.gov/eea/docs/dfg/dfw/habitat/maps-ponds/dfwquabo.pdf> 2016.

Massachusetts Division of Fisheries and Wildlife, MassWildlife. "Quacumquasit (South) Pond," www.mass.gov/eea/docs/dfg/dfw/habitat/maps-ponds/dfwquacu.pdf> 2016.

Massachusetts Heritage Landscape Inventory Program: East Brookfield Reconnaissance Report, Massachusetts DCR, CMRPC, North Quabbin Regional Landscape Partnership,Spring 2008, http://www.mass.gov/eea/docs/dcr/stewardship/histland/recon-reports/ebrookfield.pdf

"Northeastern United States blizzard of 1978." Wikipedia, Wikimedia Foundation, 15 Feb. 2018, en.wikipedia.org/wiki/Northeastern_United_States_blizzard_of_1978.

Pembassua, Quaquequunset, and Wasamagin. "Declaration of the Dealings of Uncas and the Mohegan Indians to certain Indians, the Inhabitants of Quabaug." Letter to Winthrop, John Jr. 21 May 1661.

Record Book of the Proprietors of Brookfield (Mass.), 1701-1772, Special Collections, University of Massachusetts, https://archive.org/details/PR17011772Part1,

Record of the 4th School District in the South Parish, Minutes 1820 - 1871.

Robichaud, Jean. "The Early History of the Catholic Church in Our Area." Written account from EB His torical Commission collection.

Roy, Louis E, M.D. Quaboag Plantation, alias Brookfield. Heffernon Press, Inc, Worcester MA, 1965

Roy, Louis E, M.D. History of East Brookfield, Massachusetts 1686-1970. Heffernon Press, Inc. Worcester, MA, 1970.

Saeman, Joann. Our Pynchon Family, 7 Jan. 2011, josfamilyhistory.com/htm/nickel/griffin/sheldon/whiting/whiting-pynchon-jn.htm.

Sanborn Fire Insurance Map from Brookfield, Worcester County, Massachusetts. Sanborn Map Company, Oct, 1898. Map. Retrieved from the Library of Congress, <https://www.loc.gov/item/sanborn03699_002/>.

Schultz, Eric B. and Michael J. Tougias. King Philip's War" The History and Legacy of America's Forgotten Conflict. The Countryman Press, Woodstock, CT, 1999.

Secretary's Reports, Podunk Chapel. 1896-1907.

Spencer Leader, various dates.

Spencer Sun, various dates.

"Stack at Lake Quacumquasit, Relic of Once Prosperous Plant, Felled," Worcester Telegram, September 27, 1925.

Steen, Francis F. ""The First European Contact"." Local California Chronology. UC Santa Barbara, 31 Mar. 2002. Web. 12 July 2017. < http://cogweb.ucla.edu/Chumash/California_First_Europeans.html>.

Street Railway Bulletin, Volume 14, New England Street Railway Club, 1915.

Terry, Walter, O. "Historic Podunk: Written for Meeting of Historic Society," June 23, 1926.

"The Great 1727 Earthquake and the Wrath of God." New England Historical Society, 28 Oct. 2017, www.newenglandhistoricalsociety.com/great-1727-earthquake-wrath-god/.

"The Great New England Hurricane." History.com, A&E Television Networks, 9 Feb. 2010, www.history.com/this-day-in-history/the-great-new-england-hurricane.

"The Undying Hatred of Brothers Who Love the Same Woman." The Sunday Herald, Boston, 30 July 1905.

"The Wheel: Cycling Trade Review," New York and Chicago, 1896 & 1898.)

Town of Brookfield, Town Meeting Minutes, various dates.

US Department of Commerce, NOAA, National Weather Service. "Historic Flood August 1955." National Weather Service, NOAA's National Weather Service, 21 Sept. 2015, www.weather.gov/nerfc/hf_august_1955.

U.S. Department of the Interior (2017). Geographic Names Information System. Reston, VA, https://geonames.usgs.gov/

Watkins, Lura Woodside. Early New England Potters and Their Wares. LaVergne, TN: Nabu Press, 2011.

Index

1794 Map of Brookfield, 29
1883 Baseball Championship, 126-127
308 Lakeside, 38, 63, 112, 120, 200-201
AA Putney's Hay, Grain, & Coal Store, 66
Adams Cemetery, 155-157
Adams, Abraham, 28, 49, 55, 147, 156, 160
Adams, Jr., Abraham, 156
Adams, Eleazar, 147, 156
Adams, Sr., Elijah, 156
Adams, Jesse, 156
Adams, Moses, 156
Adams, William, 156
Adena (American Indian), 10-11
African Queen, 116
Ahearn, Pat and Chris, 80
Ahearn's Market, 67, 80
Allen, Virginia, 150-151
Ayres Tavern, 21
Ayres, William, 45
Bannister, Joseph, 23
Bay Path (road), 25
Bay Path Alleys, 174
Bay Path Fun Center, 136
Bay Path Golf Course, 27, 136, 175
Beaudette, Arthur, 92
Bedard, Joan 2, 79, 84, 114, 198
Bell, George W., 194
Benoit Blacksmith Shop, 100, 225
Benoit, Ernest, 100, 132, 133
Benoit, Joseph, 89, 93
Berthiaume, Donnie, 150, 199
Berthiaume, Paul D., 96
Bhaila, Trikal, 80
Bialobrezewski, Raymond, 91
Bisbee, Reverend John, 58
Blancato, Sheryl, 191
Bodge, Leander C., 73
Bogey Lanes, 136
Bosse, Mike and Amy, 80
Boulay, Ted, 150, 199
Boulette-Skyten American Legion, 93-94, 182
Boulette, Mitchell H., 93, 96
Boulette, Wallace, 93
Bousquet, P.D., 114, 223
Brennan, Steven and Karen, 80
Brookfield Athletic Co., 66, 83, 118, 133
Brookfield Manufacturing Co., 166
Brookfield Mills, 83
Brookfield Plastic & Rubber, 83
Brookfield Town Hall, 72
Brookfield Woolen Co., 35, 66
Bugbee, Charles, 49

Burke, Raymond F., 182
Bush, Charles, 45
C.L. Moulton & Co, 32, 65, 100
Camp Atwater, 118-119
Camp Frank A. Day, 127-128
Carey Shingle Machines, 34
Carpentier, Mark, 199
Checkerboard Grain Co., 66
Civic clubs, 101-102
Civilian Defense, 91
Clary, John, 23
Cohen, George M., 143-144, 170
Cole & Gerald Manuf., 36
Cole, E.L., 36, 37
Conner, Scott & Grace, 141, 195
Connie Mack (Cornelius MacGillicuddy), 126, 134, 137, 165-172, 222
Connie Mack Day 1934, 169-170
Connie Mack Day 2012, 170-171
Connie Mack Snack Shack, 187, 199
Cove District, 28, 111
Cove District School (see District #7 School)
Crystal House, 38, 39, 63, 112, 200
Crystal Lake, 112
CSX Corporation, 79, 194
Daniels Manufacturing Co., 36, 66, 73, 75, 82
Daniels, George J., 73, 76, 173
David Prouty High School, 75, 90, 96, 106, 108, 175, 176, 178
Davidson, Theodore E., 76
Deacon Amos Harrington Center, 102
Default Brothers Counter Factory, 81
Default, Joseph, 98
Depot Square, 39, 66-68, 75, 80, 88, 92, 98-99, 137, 173, 233
Depot Square Deli, 37, 67, 79-80, 233
Depot Square Reconstruction Committee, 99
Depot Square Veterans Memorial, 98, 99
Dept. of Public Works Building, 197-198
Devil's Kitchen, 152-154
DiBara, Russell, 141
District #3 School, 50-51, 54, 55, 104, 105,
District #4 School, 51-52, 54, 55, 105
District #7 School, 52, 55, 112
District #8 School, 52-53, 55, 62
"Dolly Hazzard" (steamship), 31
Drake Family, 57, 174-175
Drake Gardens, 136
Drake, A. Howard, 73, 76, 136, 173, 174
Drake, Barbara, 136, 174, 175
Drake, Edward, 159
Drake, Francis H, 76, 174

Drake, Franklin, 13, 103, 138, 174
Drake, Howard, "Bud", 11, 174
Draper, Ellis, 147
Dunny's Tavern, 65, 87, 222
Durand, Tricia, 85, 198
E&J Hobbs, 37
East Brookfield Civic Association, 138
East Brookfield Elementary School, 55, 108-109, 170, 193
East Brookfield Literary Assoc, 38
East Brookfield Pressed Brick Co, 32
East Brookfield Woolen Co, 35
East Brookfield-Spencer Railroad, 194
EB Flatts, 141, 195
Education, pre-1920, 49-55
Education, after 1920, 104-110
Elliot, John, 11-12, 13
Eommons, Robert, 23
Ethier, Mike, 110
Evergreen Cemetery, 57, 93, 99, 130, 153, 165, 165, 232
Fahey, Charles A., 182, 193
Fay's Hall, 40, 62, 71, 88, 126
Ficociello, John, 139
Ficociello, Margaret, 176
Ficociello, Michilina, 92
Ficociello's Farm, 135
Fire Department, 36, 41, 53, 79, 84-86, 114, 121, 131, 132, 171, 202, 222, 236
Fish, Frederick, 91
Fish, Wallace, 157
Fitzpatrick, Charles J., 92
Fletcher, Glenn A., 97-98
Flood of 1955, 132-133, 186
FNT Farm, 157
Forbes & Co Wheel Manuf., 33
Forbes, George, 33, 116
Fowler, John, 149
Franklin Stones / Post Road markers, 26-27
French & Indian War, 28
Furnace Pond, 33, 57, 112, 113
G.H. Hammond & Co., 68
Gaudette, Alphonse, 87, 222
Gaudette, Frank E., 93, 100, 222
Gilmeister, Tom, 196
Gleason, H.L., 34, 37, 39, 127
Gleason, Willis, 43, 44 154, 155
Goodro, Wilrose, 92, 94
Gordon, Larry, 2, 86, 136, 171, 199
Grainger, Robert, 23
Great Depression, 35, 81, 82, 84, 105, 133, 137, 180, 185, 223
Green, Howard, 86, 91
Grey Ledge, 154, 155

Greyhound Bicycle Co, 36-37
Grimes, Sandra, 224
Grimes, Wally, 92, 157, 224
Grosvenor, John, 23
Haire Family, 111, 161
Hamiltons, Podunk settlers, 147
Hamilton, James, 157
Hamilton, John, 23,
Hare Family, 57
"Harper's Ferry", 116
Harrington St. Solar Farm, 201-202
Harrington Tavern, 43
Harrington, Amos, 30-31, 57, 102
Harrington, Ephraim, 56
Harrington, George, 42, 70
Harrington, MaryAnn, 35, 60
Hayward, Belle Howe, 103
Hayward, Dr., 76
Henshaw Tavern, 21, 43-44, 147, 155
Henshaw, Orin, 159
Henshaw, Sarah, 164
Herbert, James, 94
High Rocks, 112, 154, 176, 178
High Rocks Estates, 176
High Rocks, ore, 112
Hill, Rick, 199
Hobbs, Calvin, 154
Hobbs, Podunk settlers, 147
Hobbs, Josiah, 70
Hobbs, Moses, 58
Hobbs, Mrs. Albert, 221
Hodgkins Building, 62, 163, 178, 198, 236
Hodgkins, David Webb, 35, 60, 161-163, 227
Hodgkins School, 50, 53, 54, 55, 75, 105-105, 107-108
Holden, Frank E, 73
Hotel Pilgrim, 41, 81
Houlihan's Field, 134
Howe Lumber, 141, 186-187, 198, 199, 203
Howe, David, 187
Howe, Henry, 186
Howe, Kate, 187
Howe, Stephen, 186
Hunderup, Eric, 86
Hurricane of 1938, 101, 122, 128-131, 149, 185
Ice harvesting, 114
Ice skates, 83
Improved Order of Red Men, 40, 41, 67, 75, 88-89, 101, 138
J.N. Vaughn & Co., 34
J.Stevens Mill Pond, 112
Jaskoviak, Richard, 135, 177
Jaskoviak, Roger, 178
Jennings, Stephen, 23

Joyce, Roy, 138,
Joyce's Colonial Station, 138
Kady, Sandy, 198
Keith Block, 40-41, 46, 68, 82, 89-90, 93, 103, 177, 190, 197
Kellogg, Edward, 23
Kellogg, John, 23
King Philip's War, 19-20, 21, 24, 148
Knight, Jacob, 163, 178
Knox Trail Jr. High, 108
Knox, General Henry, 27, 177
Kowalski, Anthony, 93
L&N Warren General Store, 35, 39, 67, 173
LaCroix, Mrs. Arthur, 149
Lake Lashaway, 28, 30, 35, 38, 57, 63, 73, 77, 78, 81, 82, 111-122, 129-130, 141, 161, 178, 201, 221, 224, 236
Lake Lashaway Community Assoc, 111, 122, 201
Lake Lashaway Dam, 35, 36, 66, 122, 131, 132
Lake Lashaway Overlook, 122, 201
Lake Lashaway Park, 48, 117, 225, 229
Lake Lashaway, camps, 118
Lake Lashaway, horse races, 116
Lake Lashaway Sheep Island, 114, 119
Lake Lashaway, steamship, 115
Lake Lashaway, town beach, 121
Lake Quacumquasit (South Pond), 10, 12, 24, 31, 123, 124, 126-128, 143, 146, 236
Lakewood House, 38, 63, 76, 119-120, 200
Lambert, Dan & Amanda, 198
Lamoureux Ford, 87, 89, 188-189
Lamoureux, Lionel, 87, 91, 188
Lamoureux, Marc, 189
Lashaway Boat Club, 120
Lashaway Inn, 39, 63, 120, 121, 200
Lashaway Junior High, 55, 103, 105, 106, 108, 109, 163, 193
Lashaway Quilt Guild, 88
Lashaway Rod & Gun Club, 101, 119
Lashua Lake, 112
Lavigne, Doris, 103-104, 223
Lavigne, Jeanette, 45
Lawrence, Daniel, 22
Lawrence, John, 23
Lawrence, Thomas, 23
LeBeau, Dennis, 5, 176, 198, 199
LeBeau, Jeanne, 2, 87-88, 105, 106, 222
LeBeau, Paul, 176, 199
LeBeau, Raoul J., 177-178
LeBeau, Thomas, 178, 199
LeDoux, Arthur, 39, 73, 79, 80, 84, 137-138, 149, 233
LeDoux's Market, 67, 76, 79, 222, 224, 233

Library, town, 39-40, 64, 65, 66, 71, 90, 91, 103-104, 197, 224
Library, Podunk Branch, 104
Lindsay, Rev. Dr. John, 101-102
Linley, Richard, 31
Liquor licenses, 40, 87, 127, 227
Lofgren, John & Joyce, 186
Long John and Red Jacket, 154-155
Los's Hill, 28
M & J Hobbs, 34
Macht, Norman, 170
Maclan Hat Co., 66, 82-83, 91, 92, 93, 129, 130
Mann & Stevens Woolen Co., 35-36, 38, 66
Manning, Ephraim, 93
Manufacturing, 33-39, 42, 45
Mason, Joseph, 22
Massasoit, 14
Massasoit Art Guild, 163
McCoy, Ralph E., 92
McCrillis's Farm, 157, 224
McCrillis, George, 157
McCrillis, Josh, 85
McNeaney, Richard, 177
McNeaney, Ruth, 222
McNeaney, Tim, 99
"Meetinghouse Hill," 56
Memorial School, 55, 88, 103, 107-109, 163, 193, 197
Memorial Town Complex, 91, 104, 197
Mencken, H.L., 144-145
Messier, Heather, 110
Mettawompe, 18, 21
Mitchell, Paul & Diane, 80
Moiles, William, 144
Monyon, Robert, 201
Morgan, Debbie, 198
Morgan, James Pierpont, 47
Morse, Leander, 60, 71, 73, 76
Mosher, George, 136, 139
Moulton, C.L., 32, 65, 101
Moulton, Jesse, 37, 63, 65, 66
Neish Block, 99
New County Road, 28
New England Automotive Gateway, 193-194
New England Brick Co., 65, 173
Nipmucs, 12, 20
Norrie, Scott & Kate, 186-187
North Brookfield Railroad, 45, 46-47
Oakland Gardens, 42, 125, 126, 127
Old Engine House, 84-85
Old Podunk Church, 58
Parmenter Manufacturing Co., 33, 65, 100
Parsons Auto, 87, 99, 129, 188
Parsons, William, 87

Payne, George, 157
Pelletier Woods, 17, 50, 151, 196-197, 236
Pelletier, Richard & Romeo, 196
Perry, John, 23
Perry, Joseph, 93, 94, 132, 146
Petruzzi Farm Stand, 176, 222
Petruzzi, Louis, 135, 175-176
Petruzzi, Louis, Jr., 176
Pilgrims, 8, 16
Plimpton, Henry, 160
Plimpton, Edith Hall, 156
Plimpton, Elizabeth, 144, 160
Plimpton, James Leonard, 160
Plimpton, John, 106, 161
Podunk, 7, 11, 21, 43, 70, 132, 142-158, 160, 164, 176, 179, 180-184, 196, 218
Podunk Chapel (Union Chapel at Podunk), 59-61, 148-151, 220, 221
Podunk Community Club, 101, 148-149
Podunk Deli, 67, 80
Podunk Militia, 148
Podunk Pike (Route 49), 187-188, 224
Podunk Pond, ore, 112
Podunk Schools - see District #3 and District #4 Schools
Podunk Springs, 44

Podunk, Christmas Tree, 145, 180-184
Point of Pines, 127
Police Department, 84, 86, 90-91, 197, 224
Porter, Nathan, 31
Porter, Rosie, 178
Post Office, 40, 64, 66, 67, 80, 91, 92, 99-100, 222, 235
Post Road, 22, 23, 25, 26-27, 29, 111, 174
Pottery, 25, 30-33
Putney, George, 73, 76
Pynchon, John, 14, 16-17, 18
Quaboag Manufacturing Co., 36, 66, 118
Quaboag, Native American tribe, 12-15, 16, 17, 18, 19, 20
Quaboag Plantation, 7, 13, 16-18, 21, 113
Quaboag Pond (Lake Quaboag / Podunk Pond), 12, 13, 14, 17, 18, 31, 45, 72, 123, 125-126
Quaboag Quacumquasit Lake Assoc, 124
Quaboag Railroad, 32
Quaboag Sporting Goods, 141
Quaboag Steamship Co., 124
Quaboag Valley Hockey League, 117
Quaboag Valley Railroaders, 163
Quacumquasit Pond (South Pond), 10, 12, 24, 31, 123, 124, 126-128, 143, 146, 236
Railroad depot, 31, 32, 44-45, 46, 47, 48, 78-79

Railroad, 5, 17, 30, 33, 42, 44-47, 68, 78-79, 89, 125, 128, 129
Redmen's Hall, 67, 88
Religion, Catholic 61-62, 139-140
Religion, early, 57-62
Religion, East Brookfield Baptist Church, 56-58, 101-103, 111-112, 129, 130, 149, 150, 162, 170, 175, 220, 221
Religion, Methodist, 61
Religion, Second Universalist Society, 58, 148
Religion, St. John's Catholic Church, 62, 75, 101, 139-140
Republic Waste, 199
Rio, James, 106
Roads, construction of, 28
Rockefeller Christmas Tree, 145, 180-184
Rosen, Dick, 170
Rossi, John, 198
Sagendorph, Noah, 35
Saucony Shoe Co., 66, 83-84
Schools, map, 55
SEBRSD, 108-110, 193
Second Chance Animal Services, 191-192
Senior Center, 40, 62, 67, 71, 80, 88, 218
Separation from Brookfield, 69-76
Shattoockquis, 18
Shorty's Garage, 138
Silliman, Alva, 44, 50, 145, 146, 152, 156, 196, 222
Silliman, Alva & Helen, 142, 145, 180-184
Silliman, Glen, 2, 100
Skyten Carl F., 92-93, 96
Slab City Road, 22, 26, 43
Smith, Albert, 159
Solomon Richardson House, 179
"Spencer Corner," 52, 70
Squires, Charlotte, 151-153
Stage coaches, 26, 42, 43, 46
Stark, Mrs. Lynde, 221
Steedman Faarm, 157, 224
Stevens Pond, 33, 112, 113, 181
Stevens Tavern, 42-43, 111, 161
Stevens, Ezekiel, 30
Stevens, Jeduthan, 30, 33, 42, 111, 112, 161
Stevens, Justus, 31
Stevens, William X., 33
Stoddard Market Garden 135, 175-176
Stoddard, Emerson H. 36-37, 73, 75, 134
Summer Concert Series 198-199
Superintendency Union, Brookfields, 53, 75, 106, 107
Swan Theater, 80
Sweet, David, 150
Tarbell, Warren, 69, 71, 73, 75, 76, 79, 82, 118, 137, 173, 190

Teneriffe Hill, 93, 151, 155
Terry, James, 96-97
Terry, John, Jr., 146
Terry, Rev. Walter O., 147, 154, 155
The Flats, 77, 134-141
Timberyard Brewing Co., 186, 203
Tobin's Campground, 126,
Tower, Ambrose, 149
Town Dump, 65, 100
Trahan's Store, 64, 233
Train Crash, 1904, 47-48
Transportation, early, 42-49
Treadwell, John, 145, 176-177
Trolley Stop, 39, 64, 158, 233
Turgeon, Fremont N., 73, 157
Turgeon, Mary, 157
Twitchell & Brewster Brickyard, 31, 32, 128
Uncas, 13-14
Union Hall, 58-59, 148
Varney, Charles, 33
Varney's Garage, 87, 129, 130, 131, 188, 224, 233
Vizard, William, 41-42, 127
Vizard's Common, 98
Vizard's Hall, 168
Vizard's Saloon, 227
Vizard's Opera House, 41, 81, 225, 230-231
Von Rosendael, H. Jacques, 93
Walker, Edward, 23

Walker, Fred Jr., 91
Walker, Joseph, 28
Walsh, Gregory, 90
Walsh, J. Matthew, 76
Ward's Campground, 126
Warren, Brookfield, & Spencer Street Railway 48, 117
Western Worcester County Courthouse, 81-82, 173, 189-190
Whitney, William, 159
Wight, Abner, 31
Wilder, Bob, 27
Williams, John Brooks, 92
Wilson's Pony Farm, 140, 222
Wood, Jairus & John, 151-154, 196
Woolcot Corner, 23
Woolcot, John, 22, 23
Woolcot, Joseph, 21
Woolcot, Nathaniel, 28, 42
Woolcot, Rebecca, 23
Woolcot Mill, 33
Woolcot Tavern, 43
Worcester & Brookfield Furnace Co., 33
Young, Ernest R., 94, 96
Young, William Henry, 164-165
Zalatores, Ernest, 92
Zarif, Matt, 203

www.ingramcontent.com/pod-product-compliance
Lightning Source LLC
Chambersburg PA
CBHW061753290426
44108CB00029B/2977